THAT ONE PERSON

THAT ONE PERSON

THE TRUE STORY OF A GOD-APPOINTED
STRANGER WHO SAVED THE LIFE OF
A LITTLE GIRL WITH HER LOVE

A Memoir
by
Annie Farris

CrossLink Publishing

CrossLink Publishing
1601 Mt. Rushmore Rd, STE 3288
Rapid City, SD 57702

Ordering Information:
Quantity sales. Special discounts are available on quantity purchases by corporations, associations, and others. For details, contact the "Special Sales Department" at the address above.

That One Person/Farris —1st ed.

ISBN 978-1-63357-210-2

Library of Congress Control Number: 2019952857

First edition: 10 9 8 7 6 5 4 3 2 1

Praise for *That One Person*

"Annie Farris' story is one of the most powerful testimonies I've read in a long, long time. It's a story of overcoming and victory in this sad and broken world."
Pat Boone, Celebrity, Entertainer, Recording Artist, Minister, TV, Movies, Radio

"Annie Farris' book, "That One Person" inspired me to be more pro-active in reaching out to others with the confident expectation that while I might not be able to single-handedly change the world, I can be that one person for someone. It can even be something as simple as sponsoring a child. It's a great read, with pearls of wisdom on every page, and I couldn't put it down."
Stacey O'Brien, NY Times and International Best-Selling Author

"Annie shows in her memoir that life is all about relationships, and that one relationship (one person) can change the course of a life. She shares the healing power that God has built into relationships, to mend and heal our broken hearts and lives." 'Love your neighbor as yourself.' (Mark 12:31)
Scott Grooms, Ph.D., LMFT, Licensed Marriage and Family Therapist (21 years), ordained pastor (20 Years), Graduate Professor at Hope International University (17 years)

"Annie Farris has created a memoir that is more than a story. It is an inspiring work that will captivate you from the first page. It can make you laugh, cry and wonder how she became the incredible woman she is. The events in her life would have led most people to a life of depression, blaming others and giving up to the point of contemplating suicide. "That One Person" will give new strength to people suffering from a life of heartache and depression. It will enlighten and encourage the hearts of all who read it. As a Pastoral

Care Minister, I will be giving this book to clients who need to understand how God cares for all broken-hearted people who call on His mighty name."

Bill Nelson, Pastoral Care Minister
Founder of Fresh Beginnings Ministries

"In my thirty-year career as a teacher, counselor and assistant principal, I have counseled hundreds of students who needed the kind of encouragement that THAT ONE PERSON offers. Many came from difficult backgrounds who felt helpless as Annie did, but can be encouraged to rise above their circumstances. I believe that Annie's message is a beacon of hope for anyone who may have lived with hurt. In addition to inspiring those who are going through rough times, the story encourages all of us that we can be "that one person" to others if we will only look for the opportunity."

Dee Ransom, Retired Assistant Principal, Santa Ana High
School, CA

"a powerful reminder that God puts people in our lives at the exact right moment to not only help us get through adversity but also to encourage us to be the best we can be. The scriptures Annie uses throughout her book insure us that God loves us and has a plan for each of us. My son battled a rare form of eye cancer for 9 years and then at age 12 was told he would lose both of his eyes and be blind. During this dark time, God provided a mentor to my son that encouraged him to never give up and to always pursue his dreams. This "One Person" gave Jake the confidence to persevere through the cancer and blindness and to live a life he loves. Jake has a favorite saying "God has a plan for us, it may not be our plan, but it is the BEST plan."

Dr. Cindy Olson

"Useful and touching...this is a wonderful piece! A beautiful memoir of a human heart. As her story reveals, with God, we find the strength and peace to 'grow through' the pain and hardship. So many humans survive...in silence."

Kelli Chandler, Owner/CEO
VIVIFY-Life Elevation & Solutions

"a poignant storytelling of a girl many of us can relate to. With God at her side, her courage and loveability grew. Against all odds, she bravely leaned into life and by the grace of God, found That One Person! We all have lessons in these pages. Thanks for sharing your soul-story...it was beautiful. I loved it!

Karen Ridge, Facilitator of 'Hands of Sisterhood', helping
Women Move Forward

"a powerful example of faith, hope, and love, that readers will be inspired to recognize and act upon, in their own multiple circles of influence. It multiplies the impact of a life-changing story whose time has come to be told. As one small candle can light a thousand, in this memoir, the candle Mrs. T lit in Annie's life, sets Annie on a trajectory to light thousands more."

Marina and Scott Miller, Deputy Governor of the State of
California of the Mayflower Descendants.

"it has been a wonderful thing to read this book! It is a stunning (and sometimes shocking) testimony to the life-changing impact of simple human kindness. It encourages all of us to recognize and honor the "Mrs. T's" who have intersected our lives. Moreover, it challenges us to become a "Mrs. T" to one or more persons who need lavish and unconditional love."

Don Sewell, DMA, Pastor of Music and Worship, retired,
Huntington Beach, CA

"a captivating, informative, inspirational, and educational story. It reminds me of how friendships can have life changing impacts on others, often providing that desperately needed shoulder to lean on. Her story is full of important learning opportunities for all of us, including the importance of having God in our lives!"
Milton Wright, Historian, OCTD (Orange County Tres Dias International)

"This wonderful, uplifting book reminds us that even when we think we can't do much to help someone, we can and should. Jeremiah 21:11 says... 'I know the plans I have for you...to give you a future and a hope'. Some of us will know how we touched others. Most of the time, we never really know the "end of the story". This is one where we do. Annie is a wonderful servant of God. She watches to see where she can help and follows through. I'm sure it's all due to her own story of the one person that changed her life."
Laurey Venn, Founder of Christian Women's Luncheon Fellowship, Orange County, CA

"a beautiful story about the healing power of love and how each and every one of us matters more than we know. Annie has an incredible heart for people, and it shows through in her memoir. This book will encourage and inspire you in your relationships to become that one person that might change everything for those around you."
Scott Martin
Lead Pastor, First Christian Church
Huntington Beach, CA

"a life filled with adversity, yet ever striving, Annie overcame the hand dealt to her from a dysfunctional home. Finding "That One Person" changed everything and gave her the motivation to excel in her life. Would that we all had someone like her "One Person" in our lives. An excellent read."
Ron Maurel, Bible teacher for over 50 years. Orange County, CA

"THAT ONE PERSON at the right time can have a very positive and powerful impact on our life. Annie Farris' memoir makes this point beautifully in her interesting and attention holding life story. She reminds us of the life changing impact for good we can have on others as we take the opportunity build them up in times of need".

Dan Moss, Retired Principal Oceanview School District, Huntington Beach, CA.

"Annie's story touched me in so many ways, reminding me of what can be accomplished through our belief in Jesus Christ...that it is not the world that defines us but rather God's vision of us. All of us have gone through trials in life but Annie shows us that if we just persist and work hard, we can do so much more than we ever imagined. Thank you, Annie, for reminding me of that fact. I think Paul puts my sentiments towards Annie and her book beautifully in Philippians 1:3-6: 'I give thanks to my God for every remembrance of you, always praying with joy for all of you in my every prayer, because of your partnership in the gospel from the first day until now. I am sure of this, that he who started a good work in you will carry it on to completion until the day of Christ Jesus.' You are one of the "Victorious in Christ".

Jeanne Zenk, Women's Bible Study Facilitator, Christ Follower.

"Packed with power and wisdom for those who might question the power of One. Clear and concise, yet sensitive to the emotional turmoil of those struggling. Annie's story demonstrates how the help given to another in Christian love can make all the difference. Holds your interest."

Jerald Hollobaugh, Police Department and Hospice Chaplain

"Annie's story is awe inspiring. As a case manager at a drug and alcohol treatment center for ten years, I have experienced how one person's belief in another's broken life can make the difference between life and death."

Diane Shaw, Senior Case Manager of Cornerstone Drug and Alcohol Rehabilitation Center of Southern California.

To Maude H. Thomas, Jim and Bill Thomas, and Rich Buhler who by their love taught me how to believe in myself and trust God.

Every family is different. Families have to get by the best they can because it's a different world now. Just remember this: if you have one person in your life, just one person who loves you, believes in you and will stand by you, you are very, very rich.

- Mrs. T

Contents

FOREWARD

In life and in love, it's the little things that count. A little series of notes, one after the other, arranged just so, make a symphony. A little daily "thank you" to your child or to your parent can accumulate over time to thousands upon thousands of displays of gratitude.

My father, Rich Buhler, practiced love in the little things. He could become your friend with a smile or maintain his (many) friendships with a hug and a thoughtful question.

When I was young, my father always spoke warmly of "Producer Ann." She was, I understood, the genius behind his hit radio show. *Talk from the Heart* on KBRT had become a national success. While it gave him a name and a platform, he always humbly insisted that his producer (Annie Farris) and his station owner were the ones who took the risk to put him on the air and had the expertise to make things work; he was merely in the right place at the right time. He also gave God the credit for providentially arranging every little detail, like notes in an orchestral score.

Little did I know that "Producer Ann" was not only blessing my father's career and ministry with her expertise, but he was blessing her. He was in the group of *that one person* for her, people whose small actions have an outsized impact.

Annie's enchanting memoir articulates the extraordinary power of practicing self-sacrificial love — even (or especially) in the little things. Family members, friends, and even strangers can become *That One Person*.

Reading about those who touched Annie's life caused me to reflect (often through tears of gratitude) on those who have shown me kindness beyond what I deserve.

It also caused me to reflect, with a mixture of wonder and fear, on how I might be that person for others: Wonder because we don't always know what little act of love is going to be the snowflake that triggers an avalanche of positive changes; and fear because I may sometimes miss those opportunities out of my own ignorance or selfishness.

But Annie's story is not a story of fear. With God as the conductor, there is no need for fear. Yet she is unflinching in her description of both good and evil, kindness and indifference, love and careless cruelty. The picture that emerges is wise. Pain is real but redemption is possible. Even though life has its terrifying moments (who cannot relate to her fear of going to the cellar to get jam?) our job is to perform our part and to trust.

Her story shows how the Great Conductor can incorporate even our slip ups into a beautiful song. And his master plan encompasses more than we can imagine. Like a piccolo or chime, our part to play is small but crucial, one little note — one little act of love — at a time.

Keith Buhler, Ph.D.
Author and Teacher

PREFACE

For years, it was too painful and embarrassing for me to share how my background was so very different from the nice, normal lives of my girlfriends and friends - the traditional home lives they had with an intact family, a dad who came home every night and a mom who nurtured her kids. I was ashamed of my sorry past, of a hopeless beginning, and of being a child who had no future, who felt trapped by an abusive, alcoholic and carousing mother.

So, I kept it to myself.

But when I finally swallowed my pride and opened up in an attempt to encourage others who felt hopeless and stuck, and shared my story, I was amazed that I could actually help them by relating how God provided for me and rescued me from my dangerous life as a child. God heard my prayers in every situation and even sent a caring stranger to rescue me from the slums of Memphis, my mother and my alcoholic stepfather. God provides in different ways for different people, but he does hear our prayers.

And so, over the years, many have told me that I must write my story. Counselors, social workers, teachers, and pastors have urged me to put my experiences in writing so that they could give it to those who need encouragement. Now I am thrilled to see how being vulnerable - sharing my pain and failures - has actually helped others to hang in there and, with the help of God, get their life on track despite the many hardships they may be facing.

Now, it is a privilege to tell others who feel that they have no future that that's how I felt too, but how all that can change with God's help. It is even rewarding to share the heartbreak and successes that God brought me through. I have learned that it is never too late to overcome the past and have a happy, peaceful life.

I also hope that every reader can realize that we can each be that one person to someone else in small or big ways simply by being aware, caring and reaching out.

If my story can encourage even just one person to believe in himself and trust God with His plan, then it has been worth all the pain, the loss, the abuse, the heartbreak and finally the joy. It is humbling to think that God can use imperfect, flawed me to help someone else. He is real. He hears. He has a plan for every life. Not just for me but for you, too.

Most names in the memoir have been changed for privacy.

INTRODUCTION

Have you ever thought about that one special person who entered your world—perhaps unexpectedly—and changed the course of your life forever?

We all have one.

Sometimes, we have more than one.

Other times, we're that person for someone else.

We also have *moments* that change our lives forever; moments when the unexpected occurs; events over which we have no control. Some of those moments are happy. Others, not so much. And some moments are simply devastating.

This memoir is about those people, and those moments.

I wrote this book to encourage you during your difficult times, and to encourage you to inspire others during theirs.

My life, from the very beginning, was difficult. I was born in the ghetto of Memphis, my mother was an abusive teenager, and one of my doctors told me I probably wouldn't progress past third grade. My mother and grandmother considered me hopeless and agreed it would have been better had I never been born.

The odds of me succeeding in life were slim. I didn't know anything about faith or courage at the time—but God had a different plan. He set the miraculous in motion. He did for me what I couldn't do for myself.

Using implausible circumstances, God sent a complete stranger into my life, who, by her love, transformed everything. Against all odds I graduated from college and became a successful teacher, professional actress and singer, news broadcaster, talk show host, parent, and realtor.

My story is extraordinary, but my message is simple: no matter what you've been through, or what you might be going through now, God is with you. He can send someone into your life at any moment, from a place that might never occur to you—and he can call on you to then be that special person in someone else's life.

With that special person's help, your life can be radically changed for the better, and with your help, someone *else's* life can be radically changed for the better.

...That is, if you're paying attention.

CHAPTER 1

DANGER

Courage is more exhilarating than fear and in the long run it is easier.
- Eleanor Roosevelt

MAY 19, 1981 WAS AN ORDINARY WORKDAY—or so I thought as I drove over the Hollywood Freeway to Century City. It was a beautiful spring day. Even riding up five floors in the elevator was refreshing, with a view of the city sparkling in the sun. I looked forward to another interesting day, which would include broadcasting the news at the top of every hour that afternoon. But even more invigorating was my exciting job producing *Talk from the Heart*, a live, four-hour Christian radio talk show, the first of its kind in the nation.

Today would be especially riveting—and even fun—because I had booked one of the hottest contemporary Christian bands in the country for a two-hour interview with our host, Rich Buhler. The band was Rich's own recommendation. He would play cuts from their new album on the air and chat with the group about their next concert. I couldn't wait to hear them.

Rich had a gift for making every guest feel at home immediately with his easy going, laid-back sense of humor and genuine interest. The joke around the station was that everyone who met him considered him their new best friend.

Our day went smoothly, with the usual lighthearted off-air banter during commercial breaks as Rich and I talked through the intercom about each upcoming segment of the show. His on-air booth was next to mine and we could see each other through the soundproof window.

That day's guests—the band leader and his very pregnant wife—sat in Rich's booth close to the microphones. They chatted as Rich played several selections from their new album.

Though I could hear all that was being said on-air to our listeners, I was also busy preparing for the five o'clock news, which I would read at the top of the hour.

During the music segment, I looked over and noticed that three large men, dressed in suits, had entered Rich's sound booth. *They must be band members.* How interesting! Maybe I'd get to talk with some of them after the show.

Strange that they all had black suits on and were husky and very large. Bands don't usually dress in suits. *Do they?* I noticed that it was getting crowded in that small booth.

Something is odd here. What's going on?

I could see that one of the men had his hand in his pocket with something protruding from it. Right at the band leader's wife's head.

That couldn't be a gun.

Could it?

The music ended and I switched on a set of commercials. Rich pressed the intercom button and said, "Ann, put on some music." His abruptness startled me. Rich always called me "Producer Ann" in a relaxed, friendly tone of voice. As he turned to glance at me, his usually rosy complexion was ashen. His confident, radiant smile was gone.

What is he thinking? He knows I don't have music in my booth. This is a newsroom. He has plenty of albums right in front of him.

What's going on here?

But I did as instructed. I put on another commercial, stuck my head out the door and hollered down the hall, "Bring me some music carts fast, please."

Whenever we were live on the air, any request I shouted out the door sent everyone into a panic, running to help.

But not this time.

Rick Buhler and Annie

I saw Sam, our young program director, through the glass in the recording studio on the other side of my booth. Normally he would have come quickly, but he stood motionless at the console with yet another big burly man close beside him. This guy also wore a suit coat, and, like the others, his hand was in his pocket, pointing a sharp object at Sam.

That's when I realized something was horribly wrong.

Oh, my gosh. That is *a gun.*

Trying to appear calm, I quickly walked to the lobby and saw another huge man, arms crossed, blocking the front door to the station. Our receptionist sat stiffly at her desk facing him.

Oh, Lord. We're in trouble.

In an instant I realized the only one in the station who did not have a strange man standing over her was me.

This can't be real.

I slipped silently back to my booth, trying to be invisible.

Through the intercom from Rich's booth I heard, "You will play this tape, or I will kill you."

Rich tried to reason with the guy. "I can't do that. The FCC will cancel our license. Everything we do must be cleared and approved by them."

"Play the damn tape," the burly man said.

After more muffled conversation, Rich came back on the air and said for everyone listening to hear, "Okay. I'll play your tape. Let's listen and maybe I can help you somehow. Let's talk about it after we hear it."

He was being forced to play the tape. We had been taken hostage. I hoped his remark would make it plain to the audience that this sudden interruption was not planned. *Will they think to call the police to get help for us?* I listened as the tape rambled on and on, blaming the African famines and other world disasters on numerous Christian organizations and churches. For twelve long minutes it played, sounding more insane all the time.

What on earth is happening to our lives? How can we get out of here?

When it ended, Rich came on the air and said, "How can I help you? Why are you here?"

"You have to help us get our message out to the world about the injustice that's going on. We won't stand for it anymore," one of them said.

As the words hit me, a deep, physical stab of fear shot down the middle of my chest—a familiar feeling, though one I had not felt in many years. Feeling panicky, I started to shake all over. With my heart racing, I tried to collect my thoughts. *What should I do?*

I wondered if someone in the station had called the police, until I realized no one could because I was the only one without a threatening man hovering over me. Time seemed to move in slow motion.

I remembered that Rich had seven young children. Sam had a wife and baby, too. Those kids would need their daddies. My two daughters were grown.

Lord, what should I do?

I knew it was up to me to get help, but I was petrified. Once before, as a small child, in a terrifying moment when I needed to run to escape, I became too paralyzed to move. I had always feared that it could happen again.

Then I heard a voice in my head: *Annie, even if it's difficult or scary at times, always do the right thing. Then you'll never regret it.* It was Mrs. T, my friend since childhood, gone more than twenty years by then. How many times had she said those words to me when I was just a little girl, already afraid of so much by the time we met? Surely the Lord was watching over me just as Mrs. T had, a woman who was more mother to me than my own. Since we first met when I was six, Mrs. T was the one who always helped me feel less afraid. I was certain that's why she came into my thoughts at that moment: to help me once again overcome my fear. The very thought of her calmed me down. Even remembering the miracle of how we met still warmed my heart.

I said out loud, "God help me."

CHAPTER 2

A DIFFERENT WORLD

Some people come into our lives and quickly go. Some stay for a while, leave footprints on our hearts and we are never ever the same.
- Flavia Weedn

M Y MOTHER WAS A BEAUTIFUL WOMAN—breathtaking by all accounts—with long, wavy black hair, creamy-white skin, and bright blue eyes. With her shapely figure and long, gorgeous legs, she knew how to carry herself. When she worked at the bank as a bookkeeper, she sometimes received flowers from men she didn't even know. In later years, after *Gone with the Wind*, she was often compared to Scarlett O'Hara.

My mother, Caroline, liked men and they liked her. I was six years old when Mother, already twice divorced (from my half-sister Georgia's father and my dad), met another man. As was her way, she tended to make big changes whenever a new guy entered her life. But this time we got lucky. John Thompson, from Olean, a small town in southwest New York State, was a good person. Even before I knew his mother, Mrs. T, I liked him very much because he was so kind to Georgia and me.

John, a pilot, was a Navy lieutenant stationed at the naval base in Memphis near where we lived. On Saturday nights Mother often went to USO dances. Sometimes she gave parties at our apartment for some of the officers and their dates. John, the life of the party, was brilliant, funny, and spoke several languages. Witty, blond, and blue-eyed, he was forever laughing and always saying something outrageous. We called him Wimpy after a cartoon character who was tall, thin, and blond. He brought Georgia and me thoughtful presents, like books. From day one, from his first glimpse, he was smitten with Mother.

I met John the night I accidentally got drunk at one of Mother's parties. Our apartment was crowded with a sea of white Navy uniforms. I had wandered into the kitchen and spotted colorful bottles on the table, at eye level. I took several sips of various liquids, and even though none of it tasted good, I continued tasting—I don't know why. My next memory was waking up in the emer-

Pilot John Thompson, Georgia, Annie

gency room. I'd passed out and John found me on the kitchen floor. He and Mother rushed me to the hospital. The doctor told them that I was just drunk. The partiers explained the situation and we were sent home. I found out that there's nothing very exciting about drinking. I never lived it down though, and it became one of John's favorite stories about me.

Just when John was becoming a part of our lives, he told us that because of the war, he would soon be shipped out and he didn't know where to. Pearl Harbor had been bombed in 1941, when I was four years old. Now, I was six, and we were deep into the fighting. But John was serious about Mother and wanted her to take us to Olean to live with his mother until the war was over.

Mother explained to us that after the war, he would come home, and they would be married. John told her that if she wanted to work, she could, and his mother would watch my sister Georgia (then eight) and me. He imagined that his mom would love it since she was alone at the time.

The idea sounded good to Mother and within weeks we packed up and took our first train ride. Olean was eighty-five miles from Buffalo, known as one of the snow capitals of New York State. How Mother ever got permission to leave Memphis without my father's consent, I can't imagine. I only remember bundling up in our thin dresses and light clothes—we had no boots or leggings.

Late on a cold December night we arrived in Olean. Exhausted and hungry, I clung to Mother's arm. We tottered down the train steps, Georgia and I in our thin clothes and flimsy shoes that had cardboard in them to cover the holes, and Mother in high stiletto, open-toed shoes.

Our feet sank three inches into something cold, wet, and fluffy. Everything sparkled with white—the prettiest, cleanest sight I'd ever seen, so beautiful that I didn't mind the freezing wetness soaking through my shoes. Enchanted, I knew we had arrived in paradise.

Icy flakes had begun to come down hard. Georgia and I stuck our tongues out and caught them as if they were tiny, free popsicles. The small station looked like part of a miniature train set we had seen at a friend's house. Beyond that, to me, the whole world looked angelic.

As Mother stepped off the train, she said, "This is snow. It's cold and I hate it."

And there, standing alone on the boardwalk, as the snowflakes came down around her, was a little woman, not even five feet tall, bundled up and smiling broadly. Her blue eyes sparkled with delight at seeing us. We would learn later that she was of

New England stock and not a hugger, but we could tell that we were welcome.

We didn't know how to address her, so she suggested, "Why don't you just call me Mrs. T?" Later, we learned that friends called her Tommy because she was such a tomboy.

After we were snuggled into her big, warm Buick, she drove us through the quiet town. Everything was aglow with Christmas lights, which reflected off icicles hanging from the store fronts. Ours was almost the only car on the streets. We saw snow piled six feet high along the roadside. Mrs. T's big car had chains on so we wouldn't slip and slide on the ice. We crossed an old wooden bridge over the frozen Allegheny River and drove up the hill into a neighborhood of houses that looked like castles, like the perfect dollhouses that I had seen in toy store windows—like homes out of a fairy tale.

Every home was different, custom built, with large two-story Cape Cod estates mixed with one-story Mediterranean models on large, expansive lots dotted with pine trees. Set against a gentle, forested mountain, they reminded me of every Christmas card I'd ever seen. We drove up her steep driveway, which was sprinkled with salt to keep the car from sliding backwards.

The first thing I noticed about the inside of her home was how clear the air was. I could actually see across the room because there was no cigarette smoke. The house smelled like fresh, cool mountain air. Across the front of the house were floor-to-ceiling arched French windows, which looked out on a wide brick front porch. The snowy lawn sloped down to the street, which was lined with huge evergreen trees. Sparkling glass French doors separated the large dining room from the living room. I didn't see any raw light bulbs hanging from the ceiling like we'd had in Memphis.

"John has told me so much about you," Mrs. T said. "And you girls are just like he described. You'll love it here. But after you have some hot chocolate and cookies, let's get you to bed. You must be tired." She led us to the center bedroom, which had twin beds. I'd never seen a bed all made up and open, with not just a bottom sheet, but a top one neatly folded over colorful, plaid wool blankets, ready just for us. Georgia and I had never slept between two sheets. In Memphis, we were lucky if we had one on our bed.

"This was John's room as a boy," Mrs. T said. "One of you can sleep in here with your mom, and the other can stay in my room in my other twin bed. The third bedroom in the back of the house gets kind of cold at night."

Annie's Mother

Georgia, always more out-going, immediately grabbed Mother's hand and said, "I'll sleep in here with Mother."

"Oh, that's great," Mrs. T said. "Then little Annie can come sleep in my room with me."

Little Annie? I had never had a nickname. My real name is Anna Faith, which Mother would yell when she was angry with me. But Mrs. T actually wanted me to stay with her?

That decision, made so quickly, would eventually change the course of my life.

Our twin beds faced foot to foot. She helped me get into my pajamas, and as she tucked me into bed she said, "Now, Annie, if you need anything in the night, just call me. I'm right here." I had never been tucked into bed before, only sent to bed, and from that day on I always asked her to come tuck me in. Later, I remembered that I had never been read to either. She left a light on in the hall in case we needed to go to the bathroom in the night. And Pfeiffer, her friendly little dog, slept in the hall right outside our room.

A last thought occurred. *Uh-oh. What if I wet the bed?* But I was too tired and happy to worry about that now. For the first time in my life, I felt truly safe.

CHAPTER 3

SETTLING IN

For with God nothing will be impossible.
- Luke 1:37

T HE NEXT MORNING Georgia, Mother, and I awoke to the delicious aromas of coffee and bacon and eggs cooking in Mrs. T's big country kitchen. Georgia and I were surprised because it was the first hot breakfast we had ever had. Mother didn't think breakfast was necessary because she wasn't hungry in the mornings, only wanting her coffee and cigarettes.

We sat down to eat in an actual breakfast room next to the dining room. The bright, colorful table was already set. Yellow flowers shone from the wallpaper and there was a matching tablecloth. A large bay window looked out on the dazzling white snow piled high outside. Happy purple African violets sat on the inside windowsill, drinking in the morning sun. Carefully sliced grapefruits were placed by each of our plates, which were loaded with eggs, bacon, and toast. We could choose from a variety of jams and jellies.

The cheery room proved to be a reflection of Mrs. T's sunny disposition. I ate as much as I could, not knowing if such a special event would ever happen again. But it continued to be just as wonderful every day.

As we ate breakfast, Mrs. T said, "This morning, we'll go downtown and buy some warm snowsuits, boots, and jackets for the girls. There's a toboggan and sleds in the cellar. I'll bet you girls will enjoy sliding down the hill at the end of our street where there's a nice, gradual slope. The neighborhood kids go, and sometimes we all go over, even on a bright moonlit night."

I did not know how the clothes would be paid for, except that it would not involve Mother. Just as Mrs. T had promised, that first day we all went downtown and she bought everything we needed, including some warm school clothes. In the stores, each clerk knew Mrs. T by name and greeted her with respect. She knew all their names, too, and talked with them as if they were friends. Driving back home up the hill to York Street, now in daylight, I could see the whole

Mrs. T

mountain behind our house. I immediately said, "That's *my* backyard." Mrs. T laughed, and I called it that from then on. We made good use of our snowsuits. The pile of shoveled snow between the circular driveway of our house and the neighbor's was at least eight feet high. When Mrs. T's younger son, Paul, came home some weekends from college, he helped us dig a cave in it like an igloo, where we put our dolls and some toys. We played there for weeks with the help of Mrs. T's little dog, Pfeiffer.

Early on, as I changed clothes in her bedroom, I noticed a strange wooden contraption by her walk-in closet door. "What's that?" I asked.

"That's a device to help me take off my riding boots. They're quite tall and hard to get off. It's called a boot jack. We'll go riding someday down at the barn. The horses love getting out, even in the snow. My horse's name is Minky. She's a gentle three-gaited mare and lots of fun. We'll take her some carrots and apples for treats."

Later I learned that Mrs. T was an expert rider—just as spunky and lively as Minky. I didn't know that people could own horses for fun. The only ones I'd seen were tired, worn out nags pulling milk wagons in Memphis.

A woman of her word from the very beginning, if Mrs. T said we'd go sledding or tobogganing, we could count on it unless there was a blizzard. Georgia and I couldn't wait to come home after school every day to her cozy house, so welcoming, so sunny and bright, with her there to make hot chocolate and cookies for us. Since School Nine was only a block away, we even came home for lunch to hot soup and sandwiches. As we came in the door, her cheerful yellow canary would be singing away in his cage by the large windows that faced south. After school, we bundled up and played outside in our igloo.

Annie

One cold night I started awake, horrified that I had wet the bed. I didn't want to get up the next morning and be found out.

Mrs. T asked, "What's the matter, Annie?" My tears flowed as she walked over to my bed and discovered my shame. "Oh, you mustn't worry about that at all. That will clear up in time. I have lots of sheets and a washing machine in the cellar. Here, let's get some dry pajamas on you and I'll wrap you in this warm blanket. You can sit here in the rocking chair while I change your bed."

I couldn't believe my ears. She never told Mother, either. In Memphis I had received many spankings because of my bedwetting. Mammy, our grandmother, told Mother that I was just too lazy to get up in the night, and a few good whippings would cure that. Georgia would try to hide the sheet for me until Mother left for work.

But Mrs. T helped me figure out how to end my bedwet-ting. The plan was simple. I didn't drink any liquids several hours before bedtime. Grateful for her kindness to me, I was eager to try. The problem disappeared within weeks. *Why hadn't Mother thought of that before instead of whipping me? Why didn't she take the time to figure it out?* I had tried so hard to be good. *Why didn't Mother see my side of it like Mrs. T did?* Did Mother ever think of me at all? Did she even love me?

Sister Georgia and Annie

Mother got a job right away as a bookkeeper, but within a few months she grew tired of waiting for John to come home from the war. She was the new girl in town, and eligible men in Olean wanted to date this beauty with her stiletto heels, southern accent, and great figure. So date she did, causing a break-up with John when he heard the news from friends. Besides, she was bored with Olean and whenever she got bored, we usually moved. This time was no exception.

At the end of four idyllic months, she came home from work and announced to Mrs. T, Georgia, and me that we were packing up and going back to Memphis.

I was so disappointed that things hadn't worked out between Mother and John. Why couldn't Mother be happy waiting for a good man? Daddy was a good man who loved her, but she wasn't happy with him either.

After my parents separated and Daddy moved out of our apartment when I was three or four, I asked Mother why he couldn't live with us.

"He plays golf too much on his days off. He loves the game more than he loves me and I'm too young to be stuck at home with you kids while he's out having fun. I need to get out and have a good time. He's just too selfish. Besides, he is ten years older than I am and I'm not ready to settle down as if my life was over."

"Why don't you get back with him?" I said.

"I don't want to. Worst of all he wants us to go to church with him. I'm going to do exactly what I please, exactly when I want to. Nobody's going to cram God down my throat."

So she got the divorce. Daddy was devastated.

That Christmas morning, when I was four, Daddy knocked on the apartment door. His arms were loaded with brightly wrapped presents. Georgia and I ran to him as he stepped inside.

"Daddy, Daddy!" we yelled as we wrapped our arms around his knees.

"You can't come into this house, Ozy Blumberg," Mother shouted as she pushed him toward the door.

I looked up to see him in tears. Mother shoved him out and slammed the door. Georgia and I stood there sobbing.

Now, she was rejecting another fine man.

"Let me help you," Mrs. T said. "Caroline, let's sit down and talk about this." She paused and said, "Why don't you leave Annie here for a few months until you get settled and have time to find a job in Memphis? Your mother can keep Georgia, and when you're ready you can send for Annie."

Mother loved the idea. She and Georgia were packed and left within weeks. I felt guilty that I didn't mind Mother leaving, but I noticed that Mother showed no grief in leaving me, either. Since I'd never been without Georgia, I missed her terribly, but it helped that down the street there were some friendly playmates who took me in right away. Of course, Mrs. T had noticed the distance between Mother and me. One night over dinner a few days after they left, Mrs. T said, "Now, Annie, every family is different. This arrangement will help your mother get a fresh start. Families have to get by the best they can because it's a different world now. Just remember this: If you have one person in your life, just one person who loves you, believes in you, and will stand by you, you are very, very rich."

I knew at that moment she was *That One Person* and I realized I was very, very rich. I wasn't aware of it then, but she was launching my life with her love. Even though I didn't know how to put it into words, I loved her for it. Of course, I knew Daddy loved me, but he was eight hundred miles away.

Soon after Mother and Georgia left, Mrs. T figured out I was deathly afraid of the dark. She asked me to go into the cellar to get a jar of homemade jam from the storage shelf. The stairs were right by the kitchen stove, but I stood paralyzed looking down into the blackness. One dim light bulb hung overhead at the bottom. I worried that the cellar windows might be open because near the washing machine was an old coal bin in a spooky corner—a perfect place for someone to hide.

I refused to go down the steps. My mind was flooded with scary memories of the many times when Mother was out dancing and Georgia and I were left home alone in the Memphis apartment.

One hot summer evening when Mother was gone, our nine-year-old cousin, Shirley, babysat Georgia and me. I was five and Georgia was seven. They sent me to bed while they played in the living room. The windows were all open so we could get some breeze. I woke up to see a huge, ragged man looking at me as he cut the screen right over my bed.

I screamed. Georgia and Shirley rushed in. Georgia, seeing the man, shouted, "Get up, Anna. Let's get out of here!" But I couldn't move. My legs were paralyzed in fear. "I can't! I can't get up without my slippers," I cried, not making any sense at all. "Shirley, help me drag her out of bed," Georgia yelled.

Daddy, Georgia, and Annie

With that, they stuffed my slippers on my feet and dragged me out the back door and down the street to a friendly neighbor's house. From that moment on, I worried that if I was ever that scared again, I wouldn't be able to move.

The next morning, I told Mother how terrified I was. She said, "You're just a big baby, Anna. You're silly to be so upset. Nothing happened. You're okay." I believed she was right—that it was my fault for feeling so scared. I was being silly. But how could she have taken the incident so casually? *Why didn't she stay home with us more? Why hadn't she protected us by getting a sitter older than nine-year-old Jo?*

Mother had the screen repaired and told us not to tell Mammy, our grandmother, because she didn't want anyone to keep her from going out. From then on, we were required to keep all the windows closed and locked, even on hot summer nights. She never stopped staying out late dancing, not even when a burglar slipped in, searching for valuables, while Georgia and I shivered with fear in a closet, trying to call the operator. Finding nothing of value, he left. At that time, we lived in Lauderdale Courts—government housing in the Memphis ghetto. Four years later, a teenager named Elvis Presley and his sharecropper family would move into the Courts, too. Our paths would cross later in life through Daddy.

As I stood at the top of the stairs, another frightening memory came to mind. Mother had taught us to beware of drifters and drunks who wandered around in our rundown neighborhood. One school holiday when we were home alone, a strange man with a clipboard in his hand knocked on the door. Georgia answered.

"Hello," he said. "Smith School has sent me here to examine you." My smart sister recognized the lie immediately, because we did not attend the local Smith School. Instead, because of my poor vision, we rode three different buses across town so I could go to a special sight-saving class. Georgia slammed the door and locked it.

Mother often entertained men at night and wanted us out of the house and as far away as possible. So, she told us to walk uptown to the movies, alone and after dark. Sometimes we were followed for blocks by vagrants or drunks who crawled up out of the dry bayou. My terrified heart pounded so hard that I could hardly breathe as I clung tightly to Georgia's hand. Now and then, if we were lucky, when we saw someone behind us, we'd find a stranger's house that had a light on. We'd run up on the porch as if we lived there, then the vagrant would go away. Twice we knocked on the door and asked to come inside for a few minutes. But mostly, we ran as fast as we could to get home. We figured that even if we had stayed in our neighborhood, it would have been just as dangerous.

Mother did not seem terribly concerned about our welfare. Occasionally we came home after dark to find a note on the door: "Do not come in. I have a man visitor in here with me." So, we wandered around in the streets of the ghetto, completely unprotected. Because I was ashamed of my life in the Memphis ghetto, I did not tell Mrs. T about these things, nor did I mention Mother's fiery temper.

One Saturday night, Daddy was playing trumpet at an outdoor concert uptown and saw Georgia and me sitting in the audience. Horrified, he called for a break, got us out of the crowd, took us backstage, and drove us home. We were five and seven years old at the time. In bed that night, I asked Georgia, "How come Mother doesn't worry about us being out alone like Daddy does?"

"Mother needs time to go have fun," she said. "She works all day. Mammy says Mother was too young when she had us, so she has to get out some now."

I didn't understand. All I knew was that I was afraid a lot and Mother didn't seem to care. So, by the time I was six years old, I had plenty of reasons to be frightened, and that cellar door was just one more. Mrs. T sensed my fears and suggested I take Pfeiffer with me down to the cellar. "I'll stand here at the top of the stairs and watch you the whole time," she said.

I knew I could trust her to do that, so down I went with the dog. I grabbed the jam and flew back up the stairs, two at a time, terrified. I gradually got some control over my fear, thanks to Mrs. T's help. I loved that she never yelled at me or made fun of me when I found myself in a tough spot.

From our first meeting, Mrs. T brought light into my life where darkness had been.

We'd often take Pfeiffer for a walk around the block in the evening, enjoying the cool breeze and the peace and quiet of a starry night. Eventually, I stopped thinking that a bad person was hiding behind every bush because Mrs. T and I would talk and laugh until our walks in the evening became lots of fun—and we had Pfeiffer to protect us, too.

If only this safe and happy life could last. I never wanted to go back to living with Mother. The thought that at any time she could demand that I return to Memphis lurked like a dark shadow in the back of my mind.

CHAPTER 4

WHERE IS HOME?

Take a deep breath. You're home now.

W E DID NOT HEAR FROM MOTHER for two years. I hoped the call would never come, because those were the most contented years of my childhood. Much later, my sister Georgia told me that she and Mammy didn't hear from Mother during that time either. We never found out where she went. And here were Mammy and Daddaw (our grandparents) supporting my sister on Daddaw's small railroad pension. Georgia and I suspected that Mother had gone away with an attractive sweetheart—Phillip, whom she knew before John Thompson.

By bringing them to mind whenever possible, Mrs. T made it seem like my parents weren't far away.

"Annie, your mom and dad would be so proud of you," she'd say if I came home from school with a good picture or paper.

Daddy wrote us often and even offered to send forty dollars a month in support money to Mrs. T, but she wrote back and said it wasn't necessary, that she'd take care of everything. I guess she knew Daddy was a struggling piano salesman and musician.

Each day when I came home, Mrs. T couldn't wait to hear how my school day had gone. We talked and laughed together, which was a new experience for me. She loved to tell stories about the horses down at the stable, the squirrels and rabbits in the yard, and all about the flowers that we could look forward to in May.

* * *

A dog doesn't care if you're rich or poor, educated or
illiterate, clever or dull. Give him your heart and he will
give you his.
- John Grogan

Every afternoon Pfeiffer and I would play, chasing each other around the house, skidding on the throw rugs as she barked and wagged her tail.

On some cold, snowy days, she and I huddled under the gigantic oak table in the dining room while I read aloud to her and pretended to teach her to read. In my little wooden roll top desk, I kept report cards documenting Pfeiffer's progress. She loved the attention and affection, and Mrs. T enjoyed watching us play.

"Annie, you'd make a good teacher someday. You know, there's a state teachers' college two hours away outside of Rochester."

I changed the subject, continuing to play with the dog, because I thought there was no way I'd ever be able to go to college. Embarrassed, I didn't want her to know how poor my family was.

At School Nine, I was shy at first, but there didn't seem to be any bullies like the ones Georgia and I had encountered on the Lauderdale Courts playground. Even though Mother demanded that we stay in the apartment after school until she got home from work at six or seven p.m., and even when I didn't mean to, I managed to get Georgia and myself in trouble. "Come on, Georgia. Please, just for a little while, let's go outside and swing on the swings. Please. We don't have to tell Mother." Off we'd go, and as I soared higher and higher, I felt as though I was escaping our ugly world, at least for a few minutes.

Howard, the neighborhood bully, was always lurking around the area when we were there, but one particular day, he moved closer to my swing and stood there, watching me closely. Since I was the smallest kid in the neighborhood, Georgia had warned me to stay away from him. But I wasn't worried about him; I was swinging so high and fast, I thought he couldn't reach me.

I was wrong. He stepped right into the path of my swing. As I screamed, he knocked me flying to land face down onto the blacktop. He laughed and said, "That's the swing I want."

My nose, mouth, and skinned knees ran with blood. Georgia came to my rescue, leading me home, where she picked the dirt and gravel out of my cuts. She washed me up, put ice on my scrapes and patted on iodine.

"You stay right here, Anna," she said, with a determined look in her eye. In a little while she came home and told me, "I went to Howard's house and knocked on his door. His mother answered and I asked to speak with him. When he came to the door I said, "You leave my little sister alone, you hear me?' Then I punched him in the face and knocked him flat."

My big sister.

Happy Days in Olean

I thought we were in for trouble when Mother got home from work. I was afraid we'd be punished for leaving the apartment and I'd be sent out to gather switches for more punishment.

She took one look at my swollen lips stained with iodine and said, "What the hell happened to you, Anna?" When Georgia told her our story and how she knocked Howard flat, Mother just laughed and said that Georgia was a hero.

"It was your own fault, Anna, for leaving the apartment when I told you not to until I got home from work. You got what you deserved." What hurt worse than my cuts and bruises was that Mother had no hugs or sympathy for me.

Howard never bothered me again. For years I enjoyed reminding Georgia that she would always be my hero, and that as long as she was two years older than me, she'd always be my buffer, so I'd never have to grow old.

But the playground at School Nine in Olean was entirely different. A teacher was right there with us at all times.

In those first years of my stay with Mrs. T, I made several good friends, but Beth, a classmate, became a lifelong friend. On day one she came bouncing up to me, wanting to play. We were a lively pair, she with her long brown curls and me with my blonde braids. We giggled and laughed together and even had our second-grade crush on the same cute boy named David. Mrs. T took an immediate liking to Beth, who had to ride the school bus up the icy mountain road to get home. Several times, Mrs. T drove Beth home when she missed the bus. Pretty soon Beth's mom and Mrs. T became friends.

During the second winter of my stay with Mrs. T, Daddy sent me a three-quarter-sized violin so I could start lessons. He played violin and trumpet in a concert orchestra in Memphis. Both sides of my family were musical; my blind grandpa in Chicago, Daddy's father, also played violin.

"Oh, Annie! This is so exciting," Mrs. T said as we unwrapped the package. "Just think. Someday you could play a duet with your dad, or even a trio with him and your grandpa when you go back to Chicago to visit. If you practice and keep it up, you could do it." She had already started me on piano lessons and would sit patiently on the bench with me at her black baby grand to help me concentrate. Always looking for ways to make it fun, she'd say, "After you practice, let's sit Pfeiffer on the bench and prop her paws on the keyboard so she can play, too." And so we did. Pfeiffer got quite good at it, to the hilarity of the two of us and any friends who came to visit. Mrs. T never minded the small scratches on the backboard made by Pfeiffer's claws.

When I started violin lessons, she even hired a college student to come over two afternoons a week to help me practice. I took to it like a thirsty hiker finding water in the desert. I just couldn't get enough. I guess it was in my genes.

* * *

I'll be home for Christmas.

Where was my home supposed to be? I wondered as Christmas approached. I missed Daddy and Georgia and my Uncle Dan (Mother's younger brother), but I was so happy with Mrs. T. The war was still raging, and we weren't sure where either of Mrs. T's sons were stationed or whether they'd be shipped overseas as pilots to fight. Even though they certainly wouldn't be home for Christmas, she never complained about it to me.

Only once did I see her show any fear about her sons during the war. As we had our hot Campbell's soup at lunch, we listened to the news on the radio. The announcer said we'd be sending more troops to the front lines. She dropped her spoon and said, "Oh, no. Oh, my God." Then she immediately straightened up, changed the subject, and resumed her usual cheerfulness.

For me.

I didn't know until I was an adult that my eighteen-year-old Uncle Dan was driving ammunition-laden freight trains to the front lines in Germany. Driving with no lights in hopes that the Nazi planes wouldn't spot the train, he was instructed not to jump unless the bombs hit the coal car. The men hung out the sides of the engine until the last minute, watching the planes approach. Many lost their arms because they waited too long to jump. One of the lucky ones, Johnny came home after the war with no injuries.

But in the safety I had found tucked under Mrs. T's wings, I looked forward to Christmas. As usual, she made the best of the situation. Without my knowledge, she and Daddy had made some wonderful plans for me.

Many years later, I came across this letter she wrote to him. Her habit was to always keep him up-to-date, and that Christmas was no different.

> *Monday, December 16, 1943*
> *Dear Mr. Blumberg,*
>
> *I'm sending just a few lines to let you know that your letters arrived along with the Christmas packages. Anna was so excited. There were nine packages, all different sizes, on the front porch when she came home from school. John had sent a lot from Arizona and there were some from Memphis. She brought them in one at a time, dancing wildly around with each one, leaving the door wide open all the time. It's cold here today, but she didn't know nor care. Don't worry about that little lady. She will always find fun, wherever she is. I think your letter has encouraged her to practice her violin, because she is so eager to please you and the thought of someday playing with you set her to work.*
>
> *The doll house and also the lights have arrived. Paul, while he's home on leave, will put it all together (perhaps over at Maria's house), before he leaves to go skiing. We can carry it across the street on Christmas Eve. She will be showered with presents. It won't be a lonely day for her. I'll bring her to Memphis someday this spring for a visit if Caroline [my mother] or her brother Dan gets a house. Guess it must be crowded at Mammy's house now.*

I am sort of worried about Anna's eyes, because she gets close to her music sometimes. Guess it isn't necessary, but just that she is trying to figure it out. I'll get her to the doctor in Buffalo soon though, to be sure. Can't let anything happen to those eyes now that she is coming along so fine.

When she comes back to you or Caroline, I want her to be in A.1 condition.

Sincerely,

Mrs. Thompson

P.S. I had Anna get a present for your parents in Chicago, as they always remember her. She said, "We will have to be careful what we buy, because he is a preacher." Isn't that cute?

That Christmas Day was like a fairy tale come true. I'd never had so many wonderful gifts. The wooden Colonial-style dollhouse was the joy of my life. For many years, it was my favorite pastime. I'd imagine a real family living in it with a dad, mom, two kids, a dog, and a cat. As if the dollhouse wasn't enough, propped against the Christmas tree was a real bicycle. In my wildest dreams I never thought that I would own anything so fine.

Our happy times continued, especially on Sundays. We'd dress up and go to church together, and, even though the services were quite formal, the pastor would talk a lot about God's love, and that sounded good to me. My heart was so hungry that I latched on to every Scripture they read. I thought that there must be something special and important about church since Daddy and Grandpa honored it so much. After church, we'd go somewhere special for lunch.

CHAPTER 5

THE GIRL WITH THE GOLDEN HAIR

*Just when the caterpillar thought the world was over, it
became a butterfly.*
- Eric Carle

ONE DAY WHEN I CAME HOME from school, Mrs. T
was on the phone. I could tell it was my teacher on
the other end and they were talking about my vision.
She told Mrs. T that I was having trouble seeing the blackboard
and reading. She didn't think my glasses helped me much and
thought I should have my eyes checked. I heard Mrs. T say, "I'll
take care of that right away. Thanks for calling me. I suspected
she was having some difficulty." So, after advice from several
doctors who lived in the neighborhood, Mrs. T drove me to the
finest ophthalmologist in Buffalo.

I dreaded the trip. The only other time I had had my eyes
examined was when I was five years old. Like Mrs. T, my mother got a call from the school in Memphis. The teacher told her
I needed to see the optometrist that the school recommended.
I'll never forget that visit and still remember the optometrist's
exact words. In front of me, he said to Mother, "Oh, my dear.
There is not much hope for this child to have a normal life. Even
with glasses, with her astigmatism and nystagmus, a birth defect,
she'll be lucky if she can make it through third grade. It will be
just too hard for her. We can fit her with glasses, but she will
never see anywhere near 20/20. Any schoolwork at all will strain

her eyes." Riding home on the bus, Mother cried. Even though I didn't fully understand it all, I realized that something terrible had happened.

When we got home, I heard Mother tell my grandmother, Mammy, what the optometrist said.

Mammy said to Mother, "Lawdy, Lawdy, Caroline. I'll declare. I'll tell you right now, this child is worthless and is going to be a big burden to you if she isn't already. She'll never amount to anything."

Mother nodded in agreement.

Those words rang in my heart for years. I already knew I was a burden but didn't know I'd never amount to anything.

The Girl with the Golden Hair

Soon after that appointment, Georgia and I switched schools so I could be in a sight-saving class across town. I felt bad for her because she had to leave her friends and go on three different buses to accompany me. She was in third grade and I was in first. Mother went to work before we left for the bus, so once in a while I talked Georgia into skipping school. With no breakfast before the long bus ride, we were hungry and it was easy to fall into this routine.

"Let's take our bus and lunch money and go find something to eat," I said.

"No, Anna. We can't do that."

"Why not? Mother doesn't have to know and I'm starving."

"Well, I suppose we could walk over to one of those all-night bars near Beale Street and get a sandwich," she said.

"Goodie," I said. "We could be careful to slip in and out so the drunks in there won't notice us."

"Well, okay. We'll have to make sure we never go to the same one twice, so the bartender doesn't wonder why we're not in school."

Sure enough, there were drunks in the bars even early in the morning, but they didn't seem to care about us. My hunger overcame any concerns I had—plus, I thought Georgia would protect me if anything happened. Then we'd go home and play in the apartment the rest of the day. Mother never caught on and we made sure that we never skipped school if she was home sick with one of her migraines.

Not that she would have noticed anyway, because on those days she stayed shut in her bedroom with the shades down, taking her migraine medication.

"While I'm at work, you watch Anna," Mother said. "Do not let her read anything at home because it's bad for her eyes. If I catch you letting her read, there will be a good whippin' for both of you."

Upon hearing that, I was horrified. A "good whippin'" meant we were sent outside to gather switches that she used to hit us—hits that really hurt.

"Oh, no, Georgia," I begged. "Please let me at least read your comic books. I can see those pretty good."

Georgia felt sorry for me and would even let me read under the covers at night with a flashlight and would warn me if Mother was coming. So, early on, I learned that reading was something special to be treasured, and the more I was told not to read, the more I read.

Funny, how those memories flooded back as I walked home from School Nine to have a hot lunch with Mrs. T. As I'd think of those bar days with Georgia, I'd once again thank God for Mrs. T.

The thought of having to see another eye doctor worried me. I wondered if he would tell Mrs. T the same thing Mother had been told. *Would Mrs. T still want to have me around if this doctor said I was a burden and wasn't going to amount to anything?*

But this trip to Buffalo for an eye appointment was an entirely different experience. The exam was much more thorough than the one I had in Memphis, and the ophthalmologist spent a lot of time with us.

I told him what the optometrist in Memphis had said and asked, "Will reading still strain my eyes?"

He smiled. "Young lady, with your new glasses, you can go home and read all you want. Be sure you're in a good light, just like everyone else should do. Even though you'll never see 20/20, you'll get along okay. If you like to read, it's the greatest thing you can do to learn about this world, so have at it."

When we left his office with my new glasses, I said, "Oh, wow, Mrs. T, I can see the tiny branches on the trees, and I can see the people down the block." I felt a warm surge of joy all over as Mrs. T almost danced with me when we got in the car to go home.

"Let's celebrate," she said. "Let's go to lunch here in Buffalo at somewhere real nice." And so we did.

"Oh, my goodness," I said. "I can read the menu."

She beamed. "Good. You can order anything you want." Even while we ate, I read the entire menu over and over.

We laughed and giggled on the whole two-hour trip back home. Her excitement for me compounded my happiness. For the first time, I could read some billboards.

The icicles on the evergreen trees now took on new dazzling shapes and forms instead of being just a blur, and on the pine trees in the yard I could see needles that I had never noticed before. A wonderful new world had opened up for me.

The day after we got home, Mrs. T said, "Let's go to the bookstore so you can pick out some stories for your very own."

We bought *Black Beauty* and *Lassie*. Trips to the library became a regular treat from then on, as Pfeiffer and I spent those long winter days reading under the dining room table or by the front window, overlooking the snow.

Mrs. T's enthusiasm for making me healthy had no limits. She worried about my being thin and pale. So, off we went to the local pediatrician, who was a friend of hers.

"Tommy, Annie is behind the normal weight for her age," he said. "She needs sunshine, fresh air, exercise and plenty of good food. She doesn't have enough muscle tone. I understand her being fair-skinned, but she needs to get a little color in her cheeks. They're kind of sallow."

Oh, no.

As he spoke, I remembered the time when Mammy and I were standing at the bus stop in Memphis. We often saw some albino twins there. She whispered, "See those kids, Anna? They're freaks. You just missed being an albino yourself. That's why you're so pale and your hair is so light."

Would Mrs. T think that of me, too, and not want me with her?

But according to this doctor, I just needed to eat lots of good food, and I'd gain some much-needed weight and get some color in my cheeks.

That's what Mrs. T set out to do. In addition to a big breakfast before school, she continued to make a hot lunch every day, and oh, the dinners! I feasted on plenty of meat and baked potatoes heaped with butter and sour cream—my favorite. In season, we had fresh fruits and veggies with huge salads that she taught me how to make. Mrs. T was a fabulous cook and her holiday dinners were family legends.

After dinner she'd say, "Let's drive to the Tasty Freeze and get an ice cream cone." Or, "Hey, let's pop some popcorn and put lots of butter on it." I didn't know that eating could be so much fun.

After playing in the snow or riding my sled on the hill behind our school and walking home, I was as hungry as a bear coming out of hibernation. I headed for the refrigerator as soon as I hit the front door and I ate my way through my first few years in Olean.

Each morning before school, Mrs. T enjoyed braiding my long hair. The sun shone through the high windows in her large blue-and-white-tile bathroom as I sat on a little stool.

"Oh, Annie. Your hair is like *spun gold*. It's so beautiful." I smiled and thought, *Wait a minute. Who am I? The pale kid who just missed being an albino or the girl with golden hair?* I decided right then that I'd be the girl with the golden hair.

CHAPTER 6

MY FIRST VERSE

You must learn to paddle your own canoe.
- Mrs. T

THE SUMMER OF 1944, my second summer with Mrs. T, Daddy drove to Olean to take me to Chicago for a week to visit my blind grandpa and Grandma Anna. Daddy and I played our violins, just as we had planned, in the church where Grandpa was pastor. Even though I didn't understand a word of the Latvian they all spoke, I felt their love and basked in the hugs from all of Grandpa's friends.

I got to walk around the block with him and his white seeing-eye dog. As we strolled along, he taught me the 23rd Psalm.

The Lord is my shepherd, I shall not want. He maketh me to lie down in green pastures: He leadeth me beside the still waters. He restoreth my soul: He leadeth me in the paths of righteousness for His name's sake. Yea though I walk through the valley of the shadow of death, I will fear no evil: for Thou art with me; Thy rod and Thy staff they comfort me; Thou preparest a table before me in the presence of mine enemies. Thou anointest my head with oil; My cup runneth over. Surely, goodness and mercy shall follow me all the days of my life and I will dwell in the house of the Lord forever.

Grandpa stopped for a moment and asked me, "Does your mother take you to church Sunday mornings?" I fumbled around, not knowing what to say because Mother usually had a hangover on Sunday mornings and did not want to be disturbed until afternoon. I didn't dare say that since I didn't want to make her look bad.

After an awkward silence he said, "You know, we love your mom and we pray for her and you and Georgia every day." That night, he prayed for me and taught me how to talk to the Lord. He had such a kind, gentle manner about him that I forgot he was blind. I loved being with him.

Grandpa wrote to me for years, carefully folding the paper in horizontal lines to help him keep his place on the page, every line full of love and care.

I'm sorry I didn't keep those sweet letters.

At first, I took the words about green pastures and still waters literally, but as Daddy and I drove back to Olean he explained what the words meant, and I got it. I especially loved the part that said "surely goodness and mercy shall follow me all the days of my life." Could that really mean that with God's help, goodness and mercy would follow me all the days of my life, even though I didn't know where I'd be or with whom?

When Daddy left me back in Olean, he choked up and could hardly talk for a few minutes. I cried, too, but he loved Mrs. T and could see I was being well taken care of—certainly better than I would have been as a latchkey kid in Memphis.

I moved into the middle bedroom after Georgia and Mother left. As I lay in bed, I studied the model airplanes that hung from the ceiling. One morning, I asked Mrs. T, "Where did these come from?"

"When John and Paul were kids," she said, "they were fascinated with airplanes and they built these."

"Is that why they became pilots?" I asked.

"Oh, yes," she said. "When they were teenagers and were old enough to take lessons, I took them down to the local airport and they learned to fly the single engine Cessna. Their dad was pretty mad at me when he found out that they were flying, but it was too late to stop them then. They just loved it. That was before the war, of course. So, when they both went into the military as pilots, they didn't need much training. I didn't know until years later that John was color-blind but managed to memorize all the landing lights in order to be a Navy pilot." That was so like him. He was simply unstoppable. I admired her for supporting and encouraging her boys to pursue their interests.

When he returned after the war, John moved in with us for a while and took the back bedroom.

One day he came home with a record of *Peter and the Wolf* for me. He was all excited to teach me the musical themes for each animal.

"Annie, hum the part of the wolf for me—now the bird." I picked them up pretty quickly and he was delighted with anything he could teach me. Of course, I loved pleasing him and enjoying the music. He'd put the record on, and we'd march around the house together to the beat. Daddy would have been pleased.

Paul had gone back to college after the war, but sometimes he'd come home for the weekend and I delighted in his consistently happy disposition. He went flying at the local airport every chance he got. He met his future wife, Meg, at college. They married and came home so he could work in the family business.

One sunny afternoon, John said, "How would you like to go up in a plane with me and see what Olean looks like from the sky?"

"Oh, wow. Really? Could I?" Mrs. T nodded her approval, always eager for me to try new things.

I was very excited when he strapped me into the seat behind him. As we soared through the air, over the noise of the engine, I shouted, "Look, John. I can see our house and the mountain behind it and the mountain behind that one. Oh, there's the river road and the horse stable. It all looks like miniatures—like my dollhouse."

We buzzed low over Mrs. T's house so I could see it close-up.

"Okay, Annie. Hang on tight. We're going to roll over."

"Ohhhhh. John, don't do it!" I screamed—but only before the first rollover. After that, it was, "Ohhh! Do it again, John!"

Better than any amusement park ride, flipping upside down became more and more fun, because I felt perfectly safe with John. I never told Mother or Daddy about those flights because I didn't think they'd approve. I loved thinking about how, on the one hand, Mrs. T was so protective of me and, on the other hand, if it was safe, she was eager for me to have a new experience. I trusted her and John in every area of my life. They weren't afraid of anything. Life was a big adventure for them.

I wanted to be like that.

With his high energy level and wit, John continued to be outrageous. He had enough vitality for three of him. His high-fidelity record player was rigged up so that every morning, at exactly 6:00 a.m., it automatically blasted forth. The entire house shook with the sound of loud Sousa marches such as "Stars and Stripes Forever."

He'd leap out of bed shouting, "Come on, Pfeiffer! Let's march." Around the house they flew—John in his long white nightshirt and bare feet, and Pfeiffer wagging her tail, barking along behind him. They'd march past my bedroom. "Come on, Annie. Up and at 'em." Sometimes I'd join them, but usually, I preferred to burrow myself under the warm covers until they passed by as I enjoyed the aroma of coffee that Mrs. T was preparing for him.

At breakfast one morning, Mrs. T said, "John, why don't you go buy yourself some nice clothes for work? You don't have to wear suits, but at least get something nicer than the khaki pants, shirt, and loafers that you wear every day."

"Mater, why should I dress any differently? I'm comfortable in these clothes. Besides, this way, I don't have to figure out what to wear every morning."

She sighed.

"Plus," he added, "I don't want the people at the warehouse to think of me as higher up than them. Whenever I'm not on the road checking out the stores, I want to work alongside them."

As I got older, I drank all this in with great amusement, understanding more and more how unique he was—no arrogance, no pretention, no showing off in him at all. To everyone who knew him, he was just fearless, loveable, generous John.

Both Paul and John were working for their dad, who owned a chain of large supermarkets in southwestern New York State and parts of Pennsylvania. They would not have chosen this life. John had wanted

Annie in Chicago visiting Grandparents

to become a doctor, and Paul wanted to be a professional pilot and open a school for aerodynamics and stunt pilots.

Mrs. T and her husband had been divorced several years before I arrived and, unfortunately, she was not part of the business anymore. That seemed unfair since her brother had given her and her husband one small grocery store as a wedding gift, and through her good bookkeeping and their management, the business had expanded to over sixty markets. Eventually, once the sons took over running the business, they hired her to do quality control, checking in on the various locations unexpectedly to see if customer service was up to par.

Mrs. T and I had great fun in the spring, racing over the hills to the next grocery with a trunk full of fresh strawberries so that their store would be the first one in town to have the berries available.

Even though she had a beautiful home, it had never occurred to me that the family might be wealthy. The sons drove ordinary Volkswagen bugs and lived modestly. Paul even built his own home a few miles outside of town, where he and his wife Ruth had their three children. Mrs. T, though, was frustrated when she found out that John and Paul weren't being paid well by their father, even though they were working long hours and running the entire company.

One night when John, Mrs. T, and I were eating in the kitchen, he said, "Mater, why don't you buy a new refrigerator, for heaven's sake? This old thing is a thousand years old with coils on the top and doesn't even have a freezer section."

"Why would I do that, John, when this one works just fine? Besides, Annie and I stop by the stores every few days and we get fresh food often. We don't need a freezer."

As I began to see what a prosperous business they had, I was impressed all the more with how frugal she was. I figured out, even as a child, that her family's success was due to her frugality.

Without being taught, I was learning an important life lesson: the importance of being careful with money. Mrs. T taught me early on not to waste anything. She knew when to spend, when not to spend, and what was important to spend on. We ate almost every leftover. I had nice clothes because she felt that it was important for me to feel good about myself when I went to school.

We often talked about my future over dinner. "Annie, education is the key to being able to paddle your own canoe. If you work hard, you can take care of yourself no matter what happens to you in life. If you do the best you can and pay attention, I know you will do well."

I could easily see the benefits the Thompsons and their neighbors had from getting a good education. Money could be spent on recreation, like riding and hobbies, but never wasted on liquor or cigarettes. I did not tell her how important booze and cigarettes were to my mother's family. She always spoke kindly of Mother and I didn't want to change that impression. Mother did not smoke or drink when she stayed at Mrs. T's, which is probably one reason she wasn't comfortable there. Noticing the difference in the two families' lifestyles made me sad for Mother's family. Had I never lived with Mrs. T, I might never have known the difference.

Eventually John moved out and got his own place, but most Sunday nights he'd stop by to check on us.

With more and more responsibility at work, it soon became apparent that he needed a secretary to assist him. He came over to tell us the good news. The three of us were having ginger ale in the kitchen. "Mater, I finally found a secretary."

"That's great, John. Where'd you find her and what kind of training does she have?"

"Well, uh, it's a *he*. I went to that rundown hotel on the other side of the tracks and talked to a few alcoholics who are dried out now, but out of luck. They can't get jobs. So I hired one of them. I bought him some decent clothes for work and I'm training him myself."

"Oh, John," Mrs. T said. "What if he falls off the wagon? Can you trust him in the offices? Do you know anything about him? For goodness sake, John."

"Mater, he's doing fine. He started last Monday and he's so darn grateful that he follows me around like a puppy dog, taking notes on every word I say. He books my appointments, brings me lunch, answers my calls, and is the hardest working secretary I've ever seen. He just needed someone to give him a chance."

"Oh, John."

It didn't surprise me a bit that John loved to shock his mother whenever possible by doing the unusual. That was just like him. As the years went on, his secretary turned out to be the hardest working, most faithful employee in the company. John was right. All he'd needed was a second chance in life, just like I did, and leave it to John to give it to him. John's generous heart was more like his mother's than either of them realized.

A gold star was displayed in the windows of numerous family homes in our town. The star represented a son, brother, or dad lost in World War II. Mrs. T visited many of these families. After all, both her sons were pilots in the military and all the other families had shared in their concern for their kids.

"Do you want to go with me, Annie?" Mrs. T asked. "You go to school with some of the younger brothers and sisters of these military men."

"Well, uh, I'm not sure. I'd like to go, but I don't know what to say."

"That's it, Annie. Most people don't know what to say, and that's why they stay away sometimes. But it's not important what you say. It's caring enough to show up that matters. Just being there and listening to someone who's grieving is the best comfort you can bring. We don't have all the answers and we can't fix what they are going through, but we can sit with them, and be kind and loving."

"Then I'd like to go with you," I said.

I was deeply moved to see how grateful these families were just because we visited with them for a while. What she had said was true—they might not remember anything we said, but they would never forget that we cared enough to be with them in their time of horrific loss. For the rest of my life, that helped me to know what to do in times of sorrow.

One afternoon, John came by early after work, but he wasn't his usual upbeat self. He paced the floor, visibly upset. As we drank ginger ale in the kitchen, he said, "Mater, remember Jason? That blond kid I went to school with?"

"Sure," she said.

"I just got the call," John said. "He took his own life yesterday."

"Oh, no!"

"Yeah. Half this town believes that suicide is a mortal sin," John said, "and I think people aren't going over or calling his mom, because they don't know what to say or do. So no one is saying anything except talking behind their backs. That's not right."

"Oh, John! That's awful," Mrs. T said. "What do you want to do?"

"I'm going right over to be with them. They need support. It's not important right now to know why he did it, and I don't see it as sin. I see him as being in a world of hurt that we can't understand. I don't see him as selfish, either. He just wanted to end the pain. We don't have the right to judge him."

After a long pause while she thought it through, Mrs. T smiled. "How 'bout I fix you something to eat before you go, and you can take them some food, too. I'll go over tomorrow."

On these occasions, they seemed unaware that I, a kid, was in the room learning how to get through the really tough stuff in life. They treated me like an adult as I listened, not realizing that they were teaching me how to help out in the future, when friends faced enormous grief. It also helped me to understand the importance of having loved ones close by when my own road got rough as an adult. I thought that the Thompson theology was right on. I'd never known anyone like them and loved them all the more for living out their lives in front of me.

Several years passed. My tenth birthday came and went. Mother seldom wrote and that was fine with me. Surely, this would be my home forever. I never got over the miracle of coming home to Mrs. T after school and being greeted by her jovial disposition with Pfeiffer dancing around me, wagging his tail when I came in the door. It was such a huge contrast to Georgia and me facing an empty, cold apartment, having to stay inside until Mother came home—late, as always.

My grades continued to improve, as well as my violin and piano lessons, and I enjoyed having a few friends with whom to play or ride my sleigh.

One Saturday morning, as Mrs. T and I dusted the living room, I gazed in awe out the window at the huge Cape Cod house next door, where a surgeon's family lived. One of their sons, a friend of John's, also wanted to be a surgeon.

"How do you get to be a surgeon?" I asked.

"Well, it takes about twelve years of schooling, including medical school," she said. "Why do you ask?"

"That's a long time to go to school," I said.

"Yes," she said, "but if that's really what a person wants to do, they can find a way."

She was quiet for a few minutes as if deep in thought. Finally, she sat down on the couch and said, "Annie, did you know that you can be anything in this world you want to be if you are just willing to work hard enough to get there?"

"What do you mean?" An adult had never talked to me about such things. I stood still with my dust cloth in hand and looked her in the eye, surprised and astonished at her words.

"I mean you could be a surgeon if you really wanted to be and were willing to put in the time, but if you didn't want to study that long, it wouldn't be because you *couldn't* be a surgeon, but because you *chose* not to be. You can be anything you want if you make up your mind to commit to putting in the effort. Anyone can do the same. Hard work and perseverance will get you exactly where you want to go."

"Oh, wow. I never thought of it that way."

"Of course, you have to be wise about it and get advice and direction. For example, if you were eighty years old, you wouldn't decide to learn to ice skate so that you could compete in the Olympics the next year."

We laughed.

"But, for the most part, you can be anything, really."

I was amazed at the idea. Stunned. I thought about it for days. Months. Years. I even remember the exact spot in the living room where I was standing when she spoke. Could it really be true? My heart raced at the thought that anything was possible. So shocked was I at the idea that I sat on the edge of the couch, speechless. At that exact moment, everything changed for me. I believed her and I believed that I could do almost anything.

On that day, my mind did a 180-degree turn.

That one realization set me free for the coming years and gave me courage to explore almost anything—any education, any job, and any career I ever wanted. I believed that with enough hard work, I could make it happen.

In that very moment, I knew that it didn't matter if I came from the slums of Memphis, or that Mammy had said I'd never amount to anything. It didn't matter if my parents were divorced and my mother didn't like me. It didn't matter what I looked like, or if I wore coke bottle glasses. The only thing that mattered would be whether I was willing to work hard enough to make something of myself, to provide for myself someday as an adult.

Of all the blessings that came from living with Mrs. T, this was the most profound concept I learned. All the pain, all the fear, all the put-downs I had suffered in Memphis suddenly became smaller compared to what she taught me that day.

We finished our housework. As we ate our Campbell's soup for lunch she said, "You know, you have to learn to paddle your own canoe. I need to know that when you grow up, you'll be able to take care of yourself, Annie—that you won't have to be dependent on anyone. That if someone lets you down, you'll be okay."

Someone? Surely, I figured, she had been let down because of her divorce, when she was left on her own in a small town at a time when divorce was shameful.

At the time, I didn't understand how desperately I needed to hear her words. I'd have to find a way to make a life for myself. That night I knelt by my bed thanking God, again, for bringing me into her home.

CHAPTER 7

TWO LITTLE FROGS

A half-truth is the most cowardly of lies.
- Mark Twain

For five years I lived happy, safe, and content with Mrs. T. Mother never reached out. But finally, the dreaded call came. I was in the fifth grade.

"Anna, I have wonderful news. I just got married to a dance instructor I work with." She was teaching at Arthur Murray's Dance Studio in Memphis. "We haven't known each other very long, but that doesn't matter. I want you to come to Memphis this July for a few weeks for Georgia's birthday. You can meet Roger then, too."

Why hadn't she invited me any of the other summers before this? I didn't want to go, because I was suspicious of her motives. I mumbled something polite as she got Mrs. T on the line to plan my visit.

After we hung up, Mrs. T was enthusiastic about the idea. "Annie, it would be good for you to see your family, and especially Georgia. I know how much you've missed her. I'll buy your train ticket."

I didn't look at her as I took in the bad news.

Of course, she was eager for me to visit my family, because she didn't know what it was really like there. "I'm afraid to go. Mother might make me stay and this is my home now."

"Oh, I don't think she'd do that if she's just calling it a visit," she said.

As I felt tears well up, I raced to my bedroom and shut the door so I could cry in privacy. For several days I moped around the house, knowing that I had to go. Mrs. T, who always read my feelings so quickly, noticed my long face.

"Annie, have you heard the story about the two little frogs?" she said at dinner.

"No." *Where is she going with this?*

"Well, two little frogs fell into a bucket of cream. They swam around as long as they could. Finally, one little frog said, 'This is too hard. We're going to drown anyway.' So, he gave up, sank to the bottom, and drowned. The second little frog said, 'I won't give up. I'll keep paddling. Something will turn up.' Pretty soon he was floating on a big pad of butter. You must never, ever give up, Annie. Keep paddling no matter what happens in life. You'll be floating on a pad of butter before you know it."

I've carried the "Two Little Frogs" story in my heart ever since. It's helped me out more times than I can count.

When the time came, Mrs. T took me to the train station. As the conductor yelled, "All aboard," she hugged me.

"Keep your chin up," she said. I cried halfway to Memphis, afraid I'd never see her again.

Back in South Memphis, I joined the rest of Mother's family, hoping the visit really was only for a few weeks for Georgia's birthday. Seven of us lived in the most dangerous section of Memphis in Mammy and Daddaw's crowded two-bedroom rental: Mother, her new husband Roger, Georgia, Mammy, Daddaw, Uncle Larry, and me. Daddaw had suffered a stroke and was confined to a hospital bed in the living room.

Before I was born, my grandparents had lost their home in the Great Depression. To Mammy's credit, even though the house they rented was old and shabby, with peeling paint outside and filled with soot that blew in from the coal yard across the street, she and Daddaw had tried to keep the inside nice. They had painted and wallpapered, and Daddaw, before his stroke, had planted roses in the front yard. And yet, because all of them were heavy smokers, the house was so full of cigarette smoke that I felt like we were sleeping in a bar. I could hardly breathe, but it was worse for Georgia who coughed a lot and easily got colds and bronchitis. With no air conditioning, we lay in a pool of sweat all night, unable to sleep because of the humidity and mosquitoes.

But worse than the physical circumstances was the lack of feeling loved. Instead, there were constant squabbles as the family screamed at each other, in addition to gossiping and back-biting. Mother and Roger were heavy drinkers and often had heated arguments over money, since he'd lost his job.

Mammy's favorite remark was, "When poverty comes in the door, love goes out the window." I didn't want to believe that. I thought love was supposed to get you through the tough times and make you stronger, like in the movies. Uncle Larry was a full-on alcoholic, as was his girlfriend. Thankfully, she didn't live with us. Behind her back, Mammy called her a bad name that meant "woman of the street." But we didn't expect a lot from Uncle Larry since he had spent time in prison years ago for a teenaged robbery. At least he'd managed to get and keep a job.

When Georgia's birthday in July came and went, my worst fears came true.

"Anna," Mother announced, "You're not going back to Olean. Your place is here with your family. I'm married now and we're starting over, so dry your tears and get over it. I don't want to hear any whining."

She had lied to me and tricked me into coming for Georgia's birthday, and I knew it.

I sat on the front porch listening to the *bang, bang, bang* as coal was loaded into large trucks and driven down the dusty, trash-filled street. My heart numbed as I realized that Mother had complete power over my life and there was nothing I could do. Food tasted like cardboard to me; I had no appetite and I lost quite a bit of weight. Daddaw would kid me and say, "Anna, if you wore a white dress and drank a glass of tomato juice, we could use you as a thermometer." The family thought that was hilarious, but it only reminded me of how Mrs. T had dedicated herself to helping me gain weight.

Now I knew for sure that I could not trust Mother. I overheard Mammy telling her in the kitchen, "Anna's crying because she's a spoiled brat. All she cares about is ol' Mrs. Thompson's money and what the ol' lady can give her. She never should have been given a bike, much less been allowed to ride a horse and take lessons. Who does she think she is? Little Miss Rich B...? She shouldn't have anything that Georgia can't have."

I was right back where I had started. I knew she would never understand my love for Mrs. T and what it felt like, to me, to be loved and cared for by her, so I didn't even try to explain.

Every other Saturday, I rode the bus uptown to go home with Daddy after he got off from work. Sometimes Georgia went with me and Daddy gave us money for lunch and a movie. Afterward, she rode the bus back to Mammy's while I went home with Daddy. I was twelve years old by then. Mammy seemed to enjoy getting me alone by walking me to the bus stop so that she could tell me her little secrets that, for some reason, she wanted me to know.

One Saturday, out of the blue, she scowled at me, chuckled, and said, "You know, Anna, I'll declare, you were the ugliest baby I ever did see. You were born with black hair. It all fell out and your white hair grew in. I'd never seen anything like that. Poor Caroline! She went through such depression when you girls were babies that she left you in your crib one time and locked up the apartment while she went downtown and tried to jump off the Memphis Bridge."

I didn't want to hear any more, so I tried to change the subject. But she continued to spew her toxic information.

"Lucky for you that I had Georgia that day. When the police finally brought Caroline to my house, we began to wonder where you were. When we got there, you had been in the apartment for two days alone in your crib, hungry and screaming your head off. You were a mess to look at by then. Poor Caroline has sure had a hard time of it."

* * *

Keep paddlin'. Something will turn up.
-Mrs. T

Mrs. T often wrote to me. She even shipped my bike to Memphis. One day I asked Georgia, "Why are the envelopes to my letters all wrinkly around the glue part?"

She looked at it closely and said, "Oh, that's just Mammy. She steams open everybody's mail, reads it, and tries to glue it back together so they won't know it's been opened."

"That explains why some of my letters from Mrs. T don't make sense," I said. "She refers to something she must have mentioned in a previous letter that I never got. I guess Mammy is picking out only what she wants me to read."

I felt so violated. Now I knew that not only could I not trust Mother, but I couldn't trust Mammy either.

The summer ended and school started. After doing homework at Mammy's, Georgia and I would sneak a radio into the front bedroom, close the door, and tune in to a black music station. They played blues, soul, and spirituals—what eventually came together to create rock 'n roll. The beat was funky, and we kept listening because of the great rhythms. If only we could hear that kind of music on the white stations...but that was not to be until much later.

Mother had some secret music records which she played on Saturday mornings while we cleaned house. Some of the lyrics were dirty but she didn't know we figured out what they meant. To this day, I sometimes remember those songs and wonder why she would play them around little kids.

Unbeknownst to us at the time, a poor white guy in Tupelo Mississippi, the son of sharecroppers, was slipping into the back of an all-black Assembly of God church. Their music touched something in him, just as it had touched us. He and his parents moved to Memphis and into the projects, Lauderdale Courts, shortly after Mother, Georgia, and I moved to Olean. Across the street from Lauderdale Courts, he could hear more of the same music in that black community and began to play in his own style. The breakthrough into white stations wouldn't happen for several years, until the kid found a manager and got his records on the radio stations. He brought that style to the white world and changed the music industry forever. I'm talking about Elvis Presley, of course.

Within a few months, Mother, Roger, Georgia, and I moved to a small town an hour from Memphis, where my stepfather thought he could get work with his father. Most weekend nights Mother and her new husband continued to go out drinking, then coming back to our apartment and yelling at each other.

I asked Mother why we weren't invited to visit his parents' house more often. She said, "They're disappointed that Roger married me, a divorcee with two kids in tow, instead of his high school sweetheart that they loved."

Mother hated the little town and her in-laws, so the four of us moved back to Memphis. They rented a one-bedroom apartment over the corner drugstore down the block from Mammy's because the rent was cheap, and Mammy could keep an eye on us.

The dingy and dark building was across the street from the Southern Bell Bar, where they continued their drinking most evenings before they'd come back and argue.

They slept in the one bedroom with the door shut. We heard thumps in the night and lamps crashing to the floor. We didn't know if he had hit her or if she was hurt. I would wake up and get that stab of pain in my chest that was becoming so familiar again.

One morning, I asked Georgia, "How can they afford to go out drinking so many nights when he is out of work and they have so little money?"

"They can't," Georgia said, "they just do it anyway." She rolled her eyes as if she'd given up on them.

They found an old couch on someone's curb, tore the back and seat in half, and used that as a bunk bed for Georgia and me. Our bed was shoved against a closed door off the closet-sized kitchen that led to the hall. We couldn't see across the room because of the cigarette smoke, but at night, from my top bunk, I could open the window over the door and let in some air. Sometimes, I'd see homeless men sleeping in the hall. In addition to the smoke, the apartment reeked of stale beer and whiskey. After school, because we were ashamed of where we lived, Georgia and I would try to slip into the stairway over the drugstore unnoticed so no one from school would see us and know we lived there.

When we all had dinner at Mammy's, Georgia and I, even back when we were small, stood on chairs to wash and dry the dishes. We'd sing as we worked.

"Anna, sing the out of tune part," Georgia said, meaning the harmony that I could make up by ear. Some of our favorites were "Sentimental Journey," "Blue Skies," "Side by Side," and "Sunny Side of the Street." Singing was a great escape for us.

When we were older, we laughed at her calling my harmony the "out of tune part." Actually, we sang quite well together. She had a rich alto voice and I a soprano. I think we could have done something with our music had we been given the chance.

I even loved memorizing jingles from the radio. I learned most of the lyrics to what we now call the old standards, such as "September Song." At least I could thank Mother for sometimes having big band music playing. She had lots of records, including the best of Glenn Miller, Tommy Dorsey, Duke Ellington,

Frankie Carle, the Andrew Sisters, and the young Frank Sinatra. I had no idea what an important part of my life music would play in the future.

Nor did I realize that Roger would eventually turn his anger on us.

CHAPTER 8

FUDGE

*Sometimes God lets us hit rock bottom so we know He's
the rock at the bottom.*
- Dr. Tony Evans

A FTER SCHOOL EACH DAY, Georgia and I stayed in the cramped upstairs apartment over the drugstore. Uncle Larry's daughter, our cousin Shirley, rented the apartment next door—the same cousin who babysat us when we lived in the projects. Shirley, still just a teenager herself, was now married. She had a baby and her husband was in jail.

One Saturday night, while Mother and Roger were out drinking, Georgia and I went to Shirley's apartment to be with her and the baby.

Before they left, our stepfather hollered at us, "I'd better not catch you three making fudge again while we're out. We're on a tight budget and you're wasting my sugar. Do you understand me?"

Since we were used to his yelling, we didn't pay much attention.

After he left, Shirley said, "If they can spend money on booze and cigarettes, why can't we make fudge? We're using my sugar anyway. He's always howling that we don't show respect, but I think that respect is supposed to be earned. You don't get it by hollering at people."

Bored and alone, we three girls...well, we made fudge. You could smell it all over the second floor.

Roger came home, all six-foot-four of him, his usual Saturday-night-drunk self, roaring like a caged lion, slamming the door as he and Mother arrived.

Mother disappeared and went to bed.

Not him. Without knocking, he kicked open Shirley's door and bellowed, "I thought I told you girls not to make fudge anymore. I'll teach you to respect what I say."

Staggering, he shoved his way into the tiny kitchen. As he hollered, he yanked open a drawer. I saw the gleam of the shiny big butcher knife as he pulled it out. I froze in horror.

The next thing I knew, Shirley, with her baby in her arms, Georgia, and I were running out the door, tripping over each other, speeding down the fire escape in the back of the building and racing towards Mammy's house. Five feet behind us, waving the huge knife over his head, Roger screamed, "I'll teach you bitches a lesson you won't forget."

When we got to Mammy's porch he turned and ran away. We burst into her house, a tornado of terror, and the whole story tumbled out of our mouths. She sighed and said, "I'm not surprised. I've seen his temper before." We spent the night at Mammy's, staying until it was time for school Monday morning.

But I couldn't sleep, reliving the terrifying scene over and over in my mind. *He could have killed us. What if we hadn't had Mammy's house to run to? How could we live like this? What could I do? How could I get away? Where would I go?*

After school, I knew that I could never go back to the apartment, and I was afraid to go to Mammy's because Roger would know where I was. *If he found me, would he kill me?*

On a cold, rainy, winter afternoon, I decided that I had to run away. I reasoned that I couldn't tell Georgia because she'd try to talk me out of it. I didn't know where to go, but I knew I couldn't go home to any of them. Because it was dark and I was already in trouble for coming home late from school anyway, I hid in the alley behind Mammy's house, trying to figure out what to do. I didn't have any money to go to a phone booth and call Daddy. And, well, maybe he'd be mad at me too. *All for making fudge.*

Far into the night, I huddled behind garbage cans, shivering and wet, until I saw a drunken man stagger past. I was so scared, so cold, and so hungry, that I finally decided I had to go to Mammy's after all.

"Where have you been?" she yelled. "Who do you think you are, scaring the hell out of us? Youngin', I declare, I ought to snatch you bald for pullin' such a stunt. Sometimes, I don't think you have a brain in your head."

Mother was there, too, and gave me a hefty slap across the face for coming home from school so late. Mammy had told her about the butcher knife incident, but that didn't seem to make any difference to her.

I went to bed confused and humiliated because I couldn't figure out how to get along with any of them: Mother, Roger, or Mammy. Georgia couldn't protect me anymore; this was beyond her abilities. I felt that I was all alone, floating out to sea on an iceberg.

I pleaded with God, "Please get me out of here." I had no answers and I thought He was my only hope.

Fortunately, a few days after Mother heard about the knife incident, she and Roger separated, and she filed for divorce.

Before long, it was Christmas again. The three of us still had the apartment over the drugstore. On Christmas morning, Mother dressed up and said, "I have to go out for a while. You kids stay here until I get back. We'll open the gifts then." We waited for her all day. Georgia tried to make the day fun. We had a furry ball that had fallen off the end of a winter cap. We stood on each side of their bed and batted it back and forth for hours, keeping score. As the day slipped into darkness, we ate bologna and mustard sandwiches. It was the longest and loneliest Christmas we ever had.

Late, after we went to bed, Mother returned smelling of liquor. But she seemed happy.

She gave no explanation of where she had been.

I tried not to think about the happy Christmas times in Olean. *Why did Mother want me here?* She had no time for me and obviously didn't care.

A few weeks later, we three moved back in with Mammy. Once more, there were six of us in the one-bathroom house.

That June, I graduated from the eighth grade. It was the only time Mother ever came to my school. She made her entrance in stiletto heels, dressed in a slinky, tight black dress with slits in the long black sleeves.

Some of the other kids said, "Wow! Your mother looks like a movie star. She's beautiful." But I was embarrassed. I wanted her to look like the other mothers in nice, flowered 1950s pastel dresses with sensible shoes.

Georgia seemed to know how to get along with her. The difference between us was that I had no desire to please Mother. Whatever she or her family stood for, I would stand for the opposite. I had already seen that there was another way to live, and I thought Mother was throwing away her life, along with ours, on a lifestyle that was destructive.

If only I could get away from her! That's all I wanted. I didn't fit in. To her, I probably seemed like a boring loser, in a way that set her temper on fire. Sometimes I dared to express a different opinion from hers. When she didn't spank me for it, she took to giving me a good wallop across my face, leaving a red mark that lasted for hours. Worse than the mark on my face, though, was the hurt in my heart. *How could she love me and treat me that way?*

I thought a lot about my feelings toward her. Although I disapproved of her, I did not hate her. I was afraid of her because I never knew what to expect next. *Was it wrong of me to want to get away from her?*

One hot summer day, I walked in on Georgia and two of her girlfriends.

"What are you doing?" I asked. She was only fourteen and they were all smoking. I couldn't believe it. *Why would they do it and where did they get money to buy cigarettes?* As smoke poured out of their noses, they giggled, thinking that they were cool. I had never wanted to do the same, since Daddy told me what a struggle it was for him to kick the habit. I respected him for that. Plus, since none of the Thompson family smoked, it wasn't attractive to me.

I was twelve when I began again to wonder, *Who am I, anyway?* Mrs. T had said that I was a sweet kid with beautiful, golden hair; talented, bright, and a delight to be with. How could I also be a mean, ugly, stubborn, stupid, albino-like kid, and a whole lot of trouble? Georgia loved me. Daddy loved me. John and Mrs. T and her friends loved me. But, evidently, Mother didn't. Whatever confidence I had developed while living in Olean was fast disappearing.

On one of my trips to the bus stop with Mammy, out of nowhere she blurted, "Your mother needs a man in her life. No woman can make it, money-wise, without a man. Your mom married Georgia's dad when she was sixteen and he was twenty-eight. He went into the army and never came back to her. A year after she divorced him, she married your daddy and had you. Then she had a hysterectomy and that was a very serious surgery. Then she had a nervous breakdown."

"I didn't know that," I said. "How sad. What's a nervous breakdown?" As she explained, I began to see why Mother was unable to be a loving mother like Mrs. T. Maybe that's why Mammy told me the story, to help me understand.

But while Mother didn't want me, she didn't want anyone else to have me either. I began to think that kids who were adopted were the lucky ones. I started to like the whole idea. If only

Mrs. T could have adopted me...but I knew neither of my parents would ever have allowed that.

As I thought about Mother's past, I knew that what Mrs. T had told me was true: I would have to make something of my life so that I'd never be dependent on anyone. But I needed to be with someone *now* who really cared about me and could help me. That one person was Mrs. T. *If only I could get back to her.*

I did not understand it at the time, but God was hearing my prayers, and there was hope for a better life for me, if I could endure long enough to get to it.

CHAPTER 9

FAMILY FEUDS

A diamond is a chunk of coal that made good under pressure.
- Henry Kissinger

I LIVED WITH MOTHER FOR THREE YEARS, from ages eleven to thirteen. When I was ten years old, Daddy married Virginia, a sweet, friendly, Christian lady he met at Fisher Aircraft during World War II. He had been her supervisor as she bolted planes together—a real "Rosie the Riveter" (although she hated that nickname).

I liked her immediately because she was kind to me. She and Daddy had agreed before they married that if they ever had the chance, they'd love to have me with them full-time. They rented a one-bedroom duplex in East Memphis, a safer, newer side of town. When I went to stay with them every other weekend, Virginia and I spent hours in the kitchen talking and laughing while we did the dishes. I noticed that she never asked about Mother, nor did she ever say an unkind word about her.

Soon Daddy and Virginia had two adorable little girls, Liz and Lynn. I called them my baby sisters, even though we were half-sisters. I loved them from the first glimpse and, even though I was only with them every other weekend, I was thrilled at last to be part of an intact, loving family. Daddy and Virginia were happy without all the drinking and smoking that I saw at Mammy's.

I counted the days until I could be with them and I welcomed sleeping on the fold-out couch in their living room.

Daddy and his new family attended a little storefront church on the corner of Poplar Avenue. In future years, a much larger brick church was built across from East High School, and Daddy became their choir director and did violin solos for the offertory. I was proud of him.

It pleased me that he was never ashamed to introduce me to their church friends. After all, I was a child from a previous marriage and my clothes were pretty shabby at a time when most people dressed up for Sunday mornings. In cold weather, I wore Georgia's shiny, dirty Southside High School jacket to their church, until Virginia loaned me one of her coats that was two sizes too big. It must have irritated Daddy to see me come so poorly dressed because he was giving Mother support money, which I never saw. Nonetheless, Daddy was proud of me.

Every Tuesday, on his day off, Daddy had a maid named Lorraine babysit the little girls while he and Virginia played golf. Daddy taught Virginia how to play and she became a great golfer. I admired how smart she was to take an interest in her husband's hobby and be with him; I hadn't forgotten that Mother wanted to divorce him over golf. In later years, Daddy and Virginia acquired lifetime tickets to the Masters in Augusta, Georgia and also played in the Senior Olympics, winning many gold medals.

On a Saturday afternoon, during one of my visits, Virginia was on the telephone talking to a friend, explaining how much they loved Lorraine.

"Yes," she said, "she's a sweet Negro lady who not only watches the girls but does some cleaning and ironing, too."

When she hung up the phone, three-year-old Liz said, "Mommy, what's a Negro?"

"That's a person with dark skin."

Liz was deep in thought for several minutes as she went back to play with her doll.

"Mommy, she asked, "is Lorraine a Negro?"

Virginia answered, "Yes," and Liz went back to play again.

It pleased me that skin color made no difference to this little girl. In fact, it had never occurred to her that it would matter at all. After the cruel treatment I'd seen on the buses, my heart was warmed. My family treated Lorraine respectfully and usually sent her home with extra food for her family. *That's the way it's supposed to be*, I thought.

When I saw Negroes crowded together in the back of the bus, even when there were empty seats up front, I was confused; I had not seen anything like that in Olean. I became distressed about it. Often, I'd turn my face toward the bus window so no one could see me tear up. They were outcasts, not accepted by society. Just like me. I hated that. I knew what it felt like because that's how I felt in my mother's family.

Seeing how these Negroes endured humiliation and adversity that they could do nothing about convinced me that if they could survive their hardships, maybe I could somehow learn to handle mine.

So, I decided that if I had to live with Mother, I would *keep my chin up,* as Mrs. T always advised in her letters. I knew that I had to try harder to fit in with Mother's family if this was where I was forced to be.

I made friends with Suzy, a girl on our street who was a year older than me. She loved to tell me stories of sexy things she was doing in the dry bayou with boys, but I didn't understand what she meant. First of all, I didn't know anything about sex; secondly, I thought she was making it up because, well, she was known as a bit of a loudmouth anyway. I only knew that she was very popular with the boys.

When no one was looking, Suzy was also good at stealing makeup at the drugstore. I let her talk me into trying to steal, too.

"Anna, you can do this. Think how cool it would be to have some makeup," she said.

When I finally stole a beautiful pink handkerchief, I was ter-rified for weeks that the police would show up at our door at any moment and take me to jail. I couldn't blame Suzy because it was my decision. *I could end up in prison like Uncle Larry had. Is this how I want to live? I need to get out of this neighborhood.*

I thought I'd learned my lesson about crime. But no. One Saturday morning when Georgia, Shirley, and I were home alone, boredom trumped intelligence and an attack of stupidity took over. We three loved sharing secrets. Why not try something re-ally daring and see if we could get away with it?

"I know what we can do," Shirley said. "The school is locked up for the weekend. Let's sneak up the fire escape, pry a window open, and steal the school bell."

We laughed. Georgia said, "Ha! Imagine how surprised the principal would be when he goes to ring the bell for the start of school and at lunch time. It would serve him right for being so strict."

"We need you, Anna," Shirley said. "You're small enough to crawl through the window if we can get it open."

Oh, goodie! The big girls need me, and I want to be included on the heist.

We three thieves strolled nonchalantly to the vacant school ground in broad daylight. *I'm not scared. I can handle this.* We climbed the fire escape to the second floor. Shirley pried open the huge metal grate covering the window and pushed it open while Georgia kept watch for the janitor. Shirley helped me squeeze through the window. I ran through the dark halls to the downstairs office where the large bell was. I took the bell and back I flew, on fire with adrenaline. I crawled out the window as Shirley hid the bell in her jacket. At home, we huddled in the front bedroom, whispering.

"It was so worth it!" Shirley laughed. "Those teachers think they're so smart. They'll never figure this one out."

"And we'll be the only ones who know," Georgia added. "They won't even be able to start school for the day. That works for me."

"I can't wait to see the look on my teacher's face," I said.

Every time we thought about how clever we were, we co-conspirators giggled.

But as Sunday night approached, our laughter became more forced. A knot was forming in my stomach and I began to dread the next morning.

At bedtime, Georgia said, "What have we done?"

"Yeah. It's my school," I said. "We could go to prison for this. We broke in and that's called burglary. What if somebody from one of the houses across the street saw us? Sooner or later someone will find out for sure."

After a long pause, Georgia said, "We have to take it back."

Late that night, after the family went to bed, we snuck out of the house under the cover of darkness and stealthily returned to the scene of the crime.

Trembling with fear that someone would see our flashlight, we climbed the fire escape, pried open the heavy grate, and thanked God that the window was still unlocked. Shirley stuffed me and the evidence over the windowsill.

Oh, no. I hadn't realized how dark it would be inside. I tried to find my way alone, in complete blackness, down to the principal's office on the first floor while Georgia and Shirley stood lookout. *What was I thinking?* I tried to hurry. Halfway down the hall, I realized there wasn't enough time to run back and get the flashlight, even though I was afraid of the dark.

At night, the school was a different place. *Were there creepy people, or even ghosts, hiding in each of those empty classrooms that I had to pass? What if someone saw Shirley and Georgia? Would they run and leave me stuck?*

Scared to death, I slunk through the halls as quickly as I could, sometimes having to feel my way along the walls.

I placed the bell on the counter exactly where it had been before, wiping it down with my shirt so there would be no fingerprints, as Shirley had insisted.

Finally, I crawled back out the window. Shirley and Georgia secured the grate. We didn't see any cop cars or hear any sirens.

Our life of crime ended as quickly as it had begun.

Walking home, Georgia said, "Hey, guys, this is not the path we want to go down. It's not worth it." Shirley and I agreed. Finally, fear and intelligence trumped boredom, and we were relieved to be bored once again.

Georgia and I did manage to have some fun on hot summer nights, under the streetlamp, in front of the coal yard, playing games with the neighborhood kids. I loved Kick the Can, Hide and Seek, and my favorite, Red Rover. Whichever team Georgia was on, she always included me. I just wanted to be included, no matter what, but Georgia was the star of Trigg Avenue. The boys pounded on our door during the day, begging her to play baseball on their team, because, with no effort at all, she could hit a home run over the coal yard fence. Many years later, her son played for the Chicago Cubs.

But the family athleticism stopped with her. If only I could've been like her, with her golden tan and her natural talent in sports—but I didn't want to have a relationship with objects that flew through the air.

Years later, as an adult, a therapist asked me, "What is your earliest recollection of feeling anything like courage or determination?" I thought immediately of the Red Rover game. The way it worked was that two teams, each in a line, faced each other several yards apart, with their arms tightly linked. One person would yell out, "Red Rover, Red Rover, send Johnny right over." Johnny would run from his line and try to crash through the other line. I didn't care if the other team member broke my arm as he tried to barrel through; no matter what, they weren't getting past me. I remember the pain of holding solid as the bigger kids thundered into us. Proud when my arms ached, I thought I was finally getting tougher and becoming able to hold my own.

"What do you think is the difference between stubbornness and courage?" the therapist asked. "You said your mom thought you were stubborn."

That stopped me for a moment.

"Stubbornness," I said, "can help you stand your ground but can be a negative, too. I would not have survived those difficult years if I hadn't been stubborn. Only recently did I realize the flip side of that coin is perseverance and courage."

She continued taking notes as I spoke.

"I thought if you're scared, that's not courage. Wrong. Courage is being scared but doing the right thing anyway—pushing through the fear. I've had my tears, but I learned from Mrs. T to dry them, pull up my socks, keep my chin up, and lean into the job to be done."

In those childhood years, in my mind, I could still hear Mrs. T saying, *Annie, you have to paddle your own canoe.* I knew she was right, and even though she was not there to remind me, her ideas were permanently engraved on my heart. I trusted the way she lived—and, somehow, I would live that way too. But, finally, I could see that if I were to survive emotionally, I had to find a way to make friends with my mother's family.

* * *

There is so much good in the worst of us, and so much
bad in the best of us, that it hardly behooves any of us
to talk about the rest of us.
- Edward Wallis Hoch

My love of music came from both sides of the family. Any fun times at Mammy's house always included music. Mammy was a flapper in her youth in the 1920s and loved to dance. She taught Georgia and me the Charleston, the Fox Trot, and how to Jitterbug. Before Daddaw had his stroke, Mammy often held neighborhood Bunko and dance parties on Saturday nights while he was out driving a luxury train called the "City of New Orleans," down and back to Memphis.

Most of the time, Mother wasn't there. Mammy was slender and cute, even at her age, with gray, naturally curly hair. And even though she was the neighborhood gossip, after a little whisky or beer, she was the life of the party. She danced a thing called the Shimmy. I was embarrassed when she did it because she would lean back and shake her breasts in the face of whoever danced with her. An uninhibited grandma, she was full of fun and dirty jokes, swore like a longshoreman, and always had a cigarette hanging out of the corner of her mouth.

Her love-hate relationship with Negroes was confusing. While on the one hand, she would use the n-word, she'd also send me around the block with food for her Negro neighbor who lived over the back fence.

Even though Georgia was the darling of Mammy, Daddaw, Uncle Dan, and Uncle Larry, I tried to find a way to make friends with Mammy. I think she felt sorry for me, since, by her standards, I was an ugly duckling, and she could see that Mother didn't like me.

An old, out of tune, upright piano with yellowed keys stood in a corner of the crowded living room, beckoning me to play. When Mammy came home from the women's railroad lodge meetings humming "Alexander's Ragtime Band," "Nola," "Glow Worm," "12th Street Rag," or "The Entertainer," I could easily pick them out on the piano, because Daddy had taught me the magic of chords. I also picked out "In the Mood," my favorite.

Mammy would say, "Now, Anna Jane," (my new nickname) "if you'll play the piano for me, I'll do the dishes for you." So naturally, I was all over that piano every time it came time to do dishes. I began to call her Mammy Jane, a term of endearment.

I saw all that she had to put up with, and she was so good to my Georgia, that I couldn't help but love her for it. She worried about money all the time. Who could blame her, having lived through the Great Depression and having so many of us depending on her now?

What a good soul she was underneath her swearing and backbiting. After all, she had taken us in, again, into their small two-bedroom house, cooked for all of us, and taken care of Daddaw who was bedridden after his stroke. That's a lot for anyone.

I asked Georgia one night as we got ready for bed, "When is Uncle Dan coming home from the war?"

"Any time now," she said. "We haven't heard from him for months and we are all really scared."

"Oh, I didn't know that," I said.

"Yeah, every morning Mammy searches the missing in action list in the paper, looking for his name. Uncle Dan was their baby, born ten years after Larry and Mother. I figure that Mammy and Daddaw had finally learned how to raise a kid right by the time they had him."

"I can see that," I said. "He's so sweet, and funny—always trying to calm everyone down." Uncle Dan was cute, long and lanky with curly black hair, like Mother and Mammy. When we were small, Georgia and I adored him, enjoying his dry, mischievous sense of humor as he kept us giggling all the time.

When Uncle Dan finally came home, he arrived with a pretty, blonde, seventeen-year-old wife from Belgium named Miah, who spoke very little English. When he was out on the road driving trains, Miah was left to fend for herself, a lamb among wolves. The adults in the family delighted in teaching her swear words, which she didn't understand, to the hilarious entertainment of the entire family. I didn't think that was funny, and it served as yet another reminder that I just didn't fit in with any of them.

How often I heard Mammy say, "Anna is too much like her father."

Mammy had her dark side, though. One hot summer day, Georgia and I rescued a stray Airedale dog that we found under the house, matted and starving. We named him Buster and sneaked him food and cleaned him up without Mammy knowing, since she hated dogs and didn't want any spare food given to him.

Eventually, she found Buster and was angry with us. Daddaw, on the other hand, when he would give us money to buy an ice cream cone down at the corner drugstore, would slip us an extra nickel to get one for Buster, too. That made Mammy even madder. One day Buster disappeared. Georgia and I found his body in the back alley. Our elderly next-door neighbor, who watched everything on our street from her back window as she sat in her wheelchair, called Georgia and me over to her house.

"Girls, I'm sorry to tell you," she said, "but I think you should know I saw your grandmother feeding Buster something in the back alley. I think it was rat poison." He was the only pet Georgia ever had, and we were both devastated.

Mammy, in her spare time, liked to read her scrapbook of newspaper clippings of gory murders and crimes. She followed every case, reciting each vicious detail to us. For me, that seemed way too weird. The rest of the family accepted it as what she did for a hobby.

I finally decided that, even though it was hard at the time, not being like this family was a good idea. I gave myself permission to not feel guilty about being different from them. After all, somehow, I knew I didn't have to be like them and could be almost anything if I ever got the chance. If Mrs. T said it was so, I still believed it must be true.

My best plan to get along in this family was to keep my head down and keep my mouth shut. As Mrs. T had often said, "The least said, the soonest mended." To me that meant keeping my opinions to myself and realizing that there were areas of my family's lifestyle I would never agree with. They certainly weren't going to change, and I wasn't going to either, so it was best to let it go and say nothing.

Who says you can't learn from a bad example?

* * *

Courage is fear that says its prayers.
- Anonymous Vietnam vet

The day my bike arrived in the mail, courtesy of Mrs. T, was the day I gained a little freedom. I couldn't thank her enough. She had no way of knowing that, during those three years I was with Mother, the bike was my release to escape the dirty, trash-filled streets of Trigg Avenue, at least for a few hours. I'd peddle away for miles, to a better section of town that had pretty homes and green lawns, then turn around and ride back. It seemed that no one even noticed I was gone.

Mrs. T also mailed my violin to me. In seventh and eighth grade, I played in the small middle school orchestra. However, two of the neighborhood bullies, Doreen and Debra, walked home from school in the same direction that I did. They teased me every day about my violin. Each time, they got a little meaner.

"Look at her. White as a sheet. How ugly. Why don't you play your violin for us, four-eyes? Huh? Huh?"

I tried to avoid them, but somehow they always found me. I didn't tell Mother about them because, when I'd practice in the back bedroom, I often heard her and the family in the front room, cracking jokes about my squeaky playing. Yet if company came, she'd drag me out to make me play for them. That confused me. *Should I be ashamed of my playing or not?* When I went to Daddy's house every other weekend, he said I was playing well.

For weeks Doreen and Debra teased me as they followed me home. But one day they got more aggressive.

"Come on, stupid. Play your violin for us," they chanted over and over.

This time, they shoved me, causing me to stumble on the cracked sidewalk as I tried to get away. My glasses fell off and I couldn't see well. They thought that was funny and laughed.

"Poor old four-eyes. How can you see to play your violin for us now? Ha-ha-ha."

Something snapped inside. I turned and slugged Doreen on the arm with my violin case. They both ran away. Thank the Lord the case was hard, or the violin would have been broken.

After work, when Mother arrived at Mammy's, she called me into the kitchen where she had gathered Uncle Larry, Mammy, and Georgia.

"What have you done, Anna? Doreen's mother called Mammy and said you picked a fight with Doreen and Debra. You know you're not to fight with anyone. What kind of animal are you?"

"But Mother I didn't..."

"Shut up. Don't talk back to me. Who do you think you are embarrassing me like that? I'll teach you a lesson you won't forget, young lady. Come over here and bend over my knee and get your spanking."

To be spanked at this age, in the eighth grade, in front of the whole family was humiliating. I just wanted this all to end, so I bent down over her lap. She pulled my dress up in full view of everyone and began to pound on me. I decided that I would not give her the satisfaction of making me cry. The harder she hit me, the more determined I became not to cry. Finally, she stopped. I escaped to the back porch, where I sat shaking in anger that she was not interested in hearing my side of the story. Georgia sat with me. She didn't know what to say to comfort me, but I could tell she understood.

I heard Mother laughing in the kitchen and making jokes about the spanking. I think she was trying to prove to the family that she was good at discipline.

She said to the family, "Mammy is so right. Anna is too much like her dad—stubborn as an ox."

I decided that I wouldn't subject myself to any kind of embarrassment again, either from Doreen and Debra or the family. It wasn't worth it. I never played the violin again.

I won that day, in that Mother never spanked me again. Instead, from then on, if I displeased her, she'd slap me hard across the face, and then walk away.

Even though in some ways I felt like I went from victim to victor, I was afraid I had lost that link with my Daddy which was so dear to me. That weekend, I told him that I quit the violin because I had lost interest. With a sad look, he accepted it, even though he believed that music was in our genes.

More and more, I knew Mother did not want me. Sometimes she hardly spoke to us; she certainly didn't spend any time with either Georgia or me. But she didn't want anyone else to have me, because it would make her look like a bad mother. I knew that Mrs. T loved me and wanted me back. She was my real mother. It had nothing to do with blood lines. The more I realized this, the more I ached to get back to her.

How could things get any worse where I was?

CHAPTER 10

TURMOIL

To everything there is a season, and a time for every
purpose under heaven.
- Ecclesiastes 3:1

ONE HOT, HUMID SUMMER DAY, Uncle Larry brought a friend home from work. Tom was a machinist from the country, with little education, but a sweet guy and very handsome. Mother liked that he was younger than she was, since she looked younger and lied about her age, anyway. Staying young one way or another was part of her Scarlett O'Hara syndrome. It wasn't long before they were married. They rented the house next door to Mammy's. Even though Tom had almost no interest in Georgia or me, at least he was kind. His whole world revolved around Mother and he thought that her movie star-style pouting, hissy fits, and temper tantrums were adorable.

A few weeks after I graduated from eighth grade, we all sat down for supper to Mammy's fried chicken and a mess of greens and grits. Suddenly, Mother announced, "Tom's been laid off because of cutbacks. But, guess what? Good news. The four of us are moving to California. He can get a better job as a machinist in Burbank at Lockheed Aircraft."

Because there had been no warning that this was coming— much less any discussion, at least in front of us—we all sat in stunned silence. Smiling and triumphant, Mother and Tom left the room to sit out on the front porch swing.

While Georgia and I did the dishes, she said, "I don't want to go to California. I want to stay here and finish high school with my friends."

"I don't want you to go, either," Mammy said as she put away the leftovers. "You both belong here." After a long silence, she whispered, "I have an idea."

She shut the kitchen door so no one could hear and said, "Anna, you can stop them from going."

"What? How?"

"Your mother can't take you out of the state without your daddy's permission and he won't give it to her. Just tell him you don't want to go and then tell her, and she won't leave. She'll never give you up 'cause she doesn't want your daddy to have you."

Aha, a brilliant plan. I certainly didn't want to move yet again. If changes had to be made, I wanted to go home to Olean and Mrs. T. How could I ever get back to her from California? Wow. Here was my chance to save Georgia from moving, and save myself, too.

Armed with that, and confident that for once I was in control of my life, I proudly said to Mother later that night, "Georgia and I don't want to go to California, so I'll just tell Daddy 'cause you can't take me out of state without his permission."

To my surprise, without missing a beat she said, "Fine. Good riddance. Go live with your father. But I'll take Georgia with me. Her dad and I have no legal agreement to keep her here." Georgia hadn't seen her own dad in years. Apparently, Mother had figured all of this out before.

Oh, no. This wasn't working out the way Mammy said. "Mother, please, don't take her," I said. "She wants to finish high school here with her friends." I was going into ninth grade and Georgia would be a junior in South Side High School.

"Shut up. We have to go. Don't you hear me? I said you can go live with your father. Good riddance. I'm leaving. We can start a new life out there. I wish you'd never been born, anyway."

Too crushed to say anything, I stood looking at her in silent disbelief. The idea of moving again was shocking enough, but the sting of being told she wished I had never been brought into this world hurt the most. I knew all along that I was a nuisance to her, but her cruel words of wishing I had never been conceived cut to my heart like a poisoned spear.

For years after that, I struggled to comprehend and make sense of why she said it, even though she might not have meant it. Sure, it was said in anger, but even if she didn't like me, I hadn't imagined that her feelings went so far as to wish I'd never been here at all.

Flaxon, a Tennessee Walker

How could I deal with this kind of rejection? Maybe, someday, I'd understand her better. Maybe then it wouldn't hurt so badly. God, where are you? Do you hear me? Do you care?

I remembered, again, Mrs. T's story about the two little frogs. *Somehow, I must paddle on.*

The next weekend Daddy picked me up. All my clothes fit into one grocery bag. Saying goodbye to Georgia was almost more than I could bear. The night before I left, we snuggled close together in bed for a long time and cried in each other's arms.

Within a week, Mother and Tom left for Burbank, where he got the job at Lockheed. Georgia begged to stay with Mammy so she could finish that school year at Southside, so, for the moment, she was left in Memphis. I had to admire Mammy and Daddaw for being willing to take care of Georgia again.

Later, in the middle of Georgia's senior year, Mother sent money for her to come to California. It broke her heart. Not wanting to go, Georgia spent the money on clothes, much to Mother's fury. So, she came and got her.

At Daddy's, the five of us lived in a one-bedroom, one-bath duplex. For the next two years—my ninth and tenth grades—I slept on a sofa bed in the living room. A piano was crammed into the corner, and again I took a few lessons. The little girls' two cribs were in the small bedroom with Daddy and his wife. Even though it was crowded, what mattered most was that they loved me and welcomed me.

Yet again the new kid at a new school, I noticed that most kids already had their circle of buddies. Even though I felt shy, I realized that I'd have to draw a circle that would include them if I was going to have friends. I invited two girls who were also new to go bike riding with me on Saturday mornings. Before long, I had made several friends at the new, beautiful East High School across the street from Daddy's church.

Whenever I could, I looked for opportunities to get out of the crowded duplex. Daddy gave me an allowance and my new best friend, red-haired Jeannie, and I started roller skating three evenings a week at the local rink. We took group lessons to learn how to dance on skates. As the months progressed, she and I became quite good at dancing tangos, waltzes, and fox trots. Virginia, staying up after the babies were asleep, even made me a skating skirt. Occasionally, Daddy would drop us off at the roller rink so we didn't have to transfer two buses, but he never once came in to watch me dance or showed any curiosity about my new hobby. He was either too busy with his own concerns or, perhaps, just not interested. That hurt. The comparison between him and Mrs. T's avid pleasure in anything I did was pitiful.

Daddy became frustrated with me as a teenager, especially if I was forgetful. One time I accidentally left my purse on the bus and lost my allowance for the week. He yelled at me, chewing me out about my carelessness. I went to bed feeling stupid and embarrassed. Later in the night, as I got up to go to the bathroom, I glanced through the cracked door into their bedroom off the hall, and saw him on his knees by their bed, praying. My heart went out to him and how difficult his life must be with me as an added responsibility.

One rainy day as he drove me to school, he awkwardly brought up the divorce from my mother. "Anna, I'm sorry things didn't work out between your mother and me. I know it's been hard for you. She, uh..." As I watched him struggle to apologize and try to explain without saying anything against Mother, I interrupted him.

"Daddy, you don't have to explain. I completely understand about Mother." We never discussed it again.

Mrs. T and I wrote often. In fact, that winter she flew to Memphis to meet with Daddy privately. She stayed in a hotel so she and Daddy could have several long talks. I only got to see her for one evening. I did not hear their exact conversations, but he told me later that she wanted to take me back to Olean and finish raising me. She knew that was what I had always wanted, and she thought that now that Mother was out of the state, he might consider it. But he said he wanted to have some time with me. That seemed ironic to me because, except for Sunday afternoons, I saw very little of him.

But if I couldn't live with Mrs. T, at least Daddy let me spend the summers after ninth and tenth grade (1952 and 1953) in Olean with her. Of course, she paid the air fare.

By the time I went back to Olean in the summer after ninth grade, my skating was really smooth. I loved it; no matter how many times I fell, I popped up and tried again.

"I'll take you skating at the rink that overlooks Cuba Lake," Mrs. T said. Cuba Lake was eighteen miles away, surrounded by beautiful summer homes.

When she saw me skate, she said, "Let's get you some custom skates that are more flexible, so you can make your turns and spins easier." She also paid for me to have private lessons. She even let me practice on her beautiful new linoleum floor in her big kitchen while I hung onto the table for support. Maria, her artistic neighbor, was appalled, pointing out that I would make scratches on the floor.

"Oh, I don't care about that," Mrs. T said, "as long as it will help Annie learn."

Maria often invited us to spend the day at their cottage on the lake and have dinner with her and her husband. These were not really cottages, but big, two-story homes that were fashionably furnished, surrounded by grassy lawns and beautiful boat docks. Most residents had speed boats, and even sail boats, too. Many of the wives and kids from local towns spent summers at the lake while the dads commuted back and forth to work for the week.

Maria remembered my mother well. One Sunday as we were enjoying lunch at her cottage, she smiled and said "Annie, you look so much like your mother."

I was horrified. "No, no, no. I don't look like my mother at all." Mrs. T and Maria exchanged knowing looks, as if realizing that I did not like my mother.

"I look like my daddy."

I really didn't look much like Daddy, either. The unspoken fact was, I looked a lot more like Mrs. T's son John—blonde, blue-eyed, and skinny. The rumor around town—which I was not aware of—was that I was his love child. Years later, when I heard that story, I did the math and it didn't add up. I was not his daughter.

Sometimes, I was invited to the cottage next door where Mary Jane, who was my age, and her family lived in the summer.

I remembered her from the riding stables where her mother and Mrs. T were friends.

I noticed that Mary Jane and her group had a lot of skills I didn't have. It seemed that they had had every advantage growing up: a mom and dad at home, regular lessons in music, swimming, riding, tennis, and golf, and they knew how to sail on the lake.

Lucky me, because they were all so friendly that they invited me along to go sailing, and even taught me some of the basics. Since they'd grown up together for the most part, I was new and different. They'd gather around just to hear me talk. My southern accent took me everywhere.

Though I could read music and play a lot of piano by ear, it wasn't at Mary Jane's level. She could easily whip out the heavy classics, such as Beethoven and Chopin, and had played seriously from the time she was small. Because of my disjointed living arrangements, my lessons had been picked up here and there. She was, however, an inspiration to me, and I made up my mind that I would play well someday, too. I had a sort of a young person's bucket list.

I admired all the kids and their determination, and how their families supported them. I wished I could live that way, too.

I learned that this group was taking college prep classes in high school—Latin, French, biology, chemistry, calculus, and trigonometry. Since I knew there was no money for me to go to college, I took business courses instead. Even if I could have stayed in Olean, there were no junior colleges that I could attend while living at home. That would have a big impact on my future.

During those two summers, Mrs. T and I continued horseback riding. She now boarded her horse, Minky, outside of town, at a beautiful farm called "Sunny Acres" that was owned by her friends, the Jones family. I was encouraged to ride Flaxen, their gorgeous bronze Tennessee Walker. We all got a kick out of the fact that her mane and tail matched my blonde hair. Riding a Tennessee Walker is like a dream—like floating in a rocking chair.

They also owned Lady, a beautiful, friendly Collie. We loved each other from the first lick. Lady was one of many dogs in my life whom I loved and in whom I confided so many of my secrets. Dogs were always there for me and I hardly ever met one I didn't love.

This farm had everything: horses, a huge riding ring, a dairy farm, and chickens. Mrs. Jones enjoyed showing me how to gather eggs from under the hens while the eggs were still warm, and I even had a turn riding on the tractor they used to harvest grain for the horses. *Maybe when I grew up, I could live on top of a hill nearby and raise Collies.*

CHAPTER 11

SPIRITUAL ROOTS

God moves in mysterious ways His wonders to
perform.
- William Cowper

ONCE AGAIN, WITH THE DELICIOUS soothing smell of burning leaves and the comfort of chilly nights, fall closed in around us. With a heavy heart, I flew back to Memphis for the school year. Though Daddy said he wanted me there, I didn't see him much. He bowled one or two nights a week, had choir rehearsal one weeknight, golfed as often as possible, and practiced his fiddle or trumpet many evenings when he was home. He also worked Saturdays at the music store, on top of putting in long hours all week selling pianos, organs, instruments and sheet music. With his positive, Dale Carnegie-approach to sales, he became their top salesman.

At least we all had Sunday dinner together. Daddy, so handsome and charismatic, dressed in a crisp white shirt and tie and always smelling great of Old Spice, was very popular as the choir director at our church and I was proud of him. Some of the choir ladies had crushes on him. I thought that was cute.

Maybe God's master plan for me, after all, was to live with them. Saturated with hymns and sermons, this was the rock on which I built my belief and my relationship with God.

My middle name is Faith, but I didn't think my own faith was strong enough to live up to the name. Finally, it dawned on me that perhaps the name would help me remember that faith would always get me through.

By then, I affectionately called my stepmother "Mama." I listened from my couch in the living room as she rocked little Lynn to sleep when she suffered from numerous ear infections. While she rocked, Mama sang the traditional hymns. I fell asleep hearing her singing "The Old Rugged Cross," "It Is Well with My Soul," "How Great Thou Art," and many more. I didn't know it then, but those treasured verses were preparing me for some important years and difficult decisions that were soon to come in my life.

Mama was the first married Christian woman I had ever been around. And her marriage to Daddy was the first happy union I'd ever been close enough to observe.

East Memphis was the best end of town, with many expensive new homes and estates, so there were lots of wealthy kids in our school. Some of the girls sported pricey cashmere sweaters and owned expensive makeup. By comparison, my school clothes were pretty plain, and I was still wearing Mama's short yellow winter coat—two sizes too big—that she loaned me on cold days.

But the focus of our social life was at Daddy's church. Sundays in Memphis, then as now, are real days of rest. As we arrived home after church, we would be welcomed by the tantalizing smell of roast beef wafting through the house, which Mama had placed in the pressure cooker earlier in the morning, along with carrots, potatoes, vegetables, and onions. She made the most delicious gravy in the whole world, and at the dressed-up dining room table set with beautiful Sunday dishes we ate ourselves into a coma. Daddy and I outdid each other, sopping up the gravy bowl with our treasured pumpernickel bread, a Latvian favorite, or drowning our bread with sour cream.

A happier person now than when I was a child, Daddy was so content with Mama and his girls that he blossomed, ever the talented entertainer with his fiddle and jokes. Seeing him glow made me smile; I thought he must have had many lonely years after my Mother divorced him.

Sunday afternoons, we'd take naps, often made cozy by a good rainstorm or cold weather. After the naps, we sometimes gathered round the piano to sing, usually in four-part harmony, switching parts just for fun as one of us played the piano and Daddy played his fiddle. They enjoyed people popping by on the spur of the moment, since Memphis at that time was small enough that folks could drop in without planning days ahead. Mama was the epitome of southern hospitality, with hugs for everyone. She adored Daddy, and he raved about her cooking.

Every single pie she ever made, he'd praise as if it were the first one he'd ever eaten. "Anna, can you believe this pie? What do you know about that? For cryin' out loud. Why, this is the best pie I've ever put in my mouth. Hot dog. Have some more." And I certainly did, and so did he. Then we'd snack before going to the evening service, called Training Union, where we memorized the Bible verses that, later in life, would come to mind just when I needed them. My favorite was Proverbs 3:5: "Trust in the Lord with all your heart and lean not on your own understanding. In all your ways acknowledge Him and He will direct your path."

After Training Union, we teens stayed for a "Sing." Boy, did we ever sing. Sometimes, afterward, the youth pastor for the high school would drive us over to the poor section of South Memphis (near Trigg Avenue), where we were allowed to sit in the balcony of a black church. Small and made of clapboard, the entire building would shake with their gospel music. The emotion of their singing was very moving to all of us as they shouted, "Amen, brother!" or, "Hallelujah. Preach it brother," or, "Can I hear a witness?"

Once I'd heard one of his recordings, I realized this was the same kind of music that Elvis had heard in Tupelo, Mississippi. We had both lived in the poor part of town where gospel music flourished in little churches in black neighborhoods, so I felt a kinship with him.

On New Year's Eve, the neighbors looked forward to Daddy, ever the prankster, standing in the middle of the street at midnight playing his trumpet to welcome the new year. Well, at least we hoped they looked forward to it.

In tenth grade I accepted Christ as my personal Savior. One Sunday morning, at a service with my friend Jeannie, we listened to the choir sing six verses of "Just as I Am." The words spoke right to my heart as I realized that God would accept me just as I was. I flew down the aisle, with Jeannie right behind me, and invited Christ into my life—at just the right time in my life. A huge weight lifted from my shoulders. Jeannie and I were baptized that same night.

I finally understood that I had a personal relationship with God.

That very day, my attitude about my life situation changed. I became more accepting of my mixed-up past and didn't question God so much as to why my life hadn't worked out the way I had hoped. Whatever plans He had for me, I understood that He'd give me the strength to live them. He had so far, and I believed I could trust Him with the rest. Life might not be what I wanted or expected it to be, but I decided that, as best I could, I'd leave it in His hands.

* * *

Prayer is not getting my will in heaven; it is getting God's will on earth.
- Greg Laurie

Though I still didn't know where my life was going, for the first time, I felt like I really knew who I was. I was learning to lean on Him. I became more grateful and thanked Him for bringing Mrs.

T into my life. Even if I didn't get to live with her year round, even if I wasn't well dressed, even if I had to move a lot, even though I missed Georgia and Mrs. T, even though I thought I wouldn't be able to go to college like lots of the wealthier kids, it didn't matter so much anymore because I knew that God loved me unconditionally and understood the whole, jumbled-up situation.

He was watching. And somewhere, somehow, God had a plan for me. So, I resigned myself to my circumstances, though I continued to pray, daily and in private, that I would find my way back to Mrs. T.

CHAPTER 12:

HOME

*"For I know the thoughts that I think toward you," says
the Lord, "thoughts of peace and not of evil, to give you
a future and a hope. Then you will call upon me and
go and pray to me, and I will listen to you. And you will
seek me and find me when you search for me with all
your heart."*
- Jeremiah 29:11-13

AFTER TENTH GRADE, I spent the summer in Olean
again. Mrs. T and I resumed our riding and trips to the
lake. But, once again, in August of 1953, we could smell
fall in the air as the leaves shimmered with gold, orange, yellow,
and purple. I loved the cold nights as the days grew shorter, but
my heart ached with the knowledge that, yet again, it was time
to pack up and leave. I dreaded going back to Memphis. One
Sunday after church, I went in my room, shut the door, cried
into my pillow, and prayed for a miracle.

Mrs. T noticed how quiet I was and asked, "Why are you looking so glum?"

I blurted out, "I don't want to go back to Daddy's. I love him
and Mama and the girls, but this is my home."

"Well," she said, "you are welcome to stay here and finish high
school. You know I've always wanted you here. If that's really
what you want, why don't you call your daddy and check it out
with him? If it's okay with him, it's fine with me."

Thrilled with the invitation, I called Daddy right away. "Daddy, please, please let me stay here and finish high school. Mrs. T has invited me, if only you will let me. I want to stay so badly, Daddy, please."

"Honey, Mama and I will pray about it," he said. "We'll talk it over and call you back tomorrow. Just be sure it's what you really want."

Of course, for half a lifetime, that was exactly what I had wanted, because I had never bonded with anyone the way I had with Mrs. T.

Oh boy, did I pray that night that they would agree to my staying. *But why would he let me stay when he had already refused Mrs. T when she came to Memphis a year ago and asked to raise me after Mother left? Maybe he saw that raising a teenager* and *a small family was more than he had bargained for.* At least, that's what I prayed he would think.

Daddy called back the next evening. "Honey, Mama and I have prayed about it and talked it over. It's okay with us if you stay as long as you're sure it's what you really want and that you'll be happy there."

"Oh, Daddy! I love you so much! Thank you, thank you, thank you!"

Yippee! I was amazed at how God had put it all together. I was home at last. *Thank you, God, for working a miracle for me, for hearing my prayers.* Daddy had said yes at just the right time, in accordance with God's perfect timing.

In Memphis we had memorized Psalm 37:4, "Delight yourself also in the Lord and He shall give you the desires of your heart." The desires of my heart? *Be still, my heart.* At last, I believed that my desire must have lined up with God's will after all, or He would not have allowed it to happen.

Ironically, Mother couldn't do a thing about the decision. I could see right away how brilliantly God had orchestrated the whole thing. He had been setting it up, step by step, from the moment Mother moved to California, where she no longer had any legal say in where I lived. Voila!

And here I had been, afraid that God wasn't hearing my prayers. But, all along, He was working behind the scenes to help me. On that very day I knew that He was listening, and my faith took a gigantic leap. Compassionate and merciful—all that I had read about Him was true.

At last, I felt completely at home. I reveled in being with Mrs. T, where I knew I was totally accepted. I could tell she really wanted me there and enjoyed my company. As much as I loved Daddy and his family, and even though they never said so, I knew I was in the way. I had felt awkward sleeping on the living room sofa those two years.

Even though I had no idea what lay ahead for me, I could hardly wait for school to start.

* * *

Make the least of all that goes, and the most of all that comes.
- Ruth Bell Graham

Roller skating at the lake would end in another month since the rink would close for the winter.

All summer, I had skated a lot with an attractive guy, Stuart, as Mrs. T watched from the railing. When he learned I'd be staying in Olean and going to high school there, he asked me for a date. He politely went to the side of the rink and asked Mrs. T if he could drive to Olean and take me out.

Wow. A real date. Someone wanted to take *me* out?

Mrs. T's protective instincts kicked in. *Who is he? What is his family like? Where is he from? What are his intentions? Could she trust him?*

When it came to background checks, the FBI had nothing on Mrs. T.

She burrowed into her investigation of Stuart in top form. After all, she reasoned, she was responsible for me now.

Happily, the owners of the rink were friends of hers and knew Stuart well. He was an honor student at Penn State with an engineering scholarship, clean-cut, athletic, and of course, from my point of view, cute, with blond curly hair. I was wildly flattered that he even noticed me. This was the kind of guy I could see myself with someday.

Varsity Cheerleading, Happy Days

A go-getter, Stuart didn't seem to have any hang-ups, like heavy drinking. Even though I was tickled to be asked out by such a classy guy and wanted to date him, it all seemed a little scary to me to know that he really liked me.

Mrs. T had the equivalent of a United Nations Security Council meeting with her sons, John and Paul, and their wives to discuss the possible, alleged date. The final decision was that it would be okay for Stuart to come to Olean and take me to a movie with the stipulation that I was to be home by eleven o'clock exactly, or else.

That was fine with me.

My rules with my girlfriends were already set (of course, we didn't tell the adults). We all agreed that you never kissed good night until the third date—if then—and only if you liked the guy a lot, the reasoning being that, well, you didn't want to be perceived as cheap. You wanted to see if he'd stick around or if he was just after your kisses.

On our third date, after Stuart had driven an hour over the hills from Bradford, Pennsylvania, to take me to pizza and a movie, we parked on the River Road—an absolute no-no. The River Road might even have—my imagination went wild because it was really dark and isolated—kidnappers hiding in the bushes like I'd seen in Memphis. That alone scared me to death, but even scarier was that I had never been kissed. He slipped across the seat, gently wrapped his arms around me, and gave me my first kiss. Terrified, I sat frozen, as stiff as a piece of dry ice. Poor guy! It must have been awkward for him. While it felt good to be held, it also seemed strange. I loved his attention, but a kiss wasn't *that* exciting. Was that all there was to it? I could do without it, although it sure felt sweet to be admired. Mrs. T wasn't big on hugs, having raised two boys, so I wasn't used to those anyway. My enjoyment of warm kisses would have to come later. Stuart and I dated a lot that August and early September, and I really liked him. But with school starting soon, time was running out on us.

After going out together for weeks, on our last date before he was to leave for college, we parked on the River Road again. We talked about the future and being apart the whole next year. Quietly, Stuart took his fraternity pin out of the glove compartment. "Annie, will you wait for me while I'm away at school?"

Flattered by his caring for me, I still knew that as much as I liked him, I was not in love. After all, I'd be going to Olean High School in just a few weeks, and I wanted to leave all my options open so that, hopefully, some of those good-looking guys I saw at the lake would have a chance to chase me down.

I chose my words carefully. "Stuart, I like you so much and you're such a great guy. Let me think about it and I'll write to you next week." I did write him, saying it was just too soon to be in a committed relationship and that we each needed to be free to date others that coming school year.

I didn't perceive any advantage to being tied down to one guy. Old enough by then to have a very definite opinion of men, but tarnished by what I had seen, I assumed that men were not to be trusted. The parade of men in my Mother's life had taught me, by example, that men, after you really got to know them, were usually a disappointment. They could bring chaos rather than comfort; they could be unpredictable, or even violent.

Best not to get too close to any of them. Flirting or dating could be fun, but I resolved I would never get involved in any kind of commitment.

No sir. Not me.

Predictably, as I dated during the following year, I found that after three months with any boy, the slightest flaw made me lose interest. I began to see the connection between Mother's disasters and my attitude toward boys.

I asked Mrs. T for advice. "What's wrong with me? I know no one's perfect. Will I ever have a real boyfriend? Will I ever trust a guy?"

"Oh, don't worry about it, Annie. You're just starting out in life. Someday, when you meet the right one, you'll like him, faults and all."

Jubilant with the news that I could live with Mrs. T and finish high school in Olean, we drove to Buffalo to shop for school clothes. I had only been in Olean for two summers since the fifth grade, so I thought I'd only know a few kids from the lake, Mary Jane, and a few of her friends when school started. Nervous about the first day of my junior year, I wondered if I would even be able to find them in the large, four-story high school building that covered an entire block. *Could I find my way around? Would the other kids be friendly and accept me with my strange accent? Would I have to eat lunch alone?*

In a kind gesture, Mary Jane's mother offered to pick me up on the first day of school so I could walk in with Mary Jane. She helped me find my locker, introduced me around, and invited me to sit with her friends at lunch. I felt at home right away and was forever grateful to her for such thoughtfulness.

What a difference it made to go to school well-dressed and after a good breakfast, compared to my years in Memphis with Mother. Most mornings, as I tried to decide which of my beautiful outfits to wear, Mrs. T would say, "My mother used to say, wear the only one you have, my dear," reminding me to be grateful, since some kids had so much less.

On September 10, 1953, shortly after I started eleventh grade, Mrs. T wrote this letter to Daddy:

> *Dear Friends,*
>
> *I am up at Paul's babysitting, so have time to let you know how Annie is doing in school. She is so happy. I just marvel at it sometimes. All the years she has spent in Olean have given her more friends than she remembered. In fact, some of them are kids who recognize her from first grade, years ago, and others she knows from the rink at Cuba Lake. I guess it was a surprise to her when she walked into school Tuesday morning, because it was like Old Home Week.*
>
> *Friday night she went to a school dance in the gym and had a wonderful time. A boy walked her home and they came in so happy—except they got caught in a rainstorm just before they got to the house, walking of course, as the boys can't drive after dark until they are eighteen. So, they bounded into the house all out of breath, quite wet but laughing so hard. I took the car out and took the boy home. It was a case of "I went home with Riley, and then Riley went home with me." Have let her have a few dates the last two weeks but am very careful who the boy is, and so far, it's been double dating.*

The boys are all crazy about her, she is so cute but doesn't seem to realize it, and they love to hear her southern accent. Her girlfriends have to take a back seat when she is in a crowd, but she is always quiet and ladylike.

Even though she is having a wonderful time, she talks about you all so often. I know she misses her little sisters and is always describing some cute things they used to do. She received your check for spending money and was happy to get it. Now that school has started, I am going to get tough and let her go out only on weekends, and I am trying to get across to her that I don't just go out and pick money off the trees.

It takes a lot to clothe her, what with school clothes, gym clothes, winter coats, etc.

I don't know what church she will go to, but she can be in the choir in either one if she wants to. I'll try to write if she doesn't, so you will know what she is doing.

Love to all,
Mrs. Thompson

I don't remember being as popular as she described, and I certainly never thought I was cute, but it's nice to know that somebody thought so. Perhaps the kids liked me because I was so different. Finally, in my life, *different* was acceptable. And since the other kids had mostly grown up together, I was a novelty. While I recognized some of them from earlier years, I didn't know them well except for Mary Jane and her friends. I also reconnected with Beth, my friend from first grade.

From day one, I was outrageously, indescribably, deliciously happy.

Mrs. T and I could drive the entire length of the town in only ten minutes. We'd joke about it being so small. "Now, Annie, would you rather be a big fish in a little pond, like Olean, or a little fish in a big pond, like Memphis?"

"Oh, by far, I'd rather be a big fish in a little pond." Though the population of Olean in the fifties was twenty-five thousand, it was still considered small in comparison to Memphis. But it was just right for me.

I was home at last.

It turned out that Mary Jane's friends were some of the most active girls in school. Right away they invited me to work out with them after classes to prepare to audition for Junior or Senior Varsity cheerleading.

I told Mrs. T about it. "That's a great idea," she said. "You can meet more kids that way and get in shape at the same time."

"Oh, no," I said. "I'm certainly not athletic enough for that. I think of myself as a washed-out skinny wimp."

"What are you talking about?" she said with a look of disbelief. "You can ride horses with the best of them and can even dance on skates. You're not afraid of anything, Annie. Remember the day, on a dare, when you actually stood up on Flaxon's back and rode around the ring?"

"But, I'm not like Georgia, who can slug a baseball over the fence."

"Annie, to be athletic, you don't have to be exactly like your sister. Go ahead and try out. Remember you can do anything if you work hard enough at it."

She was right of course, and I was so flattered to be invited by the other girls that I decided to go for it. Boy, did we work. Every day for weeks, after school in the gym until 6:00 p.m., and even some evenings after dinner, we'd warm up by walking all the way around the basketball court doing knee squats, and then practice learning all the jumps and cheers.

Afterward we'd adjourn to the local soda shop and have mountains of French fries and milkshakes—and never gain weight.

Before long we were solid muscle. I'd come home so sore that I'd soak in the tub with Epsom salts to help with the Charley horses in my legs. But I saw this as a chance to do something I'd never done before, with kids I really liked.

I felt so privileged to be living my dream, beyond what I ever could have imagined. I didn't have a care in the world. I hoped it would never end.

* * *

Ain't We Got Fun

The big day finally came. One hundred of us auditioned, twenty at a time, in front of the faculty judges. The eliminations went on for several hours. Finally, the groups were honed down to just twenty girls. Out of that, only eight would be selected to be on the squad. I will never forget that when the judges called out the names of the final winners, not one of us whooped for joy until every one of our names were announced. All eight of us who worked out together made Junior Varsity that year and Senior Varsity the next year.

I couldn't have guessed the important life lessons I'd learn from cheerleading. At the time, it was all about fun and even being somewhat popular.

But cheering was more rigorous than I had imagined; we often cheered at football games when the temperature was in the teens, and sometimes even when it was snowing. We learned that no matter what, we were committed to showing up. We learned that even if our team was losing, it was up to us to rally the crowd. As you do in any sport, we learned the discipline of practice. Most of all, we learned leadership.

Before a few games, I had such severe menstrual cramps I could hardly get out of bed, but I'd take aspirin (no Midol in those days), pull myself together and arrive on time. The other girls were counting on me—I'd ruin our formations if I didn't go—and we never let each other down. Plus, of course, I didn't want to miss all the fun.

Later, I figured out why cheerleading was so important to me. This was the first time in my life where everything about me was not only accepted, but even well liked. I worked hard to get rid of my accent so I could sound more like the other girls, but nonetheless, however I sounded, and whatever I was, they took me in as one of their own.

I was one happy kid.

Those skills would prove eternally useful. Assuming leadership, being proactive, making a positive stand even when it was tough, being persistent, and cheering other people on were skills I would later need in life, no matter what I chose to do. At the time, though, it was just a hugely fun activity for me.

Both years, the school held many formal dances. I was usually invited, and Mrs. T bought me several beautiful formal gowns. Surprised to be voted onto the Student Council, I also had a role in both the junior and senior plays and loved being in on the planning of many school activities. A very active girls' club invited me to join, and, of course, I did. To earn some extra spending money, I got part-time Christmas jobs at Penny's. In the spring, I took a weekend job collecting tickets at the gate of a local drive-in theater. I wanted to contribute, even if just a little, because I appreciated all that Mrs. T did for me.

Years later, after reading Mrs. T's letters to Daddy, I came to think I wore her out. Almost every evening, she was driving me to or picking me up from someplace: rehearsals for plays, sorority meetings every Tuesday evening, the library, football and basketball games, skating and dances. I think I overdid it. I didn't care much about my grades, as long as I passed or better. I mostly had Bs, but Mrs. T never complained. If I had been her, I would have required more of me.

I wanted those two years of high school to never end because I had no further plans. *Surely Daddy would insist that I return to Memphis after high school.*

CHAPTER 13

PREJUDICE, LOVE, AND TRUST

I have no race prejudice, no caste prejudices, nor cruel
prejudices. All I care to know is that a man is a human
being and that is enough for me.
- Mark Twain

AT FIRST I DIDN'T NOTICE any prejudice in Olean, probably because it was so subtle compared to the discrimination I had seen in Memphis. Only one Negro family lived in our town. Their home was well kept, just like everyone else's, so I figured New York State did not harbor the same discrimination as Memphis.

The girl next to me in the back corner of my typing class was the only Negro in the school. Always kind and friendly, she often loaned me paper or an eraser. We chatted easily together, and I liked her.

But I was wrong about there being no prejudice. My first real crush was on a tall, handsome Polish kid who looked just like my idol, Robert Mitchem, the famous actor who played tough-guy roles. This boy's locker was near mine and we often flirted. He'd smile down at me with those blue eyes and droopy eyelids and I'd melt like butter on a hot biscuit. *My life would be complete if only he would ask me out.*

I shared that idea with my girlfriend, Carol, whose response startled me. "Annie, if you go out with him, no one else will ask you out."

"What? I don't understand."

"Well, uh, he's Polish," she said. "You're new. You don't want to be labeled."

"Labeled? For what? He couldn't be more handsome and sweet. Why would dating him label me?"

"Here, the Polish people live on the Polish side of town," she explained. "The Italians have their neighborhoods, and the Irish have theirs. If you date a Polish guy, the others won't date you."

"Huh?" My head spun around on that one for days, but I was new and didn't want to get off on the wrong foot. However, the issue never came up, because, for whatever reason, he didn't ask me out. Many of the kids' parents had thick immigrant accents, as did my Latvian grandparents in Chicago. Though I understood the desire to live in communities where the same language was spoken, it seemed to me that the younger generation should all be of one accord. After all, we admired our football team, and many of them were big, handsome Polish, Italian, and Irish boys.

Daddy, who was raised in Chicago, and Mrs. T from New York, were the least biased people I'd ever known, so it startled me to see any kind of discrimination, especially in the North.

In my senior year, our American History teacher, a tough, re-tired Marine, asked me to stay after class so we could talk. "I'd like to have a debate for the school assembly," he said, "about the Civil War between the North and the South. Since we've been studying it, I think a talk like that would help the kids understand both sides and lead to some good discussions about what is going on in our country now."

Where is he going with this?

"I need someone to represent the point of view of the Confederates," he said. "You are the only student here who has lived there, so I want you to defend their position in the debate."

There I was, the sitting duck, complete with a southern ac-cent, and the only kid in school who had spent time in the South.

He thinks I can help these kids understand why some believed in slavery back then, when I don't understand myself?

With all the courage I could muster, I said, "Thanks for the offer, Mr. Barker, but I could never defend the South. I hated the discrimination I saw there. If you must mark down my grade because I can't do it, I understand."

We never had the debate and he didn't lower my grade. But it would not be the end of the injustice I saw in our country, injustice we'd all see for many years to come.

Since I had experienced so much bias against me in my mother's family, I made a vow to myself that as long as I lived, prejudice was not going to happen on my watch. Eventually, life would show me that this was not as easy as I had hoped.

* * *

A Dream Come True

Finally, it happened. My eyes were opened to what attraction means when I met *him*. Mrs. T's prediction from a year ago was right on. Even after knowing him for three months, flaws and all, I adored him. From the first moment I saw him at school, my heart was twitterpated—the most adorable, cute, and funny guy in the world. Jamie, a charismatic Irish kid, 6'2" and brown-eyed, gazed down at me with his irresistible smile. And, best of all, he was twitterpated, too.

Hardly able to concentrate on my homework, I thought about him all the time and lived for his phone call every evening. At sixteen, when he put his arms around me, for the first time I knew what temptation was. I simply couldn't get enough of him. Because we were both naturally affectionate, it was up to me to know where to set limits, so I really had to watch myself.

Fortunately, since most of us didn't have cars, we were never unchaperoned for very long as he walked me home after a football game or a dance. When we arrived at the house, Mrs. T was always close by.

We went steady, as we called it then, and were inseparable. Jamie told me that his mom had died when he was a small child and his dad was strict and cold to him. Later, I realized that part of what I felt for him was empathy. I thought my love could make it all up to him. Even though we never discussed it, I believe we felt and shared a special loneliness because we were different from the other kids who had two loving parents in their home—that's probably why we were so affectionate.

Because of him, I learned another wonderful character trait of Mrs. T's. Jamie and I had dated for almost a year when, unexpectedly, he disappeared from school for three days and couldn't be found anywhere. Since he called me every evening, I was frantic when I didn't hear from him. None of his friends knew where he was either.

Mr. Carlson, the principal, called me into his office after school. Without even a greeting, he got right to the point. "I've just spoken with Jamie's father. Jamie's been missing for three days. Annie, where is he?"

Shaking, I sat down in front of his desk and said, "I don't know, Mr. Carlson. I haven't heard from him either. The last time I saw him he didn't say anything about leaving. I'm afraid he's walked along the frozen riverbank and slipped in." It had happened to another kid in our school the year before.

"Jamie wouldn't be stupid enough to walk on the riverbank in this icy weather," he said. "You're his girlfriend. You must know something. Now tell me where he is."

"I'm so sorry, Mr. Carlson, I really don't know anything." I could see he didn't believe me. My mouth was so dry I could hardly speak. I tried to hide my cold, shaking hands.

"Well, young lady. We'll just see about that. You'd better go home and make up your mind to tell me the truth, because when we do find him, you could be in big trouble for letting us worry like this." Abruptly, he dismissed me from his office.

I walked home scared and angry, choking back tears. The principal didn't trust me. But, worse yet, Jamie could be dead. *Had he run away?* He had threatened to take off many times because of his strict father. *If Mrs. T believes I know something and have lied, will she decide she doesn't want a troublemaker in her home and send me back to Memphis?*

As I quietly opened the side door at home, hoping to sneak into my room unnoticed, I heard Mrs. T's angry voice on the phone.

"I don't know what you're talking about, Mr. Carlson," she said. "If my Annie told you she doesn't know where Jamie is, you can bet your life she doesn't."

I quietly sat down on the snowy porch steps, leaving the door cracked open, hardly believing my ears.

"My Annie has lived with me off and on since she was a small child and she's the most honest kid I've ever met. If she knew anything about where Jamie was, she would have told me. How dare you doubt her word." Silence hung in the air because I couldn't hear what Mr. Carlson was saying.

"Let me make myself clear, Mr. Carlson," she said. "It's your job, and Jamie's father's job, to find him. Hounding my Annie won't do you any good. Do you understand me?"

Her voice deepened and sounded more heated than I had ever heard it before. I listened, stunned. "And furthermore, do not waste my time by calling me back with more accusations about Annie. This conversation is now over. Goodbye." With a loud slam, she crashed the receiver down.

I'd never heard her so upset. I quietly closed the side door and sat on the cold, icy steps. *Why did she trust me? She only knew what Mr. Carlson told her and he was the principal.* For her to believe in me, without hesitation, and stand up to him before even questioning me was an endorsement I could hardly comprehend.

Except for when Georgia and I were alone and small, no one in my life had ever defended me like that.

What kind of love was this? I had never done anything to deserve such devotion. I realized more than ever that she believed in me and was willing to give me the benefit of the doubt in any situation, even before she knew the circumstances. *This must be the kind of unconditional love the Bible talks about.* Maybe she really was an angel. At least, my angel.

Finally, weeks later, after the police had searched the river for his body, Jamie called his father. He had hitchhiked across the country to his uncle's house in California, arriving half starved, out of money, and scared. His uncle disapproved of what Jamie had done—how dare he, worrying his brother so much. Jamie was forced to fly home and return to his dad.

After Jamie returned, he told me that his father eased up on him. But he refused to talk about what had happened to cause him to want to run away, or about the weeks he spent on the road. The experience somehow changed him, and our relationship was never quite the same. He became more distant and planned to get away from home to join the Marines as soon as he got out of school.

He wasn't the only teenager with difficulties. During our senior year, my friend Mary Jane broke her leg skiing. As if that wasn't enough, her mother, who had driven us to my first day at school and was Mrs. T's riding friend, died of cancer.

Painfully, we kids became aware of the shortness of life. The grief etched on Mary Jane's face as she came down the aisle on crutches at the funeral Mass was a look of sorrow I shall never forget. How could it be, that even lives that seemed ideal could be struck by tragedy? I learned that life had its hardships, even for the privileged.

Too soon, the happiest two years of my life were coming to an end as the senior prom approached. Our dance, with a theme of "Mood Indigo," was held in the gym. We spent days decorating it in blue and purple, having no idea how lavish future proms would become, with limos, hotel rooms, and all-night parties, so we loved our party just as it was. Mrs. T bought me the most beautiful full-length formal gown I'd ever seen. Powder blue and overlaid with white lace, it had a tight waist and full-length hooped skirt. The off-the-shoulder top and hem at the bottom were trimmed with tiny blue flowers. I felt like a princess—a real southern belle. Jamie was the handsomest guy there, and we held hands almost every minute—the most romantic evening we'd ever have together.

The next week, Jamie came over to take me to a movie. As we walked home, we stopped on the bridge over the Allegheny River because he wanted to talk in private. We sat on a nearby bench.

Instead of holding hands as we usually did, he looked me in the eye and said, "You know, we've gone together for a long time and sometimes things have gotten pretty hot between us. It's about time we do something about it."

"What do you mean?"

He said, "Let me put it this way. I want you. You know what I mean. If you can't put out for me, there are lots of girls in Bradford," (the town over the hill in Pennsylvania), "who will give me what I want. I can go there any time with the guys." My heart sank. Even though he wasn't the same Jamie I'd known before he ran away, I loved him and wanted him, too. I knew if I didn't say yes, I'd lose him. *But if he loved me as much as I loved him, why didn't he want us to wait? Surely, he knew that I wanted to live according to God's will for my life. Clearly, this was not what God would want for me, and for good reason. Why was he asking me to take a risk of possible pregnancy and gamble my future for the pleasure of today?*

With so much uncertainty in both our lives, we didn't even know if we'd be together after graduation, especially since I'd probably have to go back to Memphis.

Mother's words haunted me. In our early teens, she had given Georgia and me long, boring lectures. "Stay away from men. You could get pregnant, and if you do, it will ruin your life." *Did she think that having Georgia and me had ruined her life?* She didn't explain exactly how the pregnancy thing could happen, but we knew it meant sex.

What if I got pregnant? Mrs. T would be disappointed in me and Daddy would be devastated. Besides, I wanted to do something with my life and the risk of teen pregnancy was certainly not part of my plan.

One of the most popular girls at school, a natural leader, president of several clubs and an honor student, had to drop out of school because she was pregnant. We were all shocked that her life changed so quickly. She lost all her scholarships and couldn't attend graduation either.

I decided right then that even though I loved Jamie, and wanted to be loved, I wasn't willing take a chance for his satisfaction, no matter how painful the loss of him might be. I would not let this man, or any man, be the main focus of my life, like my mother had. I would, as best I knew how, follow God and His teachings, no matter the cost. If Jamie was willing to lose me over this, then, obviously, I must not be that important to him. Mrs. T had invested years of her life in me and I would not embarrass or disappoint her by this bad decision.

I reached deep inside my lonely soul and said, "I'm sorry, Jamie. I love you but I can't do that. It's just not what I think is right."

We walked the rest of the way home in silence. He left me in a huff at the front door. I cried myself to sleep for many nights after that, but I felt a strange peace about it, too. I certainly didn't have anyone I could confide in about sex, or the lack thereof. Mrs. T had raised boys and we never talked about such intimate things.

Weeks after Jamie and I broke up, I was babysitting for friends of Mrs. T's. One night after I put their children to bed, I found a book on their shelves that explained all about sex. I studied it that evening. Finally, I knew how it all worked.

For many years, my heart belonged to Jamie. But what hurt the most was that not only had I lost him, but after graduation I'd surely be going back to live in Memphis and would not be with my beloved Mrs. T anymore.

CHAPTER 14

AN EXTRAORDINARY OFFER

The only thing that is constant in life is change.
- Heraclitus

GRADUATION WAS WEEKS AWAY. I hated to see the end of the happiest years of my life. Most of my cheerleading girlfriends had been admitted to different nursing schools across the state. We had worked as volunteer Candy Stripers at the local hospital on Saturdays. While helping the nurses, I discovered that I loved going back each week to see that so many of the patients had gotten well and gone home. I gained a better perspective on my own life, too.

My friend from first grade, Beth, was planning to go to Geneseo State Teachers' College, two hours away. Most girls at that time either became teachers or nurses.

None of the kids wanted to stay in Olean after graduation because there were so few jobs and no local colleges to attend. Some of the guys who were top students were headed for Purdue, Cornell, the Naval Academy, the Rochester Institute of Technology, and Boston University.

A few weeks before graduation, Mrs. T and I went out to dinner. I could tell that something was on her mind.

"If you could get the training you needed," she said, "what would you like to be?"

"I wish I could have gone to nursing school like some of my friends. They're already enrolled and were easily accepted months ago because they are good students and majored in college preparatory. I loved working as a volunteer nurse's aide on Saturdays. But I only took business classes, so I'm not prepared to get into nurse's training even if I had the money."

"I've been thinking," she said. "I want to help you. You know, Memphis is a medical center with many hospitals. Why don't you look around there and see if any of the nursing schools would accept you without the same requirements they have in New York State? I'm willing to pay for nursing school or college for you. You could at least apply and try to get in, even at this late date."

I sat in silence. *I can't be hearing her right.*

She told me again, "Annie, I said, I'll help you get through school. Let's figure out where you can apply. I've told you before, I want you to be able to take care of yourself after I'm gone. I have to know that you'll be okay. If you get an education, no one can ever take that away from you. But you have to promise me one thing, that whatever you start, you must finish."

I hardly knew what to say. Why would she do this? And she'd help me even if I wasn't in New York State, but in Memphis? I looked into her kind eyes. I realized that she truly did love me like a real mom loves her own child.

I sat gazing at her for a while, choking back the lump in my throat, and finally whispered, "Thank you."

Because of her, a whole new world of possibilities was opening up for me.

* * *

A Star Is Born

Daddy and the family drove to Olean in his new Oldsmobile to attend my graduation. The next day, I rode with them back to Memphis. On the way, we stopped in Washington, DC and toured the White House.

Daddy was doing so well in his sales business that he'd opened his own music store. He and Mama had bought and moved into a lovely brick three-bedroom home in a beautiful neighborhood. Over time, they were also able to purchase many acres of land outside East Memphis, the direction the city was growing, which they planned to sell when it was time to send Liz and Lynn to college. In addition, they acquired several rental properties. Eventually, the girls attended fine, private Christian colleges.

No mention was made of helping with my college expenses.

Liz and Lynn couldn't wait to tell me their favorite story about Daddy. In the early '50s, he worked at the only big music store in downtown Memphis. "Punk kids," as Daddy called them, came into the store to buy instruments, look around, get advice, buy sheet music, and hang out. Johnny Cash, Jerry Lee Lewis, and other rock and country guys dropped in, including a young kid with a jelly-roll hairstyle.

Elvis Presley was still in high school when he came into the store. He and Daddy hit it off right away. He brought in his old guitar, which would not stay in tune, and showed it to my dad. Elvis said that because his mother could not afford to buy him the bike that he'd wanted when he was twelve years old, she bought him this cheap guitar for $12.95 at a hardware store in Tupelo, Mississippi, where they had lived.

Daddy explained to him in detail why the old guitar couldn't stay in tune, then showed him some quality guitars—a Martin and a Gibson. He demonstrated how the strings on a good instrument should hit the neck of the bridge at just the right distance and how it would not warp if it was made of quality wood.

Elvis bought one of the guitars—and threw the old one in the trash. *Oh, to have that original cheap guitar now.* But at the time, neither of them thought anything more about it.

When Liz was seven and Lynn was five, Elvis had already become a big star. That September, Daddy's store had a large display of pianos and instruments at the Mid-South Fair in Memphis.

One evening, Daddy, Mama, Liz, and Lynn were at the fair together. On their way out to the parking lot, they spotted several police cars parked in a circle. Always curious, Daddy approached them to see what was going on. And there he saw Elvis, well-liked by the cops, in the middle of the group, leaning back against a police car, laughing and talking. He was known to rent the fair or movie theaters after hours for himself and his friends, so Daddy thought maybe he was waiting for the fair to close so he could go in.

The family stood there transfixed. As a crowd began to gather, Elvis spotted Daddy, walked right over to him, and reached through the crowd to shake Daddy's hand. Elvis said, "Hello, Mr. Blumberg. How are you?" Liz was so in awe that she became weak in the knees and thought she was going to faint. It's a wonder they didn't have to call the paramedics. I wish I'd been there to see that.

Daddy, disguising his surprise that Elvis remembered him, was way cool. He said, "Well, Elvis, how are you? I'd like you to meet my family: my wife Virginia, and my two daughters, Liz and Lynn."

Frozen in place, little Liz's lips were trembling when she said, "Elvis, can we have your autograph?"

He smiled and said, "Of course."

Mama quickly scrounged around in her purse and found a dental appointment card which Elvis signed in pencil.

For the next three days, Liz and Lynn glowed, practically levitating off the ground, hardly wanting to wash the hands that had touched the King. Liz took the precious document to school, guarding it like the original Declaration of Independence. But her teacher didn't believe it was really Elvis's autograph. Nonetheless, it remained Liz's prized possession for many weeks—until Lynn copied over it in ink pen, not realizing that compromised the signature. But loving Liz forgave her...eventually.

Daddy and his strolling violin trio played at some of Elvis's private parties in the '70s. When Elvis was on the road, he was famous for occasionally throwing a guitar out to the audience. Since Daddy knew exactly what Elvis wanted, Elvis's road manager would call and order another guitar from him.

Georgia, who was not with them at the fair, was one of the screaming, almost hysterical, almost frothing at the mouth—just short of having seizures—young girls when she was lucky enough to see Elvis in person at concerts. I was in Olean at the time, and while we liked slow dancing to some of his songs, we loved to fast dance to "Jailhouse Rock" and "Blue Suede Shoes."

I found these stories about my sisters very humorous and have enjoyed kidding them about it ever since.

But I also realized that the love of all kinds of music was a common thread woven through our family, creating a colorful tapestry of adventures for all of us.

* * *

Success is not final. Failure is not fatal. It is the courage
to continue that counts.
- Winston Churchill

That summer, I applied to a nurse training school at one of the major hospitals in Memphis. Through some miracle I passed the written tests—even the math and science. The next day, we applicants took a physical, which I easily passed. Then we lined up to take *the vision test*. Because I was self-conscious and nervous about my eyes, I knew that my astigmatism would get even shakier during a test. My heart was pounding as I read the eye chart with the nurse and the other girls watching. Knowing that I wouldn't do well, I was embarrassed; my face felt hot and my hands were sweating.

As I read the eye chart, the senior training nurse clucked, "I'm so sorry, Anna, but our school requires that students have 20/20 vision for the nursing program. Here is the name of a good ophthalmologist. When he fits you with new glasses, you are welcome to come back and try the vision test again."

I thanked her and quickly excused myself, hiding my tears on the bus ride back to Daddy's house. I already knew that my vision could not be corrected to 20/20 because, in addition to astigmatism, I had a congenital birth defect. *Why was I embarrassed about it? How stupid. It wasn't anything I could help. But I wanted to be like the other girls. To measure up. To not be a failure. To be accepted.*

When Daddy asked me after work how it went for me that day, I didn't tell him about the vision test. I knew that the rest of the family all wore glasses which corrected their vision to 20/20, but they did not have my birth defect. I told him that I had decided I didn't want to be a nurse after all. He and Mama seemed surprised but didn't push the subject.

I called Mrs. T and told her that after looking over the nursing possibilities, I had changed my mind.

She must have spoken with Beth, my high school friend whom I'd known since first grade, because it wasn't long before Beth called me with an enticing offer. I valued her opinion. After all, she and I shared a similar past in that we were both from broken homes, she having been raised by her grandmother and alcoholic mother and me with no mother in sight. In that sense, we were different than other kids, and we knew it. We formed an unspoken bond from the first moment we met at School Nine in first grade. She had come bouncing across the playground with her long brown curls to me with my long blonde braids, never realizing that our lifetime friendship would lead to unusual adventures.

"Annie, why don't you come back here and go with me to the State University at Geneseo? It's not too late to apply. We could be roommates. I've already been admitted. At least you could try and see if you can get in."

I phoned Mrs. T immediately. As always, she was encouraging. "Remember, Annie, when you were a little girl, from the time you pretended to teach the dog to read, I always said you'd be a good teacher. I even mentioned Geneseo to you way back then."

Within days, I flew back. Mrs. T drove me to Geneseo, two hours away, where I took the entrance exam. Much to my surprise, I passed, and I whooped with joy two weeks later when I received the acceptance letter.

Beth and I started that fall. It seemed God wanted me in New York State after all. I had never wanted to leave, and He had not forgotten my years of prayer to be there.

Geneseo, nestled in a beautiful, peaceful green valley, was surrounded by gentle rolling hills. When we moved into the dorm, the fall colors had just set in. Elegant horses and their riders came from all over the country to participate in the area's famous fox hunts.

A new, unexpected adventure was about to begin.

* * *

A friend loves at all times.
- Proverbs 17:17

Beth and I settled into the last available dorm room: a green, remodeled former laundry room, but with a beautiful view of the valley. We met girls from all over the state and even two from New York City who, unlike the rest of us, knew how to dress and do their makeup. Beth and I soon became like sisters. We shared everything, even our clothes.

The buildings were traditional red brick covered in ivy, with a bell tower at the end of the quad. Beth and I were elected secretary and treasurer of the freshman class. To relax, she and I loved to hang out in the rec room after classes and play pool or ping-pong with the other kids. We'd have a soda and sit and read magazines or newspapers.

December 1, 1955, however, will forever stand out in my memory. That day, in the rec room, as I sat in a comfortable leather chair, I picked up the paper. The headline told of a Negro lady, Rosa Parks, in Montgomery, Alabama, who would not give up her bus seat to a white passenger. Her arrest started a boycott of the city buses, led by a young Martin Luther King, Jr. I sank deep in my chair, smiling behind the paper. At last, a black person had the courage to reject the discrimination she saw. Because I had felt such rejection as a child from my mother's family, and remembered how the Negroes must have felt, I wanted to stand up and cheer for her.

I followed the story with great interest. Almost a year later, the US Supreme Court ruled that segregation laws were unconstitutional. The long journey to integration had begun.

For me, the courses at Geneseo didn't seem hard, except for biology. Most of the other students caught on right away since they had taken college preparatory classes in high school, which included biology. But even though I found most of the lectures interesting, by looking at my friends' notes, I saw that I was missing major points.

Yikes. I realized I didn't know how to study.

In high school, I had glided by with minimal effort. But I didn't know something as simple as the fact that the first sentence in a paragraph should express the main point, followed by an explanation and details. No wonder my notes were incomplete.

As fate would have it, of the two biology instructors, I got the strictest one, while my friends got the young, easy professor.

The end of the first semester came. I had straight Cs and a D in Biology, which meant I was put on probation. In orientation during the first week of class, a counselor had announced to all of us, "By spring one-third of you will be gone. Out of those who are left, only half of you will graduate in four years."

Horrified, I remembered my promise to Mrs. T that if I started college, I'd finish. I had until June to get my act together. *Could I do it?*

At the end of the semester, in late January, I went to see one of the college counselors. On that cold, windy evening with the snow coming down hard, I sat down in her office and told her how difficult biology was for me, and how my friends got the easy professor. Plus, I felt overwhelmed because there was so much homework overall.

She wasn't buying it. "Maybe you're not college material," she said. "Some people just don't have the self-discipline to study." I would never forget her parting words: "Why don't you just go home and get a job?"

* * *

The secret of getting ahead is getting started.
- Mark Twain

As I left her office, I felt numb, completely disillusioned, and ashamed of myself. *Was she trying to tell me I was stupid? Was I stupid?*

Had one of the honor students in high school been right when he said I'd probably never go to college because I'd get married right away and have lots of kids?

The building was empty as I left because everyone was at dinner. As I came out of the three-story brick structure, I stood in the entry alcove, shielded from the wind and blustery snow. I needed to gather my strength before I made a run for the dorm. Tears were freezing to my cheeks. Then, suddenly, someone was with me.

I don't know where she came from, because she arrived out of nowhere. Tall, with long blonde hair, she had a kind, soothing voice.

"What's the matter, dear?"

"I'm about to flunk out of college. I don't know where I'll go or what to do. Maybe I'm too stupid after all."

"Oh, my dear, I know that you're not stupid. This isn't worth shedding a single tear over. You will be okay. I'm sure of it. You'll figure out exactly what to do. Now dry your tears, pull yourself together, and start developing a plan to take care of this."

Since it was a small campus, I expected to recognize her, so I turned in the darkened doorway to get a better look. She was gone. No footprints marked the snow or the stairs. I never saw her again and neither did any of my friends. No tall, blonde professors taught on our campus. Had God sent me an angel?

Of course, Mrs. T was notified by mail about my probationary status. She did not even call to complain or scold. However, she must have told John Thompson about my situation, and he was not so quiet. Even though he and Paul were busy running the family-owned chain of grocery stores, John always checked in with Mrs. T to see how I was doing.

John and his wife, Teri, called, and within days drove to Geneseo to meet with me. They had married the summer I stayed to enter eleventh grade in Olean. I loved Teri to pieces because she was always so friendly. She had graduated from Buffalo State as an art major and earned a master's degree.

They arrived at my dorm, smiling, but I could see a steely look in John's eye. They took me to dinner. *What would he say to me?* I knew that I had disappointed the family that had faithfully stood by me all these years.

After we placed our order, John said, "So, Annie, tell me about your study routine every day."

"Well, each day after class, I go to the rec room to relax and play pool or ping-pong. Two afternoons a week I have a job at the soda shop downtown. Then, I meet my girlfriends for dinner in the cafeteria. After that, I go to the dorm to study."

His sober face told me that he didn't like what he heard.

"Oh, you wait until after dinner to start studying?" he said. "No wonder you're on probation. Come on. Show us where the library is. Bring your biology book and your notes."

"Now John, go easy on her," Teri said. But he wasn't listening. We finished dinner, and as we walked into the library, I felt like a kitten being hauled by the scruff of my neck.

The "eggheads" were all there, engrossed in their textbooks. In a quiet corner, the three of us sat down at one of the tables.

"From now on, after class," John said, "go directly to the library. Do not stop by the dorm. Do not go to the rec room. Tell your friends in the morning that you'll meet them in the cafeteria at 6:00 p.m., but study here until dinner time. By then, you'll be pretty much finished with your homework. Then, and only then, can you go to the rec room and party. Do you understand?"

I was hoping the "eggheads" didn't hear him. Eager not to be noticed, I meekly nodded in agreement.

"Now, show me your biology book and your notes."

Oops. I didn't want him to look at my garbled scribbling because I already knew that they were sloppy and didn't contain as much information as my friends' summaries. He opened the textbook and took out some 5x8 cards that he had brought with him.

"Annie, what is the most important sentence of this paragraph?"

"Well," I said, "it's about fossils."

"Right," he said, "but that's not enough. What about fossils? Be specific. Write it down."

Oh, dear. He was correct. I didn't care much about fossils. Since it wasn't my favorite subject, I just wanted to know enough to get by.

All of a sudden, realizing that my college life depended on it, I cared a whole lot. I knew I had to dig in and do better. With John staring at me so intently, I felt like a frog under a microscope.

"The next time we come to see you," he said, "I want to check your notes on every chapter. When you were a little kid, school was easy for you. You're a smart girl. There's no reason for you not to do well now."

He believed in me? I had to shape up.

We left the library—or rather, I slunk out, trying to be invisible. We went out for coffee. On a roll now, John shared his strong opinions about college classes and professors.

Teri looked worried and again urged him to go easy on me.

"Look," he said, "it doesn't matter if you agree with what the professor is saying. What's important is that you shovel back to him at test time exactly what he gave you in the lectures. Give him what he wants to hear. That's the only way he'll know that you got it."

I nodded in agreement.

"Most of what you will learn in college is B.S. You'll forget lots of it."

"Oh, John," his wife said.

Undeterred, John continued. "Consider yourself lucky if you come across a great prof who knows what he's talking about, and you actually learn something. But, Annie, you've got to play their game, or you'll be bounced out of here in June. Understand?"

Oh, did I! I got it big time. Here was my answer, my ticket to do better in school, to succeed. To finish what I had started, as I had promised.

Once again, I was the undeserving recipient of John Thompson's kindness. He saved my life the first time by rescuing me from the slums of Memphis when he met Mother, and now by caring enough to drive two hours each way in the snow on icy roads to help me.

What a family!

Sure, he had his early wild years in the Navy. But that was the past. I knew he was not only a very loving person, but also truly a genius. Too bad that he didn't get to go to medical school like he wanted, but instead had to come home after the war and help run the family business. By watching John all my life, I had learned that geniuses don't color just inside the lines, especially ones with big hearts. Who else would have talked his mom into taking in a divorced southern woman with two kids, sending her by train across country so he could come home and be with her afterward?

And what other kind of mom, except Mrs. T, would be open to the whole idea of accepting three strangers into her home for an indefinite period of time? Who else but her would have been willing to raise me for years, long after Mother and John broke up and Mother returned to Memphis?

Could I do what he said? Could I learn quickly enough to get off probation?

CHAPTER 15

A NEW WAY OF THINKING

Life is ten percent what happens to you, and ninety percent how you react to it.
- Charles Swindoll

B Y JUNE MY GRADES were greatly improved, so John never needed to come back. Mrs. T was right: you can be anything you want to be if you set your mind to it. When I was discouraged, I would dig into my Bible, where I found Galatians 5:22: "But the fruits of the spirit are love, joy, peace, patience, kindness, goodness, faithfulness, gentleness, and self-control." Ouch.

Since self-control and patience did not come naturally to me, in order to become a good student, I asked for His help every day. It took time, but I did grow in both of these areas.

At that time, in New York State, the legal drinking age was eighteen. I entered Geneseo when I was seventeen, so my eighteenth birthday was an excuse for all of us to celebrate.

Beth and I headed for the only local watering hole off campus, the B and C Restaurant and Bar, where I had my very first drinks—three of them, on an empty stomach. They were sweet and tasted like lemonade, and I was hot from dancing, so, not knowing any better, I gulped them right down.

We floated back to the dorm singing, but my head was reeling. We barely got to our rooms before curfew when the door was locked.

As we got into our jammies, I said, "Beth, have you ever noticed what an ugly color of green the walls of our room are?" We climbed into our bunk beds as she mumbled that we could always cover them with pictures.

"No. It's not enough," I protested. "The hideous color will still show."

Immediately, the three drinks got me in contact with my inner Michelangelo. I boldly took out some bright blue tempera paint from my art class and proceeded to write in huge letters on the long wall across from our bunk beds, *I love Jamie.*

"Annie, don't do it." Beth giggled. "Have you forgotten that Mrs. T is coming up tomorrow with a birthday cake for you?"

"Umm. I don't care. I'm too tired to think about it right now," I said as I turned out the light and snuggled under the warm covers. "See you in the morning."

I woke up hours later, having sobered up just enough to realize what I'd done. I sat bolt upright in bed. *What will Mrs. T think?* I spent the rest of the night scrubbing the blue paint off the wall. Not only had I promised her I'd never drink or smoke, I had also promised myself, as a child, that I would never do either one.

When she arrived the next day, the wall was spotless. In she came with my favorite twelve-egg angel food cake, which she had baked from scratch. She also had a large box in the car, which Beth and I carried up to our room.

"Oh, my gosh. A high-fidelity record player." (We didn't have stereo in those days.) I choked up at her never-ending thoughtfulness and, even though she was not a hugger, I flung my arms around her neck.

Later, Beth told me she saw Mrs. T tear up.

Before Mrs. T drove home, the three of us went to dinner. Remembering the night before, I was ashamed of myself. *Had I lost my mind? Didn't my mother's family wreck their lives with booze? Had I forgotten that I was drunk when I was five years old?*

From then on when we went out, I had a soda.

But I did try to smoke. Once. Beth had joined a sorority of sophisticated gals. They looked elegant sitting on a bar stool, usually in tight black dresses with just enough leg showing, head tipped towards the ceiling, right hand gracefully tilted outward, as they drew in a strong puff and blew it upward. They reminded me of the glamorous women we saw in the movies. Wow, they were sexy.

But I almost choked to death trying a cigarette.

Smoking only brought back more bad memories. I decided that I would not only keep my promise to Mrs. T, but also keep my childhood promise to myself. There were no health warnings on cigarette packages then, but it didn't look healthy to me to have smoke coming out of your nose. And the taste was awful. Later, I joined my friend Evelyn's sorority—girls who were not particularly interested in the sophisticated image that drinking and smoking projected.

I wasn't all sweetness and light, though. The second year at Geneseo, I stayed out too late several times on Saturday night dates and missed the midnight curfew when the dorm door was locked. Under the cover of darkness and bushes, my girlfriends helped pull me through the window of our first-floor room. Scary as it was, it was fun too.

Had we been caught, we would have been suspended.

Despite the dances and parties on campus, and even some dating, there was still a tug on my heart for Jamie. I missed him so much and prayed often for his safety. He had joined the Marines and was stationed at Camp Lejeune, North Carolina. Occasionally, I'd get a letter from him, which I'd read over and over.

One weekend, when he was on leave, to my joy and surprise, he came to Geneseo with a bunch of guys. I hoped he had come to see me. Even though he stopped by my dorm for a while, he made it clear that they were just there to pick up chicks. But, at least he hadn't forgotten me.

* * *

In the cookies of life, sisters are the chocolate chips.
- Author unknown

My sister Georgia, in California with Mother and Tom, had graduated from Burbank High School two years before I graduated in Olean. She married a Navy man whom she had dated for several years, and I was happy to hear that they both had good jobs with the telephone company. We didn't write much anymore. Our worlds had drifted apart—she a wife, and me a college student. Even though I hadn't seen her in years, I missed her and thought about her often. Mother wrote in the fall of my first year of college that Georgia was pregnant.

In April, Mother called. With no cell phones then, each floor of the two-story dorm had only one phone, in the hall. When someone called the main desk downstairs, your room was buzzed, and you went to the phone to answer it.

Standing in the hall to take Mother's call, there was so much noise and echo that I couldn't hear her well. So, I opened the mop closet by the phone and literally climbed into a large bucket, closing the door behind me.

"Anna, Georgia had her baby this morning. A little girl, Cindi. I'm a grandma now." Mother was beside herself with joy to be a grandmother.

"Oh, Mother, that's fantastic. I'm so happy for her. Goodie! I'm an aunt now." But I was sad to think I had missed being with her in this momentous time of her life. Eventually, Georgia and her husband had four children.

Over the years, Mother redeemed herself by being a terrific, loving, doting grandma. Though she never admitted it to us, we thought that, because she married so young, life had rushed by too quickly and she regretted not having time with us as children. Here was her chance to make up for it by enjoying the grandchildren. Since she didn't have an outside job, she had plenty of time to lavish love on Georgia's kids.

Mother sold beauty products from home and, at one time, was the top representative in the San Fernando Valley. Georgia and I chuckled at that because we suspected that customers took one look at Mother's beautiful skin and thought, "Gee, if I use these products, I'll look like her."

* * *

No one can make you feel inferior without your consent.
- Eleanor Roosevelt

That first summer after my freshman year at Geneseo, I needed a job. I had proved to Mrs. T, John, and myself that I could hold my own in college, but I needed to make money because I felt guilty for all that Mrs. T did for me. She paid for my tuition, room and board, books, clothes—everything. Even though I had had a few part-time jobs in high school, I knew that was nothing compared to what she had been spending.

But what skills did I have to offer? I could ride a horse well but wasn't sure I could teach it to anyone else. However, Mrs. T thought I'd be a good riding instructor and counselor at a summer camp. So, as usual, I figured that if she believed I could, even though I was nervous about it, I knew I could, too. With her encouragement, and several referral letters from riding instructors in Olean who knew I could ride, I applied and was accepted to teach beginning and intermediate horseback riding at a beautiful, exclusive, all equestrian summer camp, high in the Adirondack Mountains of New York State.

And so began an entirely different, sometimes nerve-wracking, adventure.

Right away, another counselor named Sue, a sweet, fresh-faced horsewoman, and I became good friends. Her family owned horses in another town and she attended Bryn Mawr College—a prestigious private women's college in Pennsylvania. We taught several courses together. At lunchtime, before we could eat, we had to run quickly from stall to stall carrying heavy buckets, watering the twenty-five horses. In addition, each of us was in charge of a cabin of ten girls.

Even though the job was physically demanding, I loved being outside, smelling the hay in the stalls, and hearing the soft neighing of the horses. Saddling them up, brushing their soft coats, discovering that each horse had its own personality, and turning the kids on to riding was very rewarding.

The camp was expensive, and most of the kids were there for the entire summer, sent by their wealthy parents to escape the sweltering heat of New York City. A few of the twelve-year-old girls in my cabin, with maids at home, had never made a bed in their lives. They expected me to be their maid.

Not going to happen.

Each cabin earned points for neatness, so the rest of my girls were not about to lose out because of a princess in their midst. Peer pressure from the other campers shamed them into learning to be tidy. I enjoyed watching all this drama and began to believe that not only would I enjoy becoming a teacher, but I might be good at it.

The challenges of camp became less difficult each week as I grew more confident in the daily routine. While I had hesitated to take the job, not knowing if I could survive the horses or the kids, I was learning that being scared is not the worst thing in the world. I could deal with it, leaning into the fear, the way Mrs. T had taught me to do when I was afraid of the dark. I could even grow from it.

Twice a week, Sue and I had the responsibility of taking ten kids at a time on overnight trail rides, which started in the late afternoon. We took turns leading the pack or bringing up the rear. I was nervous about the whole thing because I hadn't done much

trail riding, much less been responsible for directing ten campers. A fire pit, food, and makeshift stalls had already been set up
for us by the camp directors when we reached our destination at
the top of the mountain where we spent the night.

But, oh boy, did it ever rain that summer. After the girls had
their dinner and campfire and were safely tucked into their
sleeping bags, Sue and I watered and fed the horses. Their stalls
were slots of tree branches, so we had to slip along the side of
each horse to get to his bucket and take him food and water. I still
have the scar where Comanche, a huge horse that led the trail
ride, bit me on the rear when I went in to feed him. It made for a
pretty sore ride down the hill the next day, but I figured it was all
part of the adventure. In addition, because the two of us popped
in and out of our sleeping bags so often all night to check on the
girls and the horses, we got back in soaking wet. Then, thanks to
the altitude, we froze.

Back at camp on the days when we weren't on the trail, we
had to get a cabin of girls up and off to breakfast at 7:00 a.m., and
then teach our classes. I was surprised at how fond I'd grown of
my campers, and how choked up I felt the last day of summer
when their parents came to get them.

By the end of summer, either from sleeping in wet sleeping
bags or sheer fatigue, Sue and I both had pneumonia. Even so,
she and her parents invited me to go to Canada with them for two
weeks. They owned a log cabin in the Finger Lakes area that was
nine miles in by boat. Sue and I had two weeks after camp to go
home and get well. I wouldn't have missed that trip for anything,
and Mrs. T, wanting me to have the opportunity, quickly nursed
me back to health.

I can still see the shining eyes of the deer and other animals as
Sue and I canoed through the islands that she knew so well. I felt
an absolute peace in the quiet of the wilderness that I'd never felt
before. At night the sky was jet black, since there was no other
light around us. The stars popping out as bright as streetlights

and the nearest cabin being miles away gave the illusion that we were almost on our own planet.

That summer, wouldn't you know, the most popular song was "Canadian Sunset." Fiery red and orange displays streaked with gold crossed the sky at sunrise and sunset, and the nights were deliciously cold as we slept snugly inside the cabin. The smell of pine trees, the taste of dinner, sometimes cooked outdoors over a campfire, the sound of blue jays squawking as they settled down for the night and the swish of squirrels scurrying up the trees, convinced me that these woods were where God lived. I felt very close to Him in the silence of the nights.

But most of all, the hospitality of Sue's happily married parents made a memorable impression on me. *So, there are other happy couples beside Daddy and Mama on this earth.* Again, another family had blessed me with an adventure that I could not have had on my own. I remember that rugged summer as the beginning of my love of the outdoors and camping that would last me a lifetime. I did not want the Canada trip to end.

* * *

You'll have more success in life if you stop trying to include God in YOUR plan, And instead ask Him to include you in HIS.
- Quoted by Darren Brown

In my two years at Geneseo, the general education classes turned me on to subjects that I'd never thought about before. In English Literature I read many of the great classics. Even though I wasn't certain of what I wanted to be when I enrolled in college, I soon realized that I would like to be a teacher, which was the primary major there. Of greater interest to Beth was the drama department. At the time, I had no way of knowing that performing would later be part of my life, too. In our education classes we were required to observe master teachers at the local elementary school. To my surprise, I found it fascinating. I saw how one good teacher could have a real impact on the life of a child. I thought back to my favorite instructors, the ones who were kind to me during the difficult years of my life.

If Plan A, which was nursing school, hadn't worked out, perhaps Plan B stood for Better and that was what God had in store for me.

With few male students on our campus, when we weren't snowed in, I continued to date some of the guys who drove in from other colleges. But I never fell for any of them because my heart still belonged to Jamie, at that time still a Marine. I prayed every night that, somehow, he'd love me as much as I loved him and come home and marry me. I didn't know if God's answer was no, or if He meant a delay until further notice—so I kept praying anyway.

The guys I cared for at all were the ones who were good dancers. In those years, Little Richard was as hot as Elvis, Ray Charles, and Fats Domino. On weekend nights we'd all head for the B and C Bar and Restaurant and groove the night away.

I made several close friends while I was away at school, with whom I still correspond. But for the most part, it was a lonely time for me because many of the girls went home on weekends to be with their families or boyfriends. Most of the students lived within an hour of the college, but Olean was two hours away, so Beth and I had difficulty finding a ride home. At least a few of us, who had to stay on campus on weekends, hung out and went to dinner and church together, but I wished I could go home to see Mrs. T more often.

As my friends shared with me how close they were with their moms, and how they missed them, I felt a pang of guilt that I didn't feel the same way. The frequent phrases I heard in the dorm rooms were, "Mom taught me to knit," "Mom taught me to crochet," "Mom taught me how to bake," "Mom sewed for me,"

"We like to shop together," "Mom and I have fun walking together," and, "I miss my mother."

I wished I could say the same. *What was wrong with me that I hadn't bonded with my mother the way they had? Maybe I hadn't tried hard enough.*

On several occasions, different girlfriends invited me home with them for the weekend. In fact, one Christmas vacation I went by train to New York City with a Jewish friend. The Big Apple at holiday time, as her policeman boyfriend accompanied us through the city, was an unusual experience. Because my last name sounded Jewish to many people, some befriended me immediately, thinking I was part of their culture. Latvian and Jewish humor, traditions, and even foods are so similar that I felt right at home immediately. By the time they figured me out or I told them that my name was Latvian, they no longer cared because by then they were my friend. As a result, to my delight, I had many Jewish friends.

But an unexpected change was about to occur in my life.

CHAPTER 16

EAST TO WEST

Be yourself. Everyone else is taken.
- Oscar Wilde

A S THE SPRING OF OUR SOPHOMORE YEAR was coming to an end, Beth was excited because her dad, whom she hadn't seen since childhood, had invited her to visit him over the summer in California. He would pay her airfare. Another sorority sister, Allie, who had been on her own for years and was working her way through college on scholarships, told us that her mom, a chef to one of the major Hollywood stars, wanted her to come out as soon as the semester ended. All three of us had divorced parents, which was rare at the time.

When we met for lunch in the cafeteria, Beth said, "Why don't all three of us fly to California together and connect with our parents?"

"Not a bad idea," I said. "I'd love to see my sister Georgia, and even see if I could make amends with my mother. But I don't have the money to go and I know Mother couldn't pay my way."

That weekend, Beth and I went home to Olean. I was cautious about sharing the idea of the trip with Mrs. T because I didn't know if she would approve.

"Annie, that would be great," she said. "You should see your mother and Georgia and the new baby. If you want to go, I'll buy your ticket." I marveled once again at her generosity and was excited to have the opportunity.

Perhaps that nagging guilt I'd had for years of not being close to my mother could be repaired. Surely, it must be my fault. Maybe now that I was older, I could better understand her. Going to California would give me a chance to try one more time.

At the end of the school year, we each packed up our stuff, moved home, called our California parents, and set the departure date.

On the telephone, Mother sounded pleased about my coming. She and Tom planned to meet Allie and me at the LA airport, and Beth's dad would be there to pick her up. Allie was to stay with us for a few weeks while her mother moved to a different location. As the plane descended, I was amazed by this great, sprawling city. Then, as we drove over the Sepulveda Pass into the San Fernando Valley, I was dazzled by the mass of city lights surrounded by dark, rugged mountains. I'd had no idea the area was so large or so beautiful.

Mother and Tom owned a pretty two-bedroom home in North Hollywood. He had been good to her. By working a lot of overtime at Lockheed, he provided her with the finest of everything. I was surprised at the level of luxury I saw—the first plush wall-to-wall carpeting in the area, a high-fidelity entertainment console the length of one wall, fine furniture, air-conditioning, brimming jewelry boxes, and closets stuffed with cocktail dresses. Their home lacked for nothing. They didn't drink anymore, thank goodness, but they were still heavy smokers.

As a child, I remembered mother being a jealous woman, but I had no idea how insecure she still was until I brought Allie into their home. Allie, an effervescent, slightly plump Italian with gorgeous rosy skin and blue eyes, had a great sense of humor. But Mother barely tolerated her.

My first indication of trouble appeared when Allie was sitting at the dresser in our room, fully clothed, brushing her hair. The bedroom door was cracked open and she could be seen from the hall.

Mother took me aside the next morning and said, "Allie is flirting with Tom."

"Mother, Allie has no interest in Tom."

"Yes, she most certainly does. That's why she brushes her hair in front of the mirror with the door open, so he can see her when he walks down the hall.

Clearly, there was no point in arguing with her. *The least said the soonest mended,* as Mrs. T would say.

As much as I liked Tom, he was not the type of guy Allie, or any of us girls, would be interested in. Not only was he old enough to be our father, but he was married to my mother. When he came home from work late each day, always after overtime, he looked tired and haggard and smelled of machine oil. He wasn't well spoken, but I liked him because he was at least friendly to me. I'm sure he wanted to please Mother by having me visit.

Still, I could see that life for him was drudgery. Being a Tennessee country boy, he would beg Mother to let him go fishing. He went one time when I was there, and for weeks afterward she berated him. Was he seeing another woman? Where had he been for so long? Why did he want to spend any time away from her?

Because I felt sorry for him, one day while he was at work, I opened my big mouth in his defense. "Mother, Tom adores you. If you'll let him go fishing, he'll be all the more eager to come home to you."

"You're so naïve, Anna. You know nothing about men." That was probably true. Tom finally gave up his quest and never tried to go fishing again. Apparently, it wasn't worth it.

Within a week, Allie's mom had settled into her new location and Allie moved in with her. Beth was happy living with her dad in an apartment in Hollywood. She even picked up a few modeling jobs. Because she was a drama major, Hollywood was her ultimate destination.

Seeing my sister Georgia after six years was a great reunion for both of us. Her baby Nora was precious and very mellow. Best of all, Georgia seemed to be happy in her cozy apartment in Burbank and was a great mom. I wasn't surprised because I remembered how she had mothered me when we were small and left alone.

Through Georgia's best friend, Rebecca, I was able to get a job in Glendale at a manufacturing plant printing architectural blueprints, and even found a ride to work. Beth, Allie, and I rarely got together because we didn't have cars or much money, but we talked on the phone often.

Georgia fixed me up with several of her girlfriends' brothers. Her friend Rebecca's brother, Ricky, was a cheerleader at UCLA, working his way through school after serving in the Korean war. Warm and affectionate, outgoing, and full of good humor, I liked him immediately.

He invited me to my very first beach party. When I stuck my toes into the beautiful, roaring Pacific, the first ocean I'd ever seen, I was awestruck. Ricky grinned and said he enjoyed that I was so in awe of the water. Our great times together were just beginning. *Could this possibly lead to something serious?*

Ricky, always generous, got a kick out of showing me the sights all summer, and I enjoyed his upbeat outlook, so we had a wonderful time going places together. I admired the classic California girls that I saw, with their tight pedal pushers, shapely figures, and ubiquitous golden tans. Though I didn't think I measured up to them, Ricky seemed attracted to me anyway. He loved driving me around in his bright red MG as we went to the Hollywood Bowl, the Hollywood Palladium, Chinatown, and drove by movie stars' homes in Beverly Hills. We laughed and kidded a lot. A big guy, he loved to scoop me up in his arms and twirl me around in a bear hug when he came in the door. How delightful it was to finally be drawn to someone besides Jamie.

Mother was embarrassingly obvious in her attempts to fuel the fire between Ricky and me. When we went out, there was no curfew. Sure, we had to allow time for long drives home from the beach or LA, but as soon as we arrived at her house, she and Tom disappeared and didn't care if we stayed up until the wee hours. She sure didn't have the same standards as Mrs. T. I think that she hoped I'd fall in love, marry, and stay in California.

Ricky's favorite way to spend a Sunday afternoon was to take me to his mother's house so I could spend the day with her in the kitchen, while he happily worked all afternoon on his first love— his MG. *Was this a taste of what marriage to him would be like? Was this the kind of guy I should marry? Would I regret it if I didn't? My life would certainly be different if I did. Did we have enough in common?* I had to think this through because I found him to be entirely loveable.

One Saturday night, going to the Hollywood Bowl, I wore white, open-toed heels. As we got in the MG he said, "Uh, you can't wear those shoes."

"Why not?"

"In Korea, only prostitutes wear open-toed shoes."

Even though I thought that was crazy because this was America, I was so eager to please him that I went into the house and changed. *I wondered if he'd be bossy if he were my husband.* But that incident was a minor thing, considering what he had been through in Korea. One Sunday afternoon we went to the grocery store to shop for his mother. All through the market he had me paddle along behind him like a puppy. *Was he too close to his mother? Was he a mama's boy?* That all seems silly now. Of course, he would be close to her; he was her oldest son and she was a single mother, a teacher, who had raised four kids on her own, so naturally he was the man of the house. She was always gracious and welcoming to me and I didn't want to judge him too quickly.

Mother didn't like that Mrs. T and I wrote and called each other regularly. She did not even want Mrs. T's name mentioned. I couldn't understand that. *Why wasn't she grateful for all Mrs. T had done for me—things Mother could not have done? Was she jealous?*

As the hot summer progressed, Mother applied more pressure in her campaign to convince me to stay in California. Over dinner one night in July, she said, "Anna, college is a waste of time. Any true southern girl your age would be married with babies by now, like your sister. You're almost twenty years old. Do you want to be a spinster? Why don't you just stay here and keep the job you have and go on dating Ricky?"

"Lots of women marry later in life," I said. "Mama married Daddy in her late twenties, and she was a southern girl from the country. Besides, I want to finish college before I get married."

Irritated with me, she dropped the conversation—for the moment.

Finally, she arranged to show me what a true southern, genteel, glamorous woman really looked like.

Enter Mother's favorite relative, the family heirloom, my great Aunt Sarah, Daddaw's sister. She represented all that Mother held dear: glamour, beauty, money, and a little fame. To make the statement to the world that they were true Confederates, a huge, two-story-high Confederate flag proudly flew in the front yard of her and Uncle Abe's home in Van Nuys. I think they both believed in the old song that said, "Save your Confederate money, boys. The South will rise again."

To impress me with what style really looked like—or at least her idea of it—Mother invited them over to Sunday dinner. Here was Hollywood sophistication right in our own family.

Aunt Sarah had been a silent film actress and, according to family rumor, had danced with Valentino and was the mystery lady who, for years, placed flowers on his grave in Hollywood. Proof of this, Mother believed, was that in later years, after Aunt Sarah died, the lady with the flowers disappeared.

She was Swedish by ancestry, as were we, on my mother's side. Mother said that Sarah, not a doctor herself, had made a fortune by sharing her secret Swedish skin peel with several dermatologists in Beverly Hills. She brought the formula over from the old country at a time when face lifts and cosmetic surgery weren't popular yet. Good looking Uncle Abe was her charming, younger boy-toy husband.

Arriving in their Mercedes, Aunt Sarah was a sight to behold. She wore a tight, long black dress, black stockings and black high heels—in the 105-degree heat. At eighty years old, she was still incredibly beautiful, with hardly a single wrinkle on her chalk white, finely powdered face, and she still had a gorgeous figure to go with it.

I had not seen her since I was a child. Her strong perfume preceded her as she made her grand entrance into Mother's house.

"Oh, Anna, dahling!" she gushed. "I'll declare. Lawd have mercy! Bless your little ol' heart. I'm so glad to see you, child!" It took her five minutes to droll that out as we shifted from foot to foot, waiting politely to hear her out. *This was going to be quite an interesting day.* I gave her a hug and a warm smile.

"I'm glad to see you, too, Aunt Sarah! You look wonderful!"

She truly did, even with all that white powder, though a little on the vampire side.

As we sat down in the living room, Mother, pleased and proud of the family relic, went back in the kitchen to finish the spaghetti dinner.

Then the fun began.

"Anna, child," (I was twenty but never mind), "ah've been so worried about you living in the North all these years. Have they ruined you, child? I've been needin' to get over here to see what has become of you."

Hmm. With my northern ideas, this might be a good day to keep my mouth shut.

I gave her a confused look. I didn't know what to say.

"You know, I'll declare, those Yankees can't be trusted to tell the truth about how they stomped all over us in the Civil Wahr, child. I reckon no one in New York bothered to tell you our side of it, did they?"

Were we still living in 1865? To her, apparently, the "wahr" ended a few days ago, but she was still fighting it. My face went blank. I was speechless.

"Of course, they didn't," she said. "Well, I'm fixin' to tell you that the North only won the wahr because they had all the industry and wealth and we were just simple plantation folks."

"Yes, ma'am. I see," I said, wanting to avoid any confrontation. Though I was starting to feel uncomfortable, I wanted to be respectful and not embarrass Mother because she idolized Sarah.

"Northerners didn't understand," she said, "that the South could not tend all those cotton crops without their slaves. Why, youngin', it was so unfair to want to free them. How ridiculous! They were happy with free room and board provided for them the rest of their lives. Why, they didn't have a care in the world!"

Was this woman crazy? What planet was she from? How could I quickly change the subject? Even better, how could I escape?

Okay. I couldn't resist. Like a child gently dipping one toe into an icy lake, I eased into the discussion. Big mistake. I thought I could show her another side of the issue. *Foolish girl.*

"Well, but Aunt Sarah, it's morally wrong to own another human being. All men are created equal, you know, according to the Declaration of Independence."

"Ha! I knew it! They've brain washed you! Lawd have mercy. Don't start up with me, child. I told your mama years ago she shouldn't let you live in New York State!" Irritated now, she scowled at me.

Sensing trouble brewing, Mother was worried and stuck her head in the living room archway. "Anna, come make the salad."

"Oh, not yet, Caroline!" Aunt Sarah said. "I'm not finished with this youngin'."

Oh, dear, what could I do to get out of this?

Turning to me, she spoke louder, "Listen to me, you young whippersnapper, their brain is smaller than ours. Don't you know that? They don't have the intelligence to do anything but menial work. And, furthermore, you come from fine Swedish nobility stock! Can't you see the difference?"

That was it. She had pushed all my buttons and crossed the line. Upon hearing such horrific talk, no matter who she was, I would not be silent.

"Aunt Sarah, that's not true! When people of other races are given the chance and education, they can do as well as any white person. It's a cruel myth that their brain is smaller than ours. I learned that in Biology 101."

Mother's scowling red face appeared again in the doorway. "Anna, you must come make the salad. *Now.*"

Too late! Aunt Sarah had had her say and I, surely, would now have mine.

Aunt Sarah ignored Mother. Like a locomotive on fire, there was no stopping her.

"Anna, your attitude is a disgrace to our ancestors—proud southerners who had the most elegant, genteel lifestyle in the world. Back then a lady was a lady. She needed slaves to keep her plantation up and tend to the family. And the North burned it all down. We have never recovered from their brutality."

I could stand a lot of things in life, but not prejudice.

"I wouldn't want to live in a house built on the backs of slaves," I said. "And as far as the Swedish nobility stuff, how does that help me now? It's completely irrelevant. I'm struggling to get through college with help from Mrs. T—a northerner. I couldn't care less about nobility."

Her white, ghost-like face was now crimson red.

"Hush up, child. I'm disappointed in you, Anna. You've had too much education for your own good. You should be married by now with lots of children. Like your sister."

Where had I heard that before?

"Thank you, Aunt Sarah, but I choose to get my education first."

With that, head held high, I waltzed into the kitchen, to make the all-important salad.

Dinner was polite. The discussion was about safe issues: the relatives and how they were doing and the delicious meal. All through dessert, I could feel Sarah staring at me and Mother giving me dirty looks.

I had accomplished nothing. I believe she was gunning for me before she even came in the door. Neither of us had won the war.

After they left, while I did the dishes, Mother sat frowning at the kitchen table with her cigarettes and coffee. She had not spoken to me since dinner.

No wonder.

I dared ask. I had to know. "Mother, do you feel the same way about Negroes and the south as Aunt Sarah does?"

"Of course, I do."

"Oh, my Lord," I said.

"Anna, you have a lot of nerve speaking up to her like you did. I'm ashamed of you."

Before she could rip into me any further, I quickly escaped to my bedroom and closed the door.

For weeks I thought about how stupid I was to take on an eighty-year-old woman. What had gotten into me? At least that discussion with Aunt Sarah helped clarify in my mind, once again, exactly who I was and what I believed in. I had read a required reading psychology book in one of my classes that talked about how sometimes, when a person doesn't fit into their family, it's a good thing—that it's okay to be the odd man out in a dysfunctional family. Though it's miserable for you as a child, and you think you're weird for not fitting in, as an adult you can look back and see that it was better that you were different.

I thanked God for showing me that. Admittedly, Aunt Sarah was the radical extreme of the relatives, but she was greatly admired, at least by Mother. Maybe her admiration came from wishing that she had had the kind of life Aunt Sarah had lived— that she hadn't married so young and had us so early.

Too bad. With Mother's looks, she could have had any man she wanted. They certainly chased after her enough over the years. *Was it possible to be too pretty for your own good? Then you don't even have to try to be kind or gentle?*

But, after Daddy, all her husbands were uneducated, blue collar men—not that there's anything wrong with that. But she was never satisfied with any of them monetarily, and always demanded more than they could provide. Perhaps she thought she couldn't attract an educated man who could bring home the bacon at the level she demanded.

Of course, each time she searched for a new husband, even though she was gorgeous, she did have baggage—Georgia and me. Maybe, in a spouse, what she wanted was someone she could control. That certainly did not work with my dad who was his own man, talented, educated, handsome and, yes, had quite a strong ego of his own. With their opposite personalities, I marveled at how they managed to stay together for any length of time at all. But, thank God, at least they were married long enough that I got here.

The end of summer was approaching, and as I enjoyed Southern California more and more, I knew I'd have to make an important decision soon that could change the course of my life.

CHAPTER 17

TWO ROADS

Two roads diverged into a wood...and I didn't know
which one to take.
(With apologies to Robert Frost)

BETH AND ALLIE EACH CALLED in August of 1957 and said they wanted to stay in Los Angeles, live with their parents, and transfer to Cal State, LA. After getting a taste of Southern California, with great weather, lots to do, and endless opportunities, they weren't going back to the small Geneseo campus and being snowed in all winter with few guys around.

Allie had reunited with an old flame whom she'd met on a previous visit. Within a few months, they eloped. Beth was in heaven, since she was dating the handsome son of a well-known TV star.

Even when I prayed about it, I was torn and uncertain about what to do. If I stayed, I'd have to live with Mother. That would be difficult, not only because our values were so different, but because she disapproved of me going to college. Her disdain that I wasn't married yet had already caused tension between us. In addition, since she only had one friend, a woman who lived across the back fence, her plan for me being there was that I would spend my time entertaining her.

In hopes of making my future more secure, I was determined to finish school. I believed that if I had a college degree, if I ever married and something happened to my husband, as it had for Mrs. T, I'd be able to provide for myself and my children. Essentially, I'd be able to paddle my own canoe.

To become a teacher in California for grades 7-14 required a bachelor's degree, then one year of student teaching, and finally, a teaching credential. Since I loved Southern California, I thought I'd at least investigate some of the local colleges. UCLA was too far a drive, and, for me, USC was not affordable. So, I checked out the new state college campus in Northridge, a half-hour drive away. Although it was a small campus, it offered lots of interesting majors.

They even had a major in music. *Oh, boy. I could change majors to that?* I called Mrs. T. "What do you think?"

"Well, Annie, if you want to stay, I think it's a great idea. If you live with your mom and have to commute half an hour, you'll need transportation. If that's what you want to do, I'll send you enough money to buy a used car and I'll also pay for your tuition and books."

Even though I was once again grateful for her offer, I agonized over the decision. She was still very independent and healthy, but I worried about her living alone and growing old without me there to take care of her.

Finally, I decided to transfer to Cal State Northridge and major in music, with an emphasis in choral conducting, and a minor in English. Mother was happy that I was staying and, though I didn't see a lot of Georgia, she was pleased, too.

I didn't know anyone I could trust enough to buy a used car from except Ricky, who was knowledgeable about automobiles. He had fixed up an old bronze Pontiac convertible and urged me not to buy it because it guzzled gas and leaked oil. But I bought it anyway. Even though I had to put the top up and down by hand, oh, I felt like a celebrity driving it, with its abundance of shiny chrome. A few of my new friends and I had an understanding that if it started to rain while we were in class, we'd rush out to the parking lot and put the top up.

What was I thinking to major in music? I hadn't touched a piano in years, so my skills in that area needed a lot of work. I discovered that most of the music majors performed almost at concert-level with the goal of being a professional on their instrument. But I only needed enough piano skill to accompany a choir or singing group. However, tribulation produces perseverance, so, in the rehearsal rooms on campus, I played catch-up, digging in and practicing piano at least two to four hours a day. I loved my curriculum: theory, orchestration, instruments, choir, voice, music education, counterpoint, composition, conducting, and music appreciation. My passion for choral conducting was ironic since I was following in both Daddy's footsteps and those of my Latvian forebearers.

The classes were so small that there were often only ten of us, while UCLA and USC had huge classes. Still, I worried that, by comparison, I was getting a second-rate education. I would learn that I was so wrong. We had quality professors and practically private lessons.

Because Ricky's campus at UCLA and mine at Northridge were so far apart, I didn't see as much of him once school started.

I got a part-time job working in the library twenty hours a week, which felt good; it didn't seem fair to accept so much financial help from Mrs. T, especially since I didn't live in New York State anymore. So, I wrote her and said I'd try to manage on my own. Money would be tight, but between working and living at home, I thought I could make it.

With the price of gas, carpooling seemed like a good idea. But in that huge San Fernando Valley, I didn't know anyone who lived in my section of the Valley. One day I was sitting with my girlfriend, Pam, and six others at lunch in our small cafeteria, when her boyfriend came up and introduced his friend, Hugh.

Hugh had a very dark tan, offset by a crisp, white tennis outfit. He was short but very muscular, and I learned that he had been a champion gymnast in high school. Because of his dark, soulful eyes and long lashes, the kids called him Lashes. Years later, Pam told me that Hugh took one look at me and said, "That's the girl I'm going to marry." How strange, since I sure wasn't a vision of the golden-tanned California girls that I admired so much.

As fate would have it, Hugh lived in Sun Valley, near Mother's house in North Hollywood, and was eager to carpool with me. We had everything in common. Both dads were professional musicians and had played in the big bands. Hugh loved music and had won a scholarship to USC in French horn, but he didn't want to go into music full-time. His dad had been one of the top big band drummers during the swing era, performing with Horace Heidt and Frankie Carle, and now had a studio in Sun Valley with teachers for many instruments. He did gigs on the weekends. All three sons played drums well, and Hugh also blew a hot trumpet.

Soon we were dating, and the more time I spent with Hugh, the less time I had for Ricky. Since Hugh was so persistent, the distance between Ricky and me grew wider.

Hugh and I were broke most of the time, using every penny we had for gas money to get to school, so we spent a lot of time at his house and in his family pool. His kind parents often invited me to stay for dinner. Since his mom was a fabulous cook, I couldn't resist. Later, I learned that they were eager for us to date, since they saw me as a clean-cut girl and they did not approve of his uncle in Vegas matching him up with showgirls. Hugh's dad and I were buddies from the start. Gentle, handsome, and always smiling, he was devoted to his family, which, of course, impressed me.

Saturday nights, whenever Hugh and I could scrape together enough money to go to a drive-in movie, his little brother, who was eleven years younger, would volunteer to contribute the last dollar or two if we'd take him along. As the evening dew descended on the open convertible, the three of us huddled under a blanket in the front seat—with him in between us. It kept us pretty innocent, but he was a sweet, unspoiled kid and we enjoyed him.

Hugh encouraged me in my music and loved hearing about every class. After six months, we were going steady, and in a year were engaged. We went together for two more years and couldn't wait to finish school so we could be married and finally be on our own. Meanwhile, I was pleased that we were both believers and on Sundays we often attended Grace Community Church, just down the street from Mother's, where John MacArthur was pastor.

* * *

Experience is the hardest kind of teacher. It gives you the test first and the lesson afterward.
- Oscar Wilde

Even though my romantic life was great, life wasn't going well between Mother and me. By the end of each week, after classes, practicing two to four hours a day, carrying a full load of eighteen units, doing homework, and working twenty to thirty hours in the library, I was exhausted. I also had a few classes on Saturdays, and, in addition, had to rehearse even more in preparation for my senior recital. Mother was angry that I wasn't enough of a companion to her while Tom worked overtime.

I was concerned about doing my best in my senior recital, which involved accompanying a string quartet. If I didn't pass that, I wouldn't graduate, which would set me back a year before I could even start student teaching. The pressure was on to make every minute count.

Mother, who never made breakfast, was a late sleeper, so I always tried to sneak out of the house to drive to my early 8:00 a.m. classes before she woke up for her coffee and cigarettes.

Before I left, I'd quietly slip into the kitchen to grab something to eat. Then she'd call to me from her bedroom, "Anna, won't you fix Mother some breakfast, too?"

"Mother, I'm on my way out the door. I'll be late to class if I do."

"Don't you love Mother?"

So, to keep the peace, I'd cook an egg and make some toast and coffee for her, then fly out the door for school, speeding all the way. *Why didn't she care that I would be late?*

I fumed as I sat in heavy traffic in the half-hour drive to Northridge. *Did she have no concern for my safety, having to rush to get to class on time? How could she be so self-centered? What was the matter with her?*

I tried once again to figure her out. *Was she jealous that I was having a better time at the age of twenty than she did? Since she had Georgia at sixteen and me at eighteen, and had a hard life, why didn't she want a better start for me? Is she against my going to college because Georgia didn't?* But Georgia didn't want to go and preferred to get married.

Or was it that she was jealous of what Mrs. T had done for me? Why wasn't she grateful instead? Oh, God. Why couldn't she just love me for who I was? Why did she still resent that I was like my dad?

Most hurtful of all was realizing that she just didn't care—that she was incapable of caring. *But didn't I know that before I came to California?* And here I was again, under her control just as I had been as a child. *How stupid that I came out here. Why did I do it?*

I usually arrived on campus still fuming, my class serving as a great distraction—a great escape. When I parked my car and entered the campus atmosphere, I felt a warm glow of determination rise within me.

I'll show her. I'll show the world that this girl will succeed, no matter the price, no matter the effort. God be my witness. I will, I certainly will.

I began to accept the fact that if we missed bonding together when I was young, it was too late now. Even though I'd come here to try to work things out between us, I slowly realized that nothing I did now was going to change the dynamics that had been set in motion even before I was born. She and I had traveled two entirely different paths in life and there was no way at this late date they would be able to converge. *Couldn't we at least just get along?*

But we were hopelessly different. My whole philosophy and outlook on life came from the Thompson family and was directly opposite from hers. Mother was not going to change, and I certainly wasn't going to change, either.

Poor Mother. If I had grown up with her, maybe I wouldn't have been so critical of her lifestyle and outlook. If I'd never lived with Mrs. T, I would never have known the difference. Georgia, on the other hand, knew how to get along with her. Of course, it helped that Georgia had children, making Mother a happy grandmother.

Disappointed in myself, I wondered what was wrong with me. *Maybe I'd better not have kids, since, apparently, I had no idea how a normal family worked.* The only time I'd been in a two-parent family was the two short years I lived with Daddy and Mama. Thank God, they were happy.

As Mother and I worked together in the kitchen, the comparison was painful. To my horror, she would throw enough leftover food down the garbage disposal to feed a family of four, whereas Mrs. T and I ate almost every leftover. Maximizing charge cards to buy lavish purchases, Mother and Tom lived from paycheck to paycheck. Since Mother's family had been poor, I would have expected her to be more careful. After living with Mrs. T, who was so frugal but not poor, I couldn't make sense of it. My sister and I reasoned that since Mother was raised in the Great Depression, somehow, in her mind, being lavish now was making up for the difficulties of her past. But that didn't make sense either, since

Daddy and the Thompson family had lived through the same era and were the opposite of Mother.

Months passed, and the situation grew more tense. I stayed away from home as much as possible, staying either at school or at Hugh's house. My senior year, as soon as the first dorm was built at Cal State Northridge, I moved in and added more work hours to pay for it. Handling expenses all on my own made me proud.

Life was exhausting, though. Tired all the time from never getting enough sleep, and often coming down with colds or the flu, I still wondered if I'd made the right decision by staying in California. But it was too late to turn back now.

I missed Mrs. T, especially in those stressful years, even though I called her often. What if she got sick at home alone? I agonized about that for months, wanting to be in both places. Though Mrs. T cheered me on from a distance, I couldn't imagine my life without her. What would I do when she was gone? Always thinking ahead of what would be right for me, she rarely thought of what would be best for her.

But graduation, student teaching, marriage, and a job were now within sight. Soon I really would be able to paddle my own canoe. I was determined to be a success, not only for my own sake but also because Mrs. T believed in me. I didn't have the heart to let her down.

CHAPTER 18

PADDLIN' PAYS OFF

A Sentimental Journey

I WAS IN LOVE WITH HIM and loved his family, but I thought a lot about the decision to marry Hugh, nonetheless. Our wedding was to occur during the semester break right after my graduation in January of 1960. Mrs. T invited me back for a few weeks the summer before. She wanted to be sure that I was solid in my decision to spend the rest of my life with Hugh.

I glowed with pleasure to see her waiting for me at the airport, all smiles, just as she had been waiting when Mother, Georgia, and I arrived as complete strangers, by train, that snowy, cold night when I was five years old—that magical moment when my life was completely transformed by her love.

After four years in the Marines, Jamie was in town. He had come by the house often before I came back, visiting Mrs. T and asking about me. Having raised two sons of her own, she had always loved and even understood him. But he and I had not written since I moved to California three years earlier.

Mrs. T thought it was important that I see him one last time, just to be sure that I had no lingering feelings. I certainly didn't want to feel anything for him because here I was, engaged. He called and came over one afternoon. We sat on the front porch steps and visited for a few hours, making small talk and catching up on what each of our friends were doing and where they all were. As he spoke, I was impressed with what the Marine Corps had done for him. And, unfortunately for my guarded heart, I saw that he was still as handsome as all get out—all grown up, the respectful, gracious smiling Marine. *Darn it.* The strong attraction to him was still there. My heart skipped a beat when he reached over and took my hand.

"Annie, I've thought about you all this time."

I smiled at the words I had yearned to hear years ago.

"And, well, I figured when I got out of the Marines, you'd be back in Olean from Geneseo and, we'd get together again and, uh, well, end up getting married."

What? How ridiculous. Did he actually assume I'd still be available after not hearing from him all this time? I couldn't believe it. Still, I was flattered.

I could tell that even though he was unrealistic, he was sincere. Too many emotions were tumbling around in my head at once, including pain and anger because he had let the years slip by while I longed for him. Still, I didn't want to hurt him, so I spoke my words slowly.

"You know, Jamie, you didn't get in touch with me for three years and it broke my heart because I loved you so much. You never asked me to wait for you."

He gave me a weak smile, probably wondering what was next.

"But I finally moved on with my life. Now I'm engaged to a wonderful man."

I felt sad realizing that if he had truly loved me all that time, he would have reached out to me while I still loved him. *He had been pretty casual about it all—and immature to have taken me for granted.*

But it was too late for us.

"You're a great guy," I said. "I loved you for so long but always knew that I loved you more than you loved me. Now, my life is in California and I'll be getting married this January. You will always have a special place in my heart and I'm so sorry it didn't work out between us."

As we hugged, I didn't want to let go, knowing that I was releasing an important and emotional part of my past. He tried to save face by being casual. "Okay, I understand. I wish you the best," he said.

Smiling a friendly goodbye-and-good-luck, he drove away. I waved to him, hiding my tears of regret. *Had I made the right decision? Of course, I had. Keep thinking that. Use your head. Those precious words he had spoken weren't important to me anymore. Yes, he had loved me—but not enough. My life was in California with Hugh.* I believed I'd made the right decision.

I'd knew I'd never see Jamie again.

Being at home again with Mrs. T was wonderful. Lively as ever and very involved with her three grandchildren, she often babysat for Paul and his wife so they could get away. I hoped that it was a relief for her to no longer be responsible for me. As I headed back to California, the drive to the Buffalo airport was gloomy. I did not know when I'd see her again.

That fall, I returned to the Cal State Northridge dorm. Events were happening quickly then. In December, I accompanied a string quartet on piano for my senior recital. Thanks to many hours of practice with the group, I did better than I expected and even enjoyed performing.

Two weeks later, doubling over with severe stomach cramps while working in the library, I was rushed to the hospital and had an emergency appendectomy. But I recovered just in time to participate in my graduation ceremony to celebrate a bachelor's degree in music and a minor in English. Mrs. T, calling from Olean, was jubilant, realizing that I was the first person in my family to graduate from college and excited that I was getting close to becoming a teacher. The next step would be two semesters of student teaching in order to get my teaching credential.

A week after graduation, in a little chapel in Burbank, Hugh and I were married. Daddy flew out to meet Hugh and his family and to walk me down the aisle. A friend of Georgia's loaned me her wedding dress, and my three bridesmaids were a Catholic (my sister, who had converted to her husband's faith), a Jew (my roommate), and a Protestant (my friend Allie). I liked that.

Mrs. T, not wanting to overshadow anyone—especially my parents and Hugh's—didn't come to the wedding. I missed her so much on our special day and had to fight being depressed because I would have loved for everyone to meet her. But, as usual, she was forever thinking of others and not herself.

Georgia had given me a lovely shower a week before where, thank goodness, we received much needed household items. Mother, meanwhile, figured out how to use the wedding to her advantage. For years she had wanted to add on a large, wood-paneled family room to their house. I didn't understand why, since only the two of them lived there. But my wedding reception was the perfect excuse to talk Tom into doing it. I tried to convince her that cake and punch in the church hall would be just fine, but she insisted. The expense of the room addition? No problem. Tom could just work more overtime.

My bridesmaids told me later that Tom circulated among the guests, proudly announcing what sacrifices they had made to send me to college. Whatever. Everyone knew better. I decided, again, that the least said, the soonest mended, so I let it go.

* * *

Letting go means to come to the realization that some people are a part of your history, but not a part of your destiny.
- Sam Maraboli

Before our wedding day, Hugh and I discussed what an appropriate relationship with Mother would be. Hugh, being a psychology major, had unceremoniously told me on several occasions—because he saw what he called Mother's passive-aggressive behavior—that my mother was "nuts." We made the decision to take the high road by visiting on the usual holidays. Even though their house was filled with cigarette smoke, we would stay a respectable length of time. Whenever appropriate, we would have them over for dinner along with Hugh's family.

Hugh's parents gave us a wedding gift of a three-day honeymoon at Lake Arrowhead, for which we were very grateful. As a gift, Mrs. T sent us some money, which she knew we were much in need of.

After the honeymoon, it took me months to get over the wonder of coming home every night to the same house to be with the one I loved. During the long three years before the wedding, that had seemed like it would never happen.

We settled down in a tiny one-bedroom guest house in someone's backyard where the rent was cheap. Close to Birmingham High School (where I would later student teach) and the freeway, we could commute quickly to work and school.

Hugh was eager to start his new job and get in on the ground floor of training in the world of computers. He took employment with an insurance company in LA even before he had finished his degree. His friends laughed at him for taking such low paying, entry level work, but he was smart enough to see that computers would be the future. How right he was.

We didn't have much money, but hardly noticed it because we were so in love, and we felt that we were building our futures. So, we managed well by taking sack lunches and driving our old cars.

A year later, Hugh got a better job at JPL—the Jet Propulsion Lab, in Pasadena, which is part of Caltech. Almost everyone there had a PhD but no knowledge of computers, so with his experience, they needed him.

That next December, Mrs. T flew out and stayed at a local hotel so she could visit us for a few days and go to the Rose Bowl Parade. The tiny, old guest house that Hugh and I rented was embarrassing to me, but she thought it was a wonderful start for us.

I spent two semesters student teaching: one semester at Sequoia Junior High directing a girls' chorus, and one semester at Birmingham High School with an English class of gifted tenth-graders.

Since we didn't have a piano, I had to rent a small spinet for six dollars a month so I could go over the music at home for my girls' chorus. Eventually, the rental money added up to a down payment so I could buy it.

We attended a large church in Van Nuys where I led a junior choir of one hundred kids. I loved directing that many children in a youth-oriented congregation and was inspired as I learned that I could really get them to sing.

In the spring of 1961, I earned my General Secondary Credential for teaching grades 7-14. *At last.* Finally, no matter what happened in life, I'd be prepared to paddle my own canoe.

Mrs. T was proud.

* * *

I've suffered a great many catastrophes in my life. Most of them never happened.
- Mark Twain

The interviews for finding a teaching job began. Memories of not getting into nursing school still haunted me. I had worried all the way through college that a school district would, before hiring me, require me to take a vision test. *Would I be rejected again because I didn't have 20/20 vision?* What a relief that I was only required to take a chest x-ray. I guess the thinking was that if you could see well enough to get through college and earn a driver's license, you were okay.

I didn't want to work in a big district like Los Angeles City, because they could place me anywhere and a long commute wasn't appealing. So, I interviewed in several smaller districts. We really liked Burbank; it was an easy commute for both of our jobs and even close to Georgia and her family.

After the principal of Luther Burbank Junior High interviewed and hired me, I was flying high. I would start in the fall.

Right away, I called Mrs. T. Thrilled and happy for me, once again she reminded me, "Now, Annie, you've got something that no one can ever take away from you—a college education. That's your insurance. You've stuck with it against all odds. I won't ever have to worry about you. You can take care of yourself now, no matter what the future brings."

In August, as I prepared for school, I wrote her a long letter. Pouring my heart out to her, I explained that none of this would have been possible without her lifetime commitment to me. I spelled it out carefully, so she would know for sure what she meant to me and how much I loved her. I credited her for teaching me all my values, including any drive and every bit of confidence I had.

It would be the most important letter I would ever write.

All summer I worked on lesson plans for the courses the principal gave me to teach. Oh, wow—my assignments were quite a mixture, including social studies, several ninth grade English classes, and music appreciation. I hoped someday to teach only music.

The week before school started, the principal called me into his office. "Ann," he said, "I'm giving you one class of ninth-graders who are C, D, and even F students, many of whom still cannot write a simple sentence. I am placing eight boys in your class who have been troublemakers for two years. Here's a list of their names so you can look for them. If you get them through ninth grade and they graduate, you will have earned your salary."

I thought he was kidding. I learned later that principals often gave new teachers the problem kids that others didn't want, to see if the new hires could handle it. The administration needed to find out before they earned tenure, which happens after five years of teaching. After that, it was difficult to fire anyone.

During the weeks before school, I spent long days in my classroom after everyone else had gone home, preparing and decorating bulletin boards. Once the semester started, a master teacher would occasionally sit in the back of the room to see how I was doing.

With so many lists to keep track of, I lost the list of troublemakers. And I sure wasn't going to go to the principal to admit it.

On the first day, I introduced myself to each class. I said, "Having a new teacher can be a great advantage to you students, because I don't know anything about you. I will only know how you behave in my room. That's all that matters to me. So, if you need a fresh start in this school, here is where you can have it."

For the most part, it worked.

On day three, in the class that had so many low achievers, I noticed as they entered the room that some of the boys were showing off their switchblades to everyone. That would not do.

When the bell rang and class started, I said, "I see your switchblades, and I could send you to the office or report you to the principal, and you'd be in big trouble."

Beneath their cool exterior, the boys looked worried.

"Let's do this instead. Bring them up to my desk and leave them here. After school you come pick them up, take them home, and don't ever bring them back."

It never occurred to me what I'd do if they didn't cooperate. But, to a one, they brought them to my desk, came after school to pick them up, and as far as I knew, never brought them back.

On day four, the ringleader, who sat in the front right desk making wisecracks to get attention from everyone, continually interrupted me. As I was working on the board explaining the parts of a simple sentence in as many ways as I could think of, he made a remark that was really funny. I don't remember what it was, but even I laughed. He didn't know what to expect when I spun around on my heel and walked over to him.

"Jose, you have a great sense of humor. If only we could capture that on paper. Say it again, Jose. I'll write it on the board. The only rule is, no swearing. Help me, class, to clean up his sentences and we'll have something here."

All aglow now, he had the attention he needed, and suddenly it was important to all of them to find a way to put his words together. Once they saw that I wasn't going to condemn them for what they didn't know, they opened up to me with their stories and we had a great time fixing them. Slowly, tediously, these students learned to write, not only a sentence but even a paragraph. Thrilled, I couldn't believe they were learning from me, a new teacher. After school, on the fourth day, I rushed to the phone to tell Mrs. T how well it was going.

"Annie, I got your letter," she said. "I'm pleased that you remember our years together. But remember that much of your success is because of your own hard work. I always knew, if given the chance, you'd do well."

Before the first week was over, I went into the office records after school and looked up the history of all the students in that special class. From the files, it became obvious which were the eight troubled boys. These kids had a long history of suspensions, truancy, moving a lot, grandmothers in and out trying to help them, uncooperative parents, many single-parent homes with lots of siblings, and some large families on welfare. Jose had had six or seven "dads" in his mom's home in just the last two years. Many of the parents' comments when past teachers had called were, "I can't do anything with him. That's your job." In short,

172 • ANNIE FARRIS

they had given up on their own children. Memories of Mammy, who said I'd never amount to anything and gave up on me so quickly, flooded my heart.

Feeling helpless, I went home to our apartment, got down on my knees beside the bed, and said, "Lord, I only have them an hour a day. How can I possibly be of any help to them in the long run?" Their situations moved me because I understood much of what they were going through.

Now that I knew the kids better, I worked enthusiastically all weekend, throwing out some of my old lesson plans and developing new strategies. Somehow God changed my heart from, "I only have them an hour a day," to, "I have a chance to help them an hour a day and I'm up for it." I especially looked forward to that difficult class each day as I realized that God was using my life experiences and Mrs. T's can-do attitude to help me care for them.

At that time, I figured it was a blessing that my husband was rarely home. He, too, was completely consumed with his new job. I thought he was an Einstein in his field, and he thought I was a Leonard Bernstein because I could get a bunch of kids to sing. I was happy to see him apply his intelligence in work that he loved. Even so, days were sometimes lonely as I saw so little of him. We were living in two different worlds.

CHAPTER 19

THE WIND BENEATH MY WINGS

Trust in the Lord with all your heart and lean not on
your own understanding. In all your ways acknowledge
Him and he shall direct your paths.
- Proverbs 3:5

I COULD HARDLY WAIT for Monday morning, to try out my new ideas for my classes. I was enthusiastic and so were my students. To my delight, the day went well.

That day after school, as I climbed the stairs to our apartment at 6:00 p.m., I could hear the phone constantly ringing. Whoever was calling wasn't hanging up. Hugh wasn't home yet. I unlocked the door, threw my books down, and rushed to the phone.

"Hi, Anna. This is John Thompson. How are you doing?"

"Great. It's good to hear your voice. What's going on?"

After a long pause, he said, "Uh, you need to sit down."

John never called me. Something must be wrong.

"What is it? Is Mrs. T sick?"

"Well, she rode her horse Saturday morning and was fine," he said. "Sunday morning in church, she lifted up her arm to put her coat on and keeled over with a heart attack. She was rushed to the hospital and they thought she'd be okay, so we didn't call you right away, what with it being your first week of teaching and all."

"Oh, no. How is she doing?"

I held my breath as seconds passed with no response from John.

"Well, she didn't make it. She's gone."

"No. No. Please, no," I said.

"I'm so sorry we didn't call you sooner."

"I can't believe it. She's been so healthy."

"I know. We're all in shock here."

He paused again as if thinking to himself. "Look, we don't expect you to come back for the funeral, but if you can, I'll buy your ticket and pick you up at the Buffalo airport."

I needed to calm down and be coherent. *This can't be happening.* As the reality sunk in, too weak to stand up, I dropped to my knees by the couch.

"Thanks, John. I'll be on my way as soon as I can call my school and book a flight."

It doesn't matter if the district approves of my leaving—a new teacher on the sixth day of classes—I'm going.

I don't remember making the reservation or Hugh driving me to the airport. I only remember how kind my principal was when I called him. *How was I to explain? She isn't my mother or even a relative.* I just said she was the lady who raised me.

"Then you must go," he said. "We'll cover for you while you're gone. Don't worry."

On the flight back to Buffalo, in my head, I was magically wrapped in a cocoon of my most beloved music, as if I had on earphones. I heard some of my favorite hymns, such as "How Great Thou Art," "Great Is Thy Faithfulness," "This Is My Father's World," "Fairest Lord Jesus," and even some parts of "The Messiah."

I looked out at the night sky and thanked God that she did not die at home alone, as I had feared. She always said she wanted to die with her boots on and be active until the last breath, and she was.

I tried to be glad for that, repeating it over and over in my head. But I was overwhelmed with the loss of her, the love of her, the kindness of her, the humor of her, her brightness, and her totally unearned, undeserved devotion for me. I should have called her more. I should have stayed with her.

Oh, God, what will I do without her?

John drove me directly to the house. Nothing had changed since I'd been gone. It seemed so good yet so awful to be home, because she wasn't there and never would be again. I gently touched the huge oak dining room table that still had her favorite lace cloth on it, the table I had spent so many happy, snowy days underneath, playing with the dog. On the corner of the table in their usual spot were her reading glasses. She'd never need them again. I held them reverently in my hands, turned away from John, and wept. Kindly, he left me alone for a while.

"Walk through the house," he said as he came back into the dining room. "You can have anything here that you want—the baby grand piano, any of the furniture, any of the china and silver. You just make a list and we'll ship it to you."

Wrapped in memories, I went back to her bedroom. I thought of my first night there as a child when she said, "Little Annie can sleep in here with me." How kind she was when I wet the bed, wrapping me in a warm blanket while she changed the sheets. There in the corner by her walk-in closet were her boot remover and her riding boots. I sat on her twin bed, buried my face in her pillow and sobbed. I went into the kitchen. The old refrigerator with the coils on top was still there. I opened it and there was her little glass of grape juice, which she sipped every night before going to bed.

Death and I had never been this intimate before. Each of my grandparents had passed away, back when I was in high school. I loved them and was sorry, but I was not as close to them as I was to Mrs. T, and I was not able to go to their funerals in Memphis and Chicago.

But this was different. She was that one person who was a mother to me.

To see her looking so peaceful in her casket at the funeral home gave me some comfort. Hers was a life well lived and I knew she was in heaven. I'd see her again someday. Grandpa's verse that he had taught me, from Psalm 23, carried me during those three days. *Yea though I walk through the valley of the shadow of death, I will fear no evil, for thou art with me; thy rod and thy staff they comfort me...Surely goodness and mercy shall follow me all the days of my life and I will dwell in the house of the Lord forever.*

At the funeral service, Mrs. T was praised for her generosity, not only to her family and friends, but for helping the needy and numerous organizations close to her heart. Active on the music committee of her church and on the board of directors of an orphanage, she also belonged to the Olean Association for Aid to the Blind. I didn't know all that. No wonder she had such kind regard for my blind grandfather.

After the service, we drove to the cemetery through the main street of town. Busy shoppers were rushing around as if nothing had happened. *Didn't the whole world understand that the finest person I ever loved was gone?* We crossed the Allegheny River Bridge, the route I'd taken walking home from high school. *I'd lost my rock, my friend, the person I trusted the most in my whole life, the person who loved me unconditionally and stood by me no matter what.*

Why did she have to die now?

I don't understand. This isn't fair. She was only seventy-three. I knew that somehow, I had to trust God now more than ever. I turned to Proverbs 3:5 for help. "Trust in the Lord with all thine heart and lean not unto thine own understanding. In all thy ways acknowledge him, and he shall direct thy paths." *Maybe someday, when I get to the other side, I'll understand God's plan.*

We live life looking forward, but understand it looking backward.

At least I knew she was with the Lord. But even with those words of comfort, I wondered how I'd get through the days and weeks ahead because the grief was so severe. I had wanted her to live to be very old, to be a grandmother to my future children. I wanted to be good to her in her old age. But it was not to be. *Would the pain ever stop and give way to happy memories?*

For me, the cemetery was filled with fond recollections. When I was small, we went there often to water the pot of geraniums on the grave of her first child, Charles, an infant who died of pneumonia. She would be buried beside him. Years ago, she had enjoyed my enthusiasm as I ran all over the hillside carrying buckets of water to the thirsty plants on the other graves that were hardly ever visited.

After the funeral, at a buffet, Maria, her beloved and artistic neighbor from across the street, spoke with me privately.

"Mrs. T came over to read me the letter that you wrote to her," she said. "She was so happy to see that you appreciated all that she did for you and that you never forgot her. You know, you were the daughter she never had."

"Oh, thank God. I hope she got something out of our relationship other than just doing so much for me."

"Did you know," Maria said, "that they're one of the wealthiest families in the southwestern part of the state?"

"No, I didn't. There was no way to tell, because they lived so modestly. She never bragged about what they had."

"She had a hard life," Maria said, "what with her divorce when the boys were away at school. You know, divorce was a scandal back then. Rumor has it that her husband had an affair with the local dance teacher, twenty-five years younger than he."

"Oh, my gosh. I had a few lessons with her when I was a child."

"We all thought the woman married him for his money," Maria said, "because she sure wasn't happy with him as he got older and had heart trouble. She didn't like nursing him at all. He died a few years back."

"How sad," I said, remembering that if we saw his car parked in front of one of their grocery stores, we didn't go in. I saw the pain in Mrs. T's eyes those times, so I never asked her about their marriage. "Now I understand. Because of her own divorce and being on her own, that's why she was determined to prepare me to paddle my own canoe and be independent, so I'd be able to take care of myself no matter what happened in the future. I only wish I had gotten her advice about marriage, but it didn't occur to me then."

"She worked very hard," Maria said, "in the early years of the marriage, helping build up the business and raising the boys. Mr. T went to New York a lot, supposedly on business. We neighbors wondered what he did there, since the grocery stores didn't require trips to New York. Rumor had it that he was seeing several showgirls there. It was all very strange. But Mrs. T held her head high all those years. Then, after the divorce, he tried to keep her out of the very business she had built up."

"How unfair. I never knew that either."

"She had a brilliant, operatic, soprano voice," Maria said. "When she was young, her parents wanted her to study in New York. After the divorce, she lost her singing voice and never sang again. It was just gone."

That explained the stacks of music solos and oratorios on the back of the piano, including "The Messiah."

"And then you came along, Annie. The boys thought you were so good for her. She loved you from the first day."

"I'm glad to hear that," I said. "To think that I could have been good for her, too, helps a lot."

* * *

You'll Always Be My Hero.

I had to get back to my teaching job soon. John and I went to the house one more time. "Remember I said that we can ship anything to you?" he reminded me. "We both have homes of our own now and don't need anything. She'd want you to have whatever you want."

Touched by their generosity, I had thought about his offer for two days. She had given so much to me, not only as a child, but had helped me through high school and college, both financially and emotionally. How could I take anything more from her?

"The only things I want are her pillow and the two silver candelabras that sat on the dining room table my whole life," I said.

"Are you sure you don't want the piano?"

"We just don't have room for it in our small apartment and we can't afford to store it."

I would have loved to have the baby grand because of the happy memories I had with her patiently sitting on that stool with me, helping and encouraging me with my first lessons. But it wasn't practical. I had no way of knowing at the time, but my heavenly Father made a mental note of that.

I didn't know when I left Mrs. T's house whether I'd ever be back again. My home, my backyard, my mountain, where I had learned what unconditional love was all about.

The day after the funeral, John drove me to the Buffalo airport. I wondered if I'd ever see John again—the guy who had transformed my life by meeting Mother when he was a Navy pilot.

The flight home was a gray blur to me, as were the coming weeks and months. I struggled to regain enthusiasm for teaching when all I wanted to do was to go somewhere and be alone with my thoughts.

On the first day back at school, I didn't know what to expect. The principal had told my classes that I had gone back east because of a death in the family. They were just young kids. *How would they treat me? Would they take advantage or make remarks to me?*

The students were kind. I felt as fragile as an eggshell and it would not have taken much to upset me. But my grief fog carried me, as I walked through those early months of teaching with the joy knocked out of me. For a long time, I didn't care about anything. But I knew I must go on. She would expect that of me, and she had put so much of her life into mine that I wanted to do a good job and live to make her proud.

I discovered that most of the kids in my class who had poor grades had never read a book. Finally, I decided we'd read one together, a chapter at a time, at the end of each class session. They needed to see what it felt like to enjoy reading.

I checked out thirty copies of *The Yearling* by Marjorie Kinnan Rawlings. Being poor readers, very few students were willing to read out loud in front of their classmates. They were embarrassed, so I kept their turns very short to ease their discomfort.

The Yearling is the story of a poor family on a farm in the backwoods of Florida, barely surviving in the depression of 1938. A yearling is found eating in the family's garden—their only source of food. The twelve-year-old son is very fond of the yearling—his only pet. But as the fawn grows quickly, it begins eating too much and something needs to be done. Finally, the father tells the young son that if the family is to survive, he will have to shoot the yearling.

As we came to the final chapter, the kids took turns reading out loud, a few sentences at a time. I read the very last pages. Sadly, the dad shoots the yearling and explains to his son that life knocks you down, but you take it, get up again and go on.

As I looked up from my reading, I saw that many students had tears in their eyes. They could relate to the harshness of life. I could, too. As a new teacher, I was happy that in some small way, I could care about them like Mrs. T cared about me. I also could take what life threw at me and go on.

They got it. Finally, the students could see the value of reading a book. As the semester progressed, the class read better and better. It was magic to see them grow. I loved them, every one. *I can do this. I am really a teacher, just as Mrs. T said I would be. With the work ethic and values she taught me, I will succeed.*

I stood in the back of the auditorium with sunglasses on so no one could see me misty-eyed as I watched my students graduate in June, including the eight boys who were supposed to be so terrible. Proud of them and of myself, I thought that perhaps if I could help *them*, maybe I did know enough that I could qualify to be a mom myself someday.

CHAPTER 20

MUSIC IN OUR GENES

There are only two ways to live your life. One is as
though nothing is a miracle. The other is as though
everything is a miracle.
- Albert Einstein

IN EARLY JUNE, A BREAKFAST BANQUET WAS HELD at
the Smoke House in Burbank to celebrate the retirement
of the head of the music department at our school. To my
amazement, the principal offered me the job. Since there were
other teachers who had been there much longer than I had, I
was surprised and elated. At last, in the fall, I'd have all music
classes.

As we waited for the food to be served, whenever I tried to
talk to anyone, I kept gagging. A week later, a trip to the doctor
revealed that I was pregnant. Hugh and I were thrilled. Our baby
was due in February.

I asked Hugh, "Should I go back in the fall and teach? It's my
dream job—all music."

"Do what you want," he said. "Think about it. But you'll be
putting in long hours again. I'm not sure that's a good idea."

"If I return," I said, "I could have a solid career that I love, with
good benefits and summers off. But I want, at least for a while,
to be a stay-at-home mom. No latchkey kids for me after having
been one myself. I understand that there are situations when a
woman has to work, but that's a different story."

"Maybe you could take a year or two off," he said.

"We've saved most of my salary and, even though your income isn't a lot yet, if we're careful, we can make it," I said. "Then I could be home with the baby, at least for a while." So, after much prayer and discussion, I decided not to return to teaching in the fall and stay home, take it easy, and prepare for the baby.

Once again, Mrs. T and her generosity helped us make that decision. She had left me $5,000. With that money and most of my year's salary as a down payment, we bought a small, brand new, three-bedroom tract home in the Lakeview Terrace area of the San Fernando Valley, not far from Burbank.

But during the early months of pregnancy, as I felt my body change, my worst fears haunted me. I realized that this was a *baby*, a real human being, growing inside me. *What have I done? I don't know how to be a mom. What was I thinking? I don't know how to raise a healthy, happy child. I have no background for this, no example to follow. Having been a teacher, where the kids were in my classroom only one hour a day, and went home to their parents, who were responsible for them, was not the same as raising a child 24/7 for eighteen-plus years. Could I do this right? There were no guarantees. Teaching was easy compared to parenting.*

Taking care of a baby's physical needs would be daunting enough. I hadn't even been around enough babies to know what to do. But worse yet was wondering if I could be a loving, patient, and kind mother.

Will I be like my mother? Impatient and eager to dump my child with someone else so I can focus on my own interests—dump her with just anyone else if times get rough? Will I be able to look beyond my own interests and put this child first?

What makes me think I can do that? I didn't know. I was scared.

I spent many sleepless nights thinking about my mother in a whole different light. *How could she have left us alone at night in such a dangerous neighborhood, when we were so young and vulnerable? Why did she hate me one minute and ignore me the next?*

Would I be like that?

Why did she seem so eager to leave me with Mrs. T and not contact me for two years? In a new and different way, the pain stabbed my very soul. For most of my life, I had been so grateful for the love of Mrs. T that I hadn't thought much about Mother's role in leaving me behind. *How could she have done that to her own child? How could she have not loved me?*

Would I be like that?

Then, through my tears, I loved Mrs. T all the more. I remembered her getting up so early on those cold winter mornings to make me a hot breakfast before she drove me to school. I remembered how she enjoyed braiding my hair and shopping for just the right ribbons to match my outfits. I remembered how proud she was that I had musical talent, like my daddy, when I played my violin well. I remembered what a good grandma she was to Paul's kids, always so eager to have them over for the weekend, so Paul and Ruth could get away. Even though she was exhausted when they left, her joy in being with them shone in her eyes.

In the dark of the night, I resolved that I could not—I *would* not—be like my mother. *I will prepare.* I attended a parenting class and read every book I could find on child rearing. I even practiced cuddling on our little collie-shepherd puppy—but he was easy to hug and play with. I walked him and took him to obedience training until I was so large I couldn't waddle to the class. Hugh took him to the last class, where our dog won first prize.

Through my reading, I learned that a child is influenced partly through heredity and partly through environment. I vowed I would create a loving environment for our baby. *I can do it. I will do it.*

So, I sang to this little person who lived inside my belly. She or he was real to me now, and I could hardly wait to meet our baby.

I wondered if Hugh would be able to help me. His long hours kept him occupied, and he was tired when he got home. Quiet and reserved as he was, and with insomnia keeping him up reading most of the night, would he be a good dad?

It's a good thing I hadn't gone back to work. I often took long naps, worked on the new house, planted geraniums, and ate like a starving puppy.

The big Christmas concert at church was in early December. I was very pregnant, since the baby was due in a little over a month. I waddled to the podium, feeling like a small elephant, then led my children's choir in a few Christmas carols. When we were done, we sat in the front rows while the adults sang. Seated in the orchestra, right in front of the timpani—the big kettle drums—I could feel every vibration. At the end, as the hundred-voice adult choir sang the Hallelujah Chorus, the timpani pounded out every beat of the last five Hallelujahs—and exactly on the beat, the baby kicked from inside my stomach. Right then I knew we had a musical child.

In that big congregation, some of the kids' families didn't attend church and hadn't had a pastor, or anyone, come by and see them. I decided that before the baby was born, I would personally visit the home of each of the kids in choir so their family would feel welcomed. I went out two or three afternoons a week in the hours after school or early evening, so that by the time our baby came, I had seen them all. Of course, toward the end, I could barely roll myself through the door, but I laughed about that and was tickled to have done it.

In February, right on time, our beautiful baby girl, Shannon, was born. Awestruck the first time I held this tiny pink bundle, I immediately knew unconditional love. Hugh and I counted all her fingers and toes just to be sure they were all there. My fears of being a good mom faded as I could hardly wait to take her home, care for her when she needed me, and love her every day of my life.

How could any mother hold a helpless baby and not want the best for her? How could our own mother have not cared enough to shield me and my half-sister from the dangers that life brought us? How was it that she had not cared enough to protect me, as Mrs. T had? Mrs. T was the exact opposite of my mother, and as I remembered her, I loved her all the more.

That spring, Daddy and the family drove out to see Shannon—a bright little blonde who never missed a thing as she smiled and cooed. Because she was fascinated from the start with every living creature, including our dog and even tiny bugs in the yard, we should have known she'd grow up to be a biologist.

Two years and three months after Shannon was born, along came our Gina. A smiling little gal from the first moment, she was alert to everything around her. We could not have asked for more, as she was a mellow, happy baby. We were glad to see that our devoted collie-shepherd chose to sleep under their cribs as chief guard dog.

With our new family, God had given me what I had always wanted—a new life and a chance to have a happy home.

As soon as she could crawl, Gina was climbing everything within reach, a natural born gymnast like her dad had been. When she was four, I plucked her off the bookcases and took her to Tiny Tot Tumbling and, later, to ballet. When she was older, she also became a champion gymnast.

I thought my job as a parent was to cultivate any natural talents the girls had, just as Mrs. T had done for me. Much like it is with teaching, you start where the kids are and build on that. Even though I wanted to develop their strengths, I felt that it was important for them, when they grew up, to choose what they wanted to do. I wished Mrs. T could have been there to see them and advise me.

When Shannon and Gina were three and six-months old, because it was closer to JPL and had a good school district, we moved to La Crescenta.

* * *

God gave us music that we might pray without words.
- Author unknown

When the girls were preschoolers, after their afternoon naps, I'd open the patio door and let them play in our fenced yard with their toys and our dog. Meanwhile, I'd be right inside the sliding glass door at the piano, singing, sight-reading music, and vocally running scales. I hoped, eventually, to pick up some part-time work doing studio background singing and commercials. I loved those brief moments each day, remembering Mrs. T sitting at her baby grand, helping me learn to read music.

But, well...it didn't work out exactly as I had planned. When Shannon and Gina heard me singing, they would come in, crawl up on the piano stool and say, "Show me, Mommy."

"No, this is Mommy's time to practice. You go play with the dog for a few minutes while I sight-read."

"No, Mommy. Show me."

Gee, can't I have just a few minutes to myself? But I knew that the best time to teach a child is when they are curious, and I should offer them whatever they wanted to learn.

So, I showed them the keyboard. "Okay. Line your belly button up right here to the middle of the piano. That's called C. To the left you have A, B, then C."

Then, on some large notebook paper, I drew a staff and notes. We'd only spend a few minutes a day doing that, but they just couldn't get enough of it. Before many weeks, they were sight-reading music even before they learned to read. Because I didn't know any better, and didn't think anything about it, it never occurred to me it might be hard to teach such small children to read music. But like two eager little sponges, they soaked up anything I showed them.

I also noticed what clear, sweet voices they had—right on pitch—and how quickly they picked up any of the fun songs and hymns we sang together. Just as my sister and I had when we were little, they were even able to harmonize by ear. I should not have been surprised, with musicality on both sides of the family.

At that time, I had no idea what exciting adventures lay ahead of us with our music.

When Hugh's dad—my California Dad, as I called him—asked me to join him and his keyboard player to form a music trio, I was ecstatic. They already played around Southern California for large parties on the weekends—weddings, bar mitzvahs, and other celebrations, at some of the ritziest hotels in Beverly Hills and the Valley. These men were two of the finest professional musicians I'd ever heard. Dad, who had been a famous drummer in the big band era, and Frank, a keyboard player who could improvise anything, had a huge fan base and they were making some good money.

I became their lead singer and master of ceremonies (MC), humbling to me because even though I had a pleasant singing voice, I was not in the same league as a Streisand or Kelly Clarkson. Hugh was satisfied to see me out on weekends contributing to our finances. Meanwhile, to bring in extra cash during weekday afternoons and Saturdays, I taught folk guitar classes at home. My theory was that as long as I could bring in some extra income at home, I wouldn't have to go back to teaching while the kids were young.

Having learned from Mrs. T that if I was going to do something, I must do my best, I wanted to improve my vocal technique, so I started taking voice lessons in Hollywood from Margaret, a well-known voice coach. Even though Mrs. T had lost her big, operatic voice, she used to sing softly with me when I was a child and had given me confidence that I had a pleasant voice.

As I practiced vocal exercises at home, running scales, I laughed out loud because as I sang higher and higher, our collie-shepherd howled mournfully and clawed frantically at the patio door to escape. I guess it hurt his ears.

At one of my lessons, I said to my coach, "Margaret, my little girls are four and six. The three of us sing at church and for lots of kids' gatherings. They can read music well. I wondered if I could bring them with me next week so you could give us some tips. We're having fun harmonizing in three parts. They also have taken my guitar classes at home and sometimes we accompany ourselves."

"What?" she said. "I'm sorry, but I don't believe that children this young can hold a harmony part on their own, and I've never heard of a child that little actually being able to read music."

Surprised that she didn't believe me, I felt kind of stupid. Singing harmony in my family, even as a young child, was the most natural thing in the world to me.

"You bring them with you next week," she said. "I want to hear them."

With the girls and their two guitars in tow, we arrived the next Monday. First the three of us sang "Amazing Grace" in three parts. Then they sang some other tunes together: "Yellow Bird", "The Lion Sleeps Tonight," and our own arrangement of "Side by Side." They had Margaret one minute into the first song. She teared up.

I wondered what she was thinking.

When they stopped, she said, "Oh, my dear girl! You must get them to Bart James right away so he can hear them. Here's his number."

Right. I didn't know who Bart James was. *Was this some sort of compliment or Hollywood gimmick?*

After we got home, I didn't call this Bart. In fact, even though I was flattered, I forgot about it. But within the week, he called me. It turned out that he was the top contractor in Hollywood for using children's voices for commercials and background singing for albums, movies, and television. His own sons had been some of the voices in *The Sound of Music* and *It's a Small World*, but they were older now and he was looking for younger singers.

"Could you bring the girls to our house tomorrow after school so my wife and I can hear them?" he asked. "We're up here in the Hollywood Hills. I don't have any kids that young who can read music. Margaret tells me they are right on pitch and can hold a harmony part, too. That helps a lot when we're recording commercials."

So, he was the real thing after all. *Oh, ye of little faith.*

The girls and I had a great time at his house. Since we didn't understand the magnitude of what he was considering, we weren't nervous at all.

Within weeks, Gina and Shannon were recording commercials for McDonald's, Baskin-Robbins, Knott's Berry Farm, California Raisins, Bekins Moving, John Denver, Helen Reddy, and dozens of others. They did that for many years, into their twenties, including nine sing-along albums for Disney, which included four other kids' voices. In some they were as young as four and six years old. They also sang backgrounds for Glenn Campbell and Barry Manilow, and appeared on numerous TV shows. Because they grew up in the music world, they were never starstruck. Shannon and Gina were now eligible to join SAG (the Screen Actors Guild) and AFTRA (American Federation of Television and Radio Artists), which brought them even more opportunities.

During the winter months, the girls and I would often be leaving different recording studios, located on side streets in Hollywood, when nighttime closed in around us. These studios were not always located in the best parts of town, so once again, my old fear of the dark reappeared. I thought Mrs. T had cured me of that, but I was wrong. I still remembered vagrants in Memphis crawling out of the dry bayous and the burglar who had tried to break in while I was sleeping as a small child. But now, I felt even more concerned since I had my own children to protect.

I didn't want to pass my anxiety onto Shannon and Gina, so I struggled to find balance, asking God to show me how to be cautious but not fearful. The girls had already noticed that even when parking the car at home in the driveway or garage, I had an eye out for dark bushes where someone could hide.

Worse yet, during those recording years in the late 1970s, the Hillside Strangler was terrorizing Southern California. So, in addition to raising the biggest Malamute watchdog we could find, we three attended a self-defense class at our local YMCA taught by three big, burly experts.

In the YMCA gym, three large circles were formed with adults and kids, with an instructor in each. We were taught how to break loose from a stranglehold from behind. Gina and I were across

Music in our Genes

the room from each other in different circles.

Her instructor, knowing she was an agile gymnast, chose, with her permission, to demonstrate a hold and flipped her over in one quick move. I do not even remember flying across the room. Without saying a word, I found myself standing by her side to be sure she was okay.

Her coach stopped the class and said, "This is a classic example of instinct in action. Mama Bear appeared out of nowhere to protect her cub, her baby. This is why you rarely hear of a child being attacked when she is with her mother. All of you need to not only be cautious but trust your instincts. Look behind you. Park in well-lit areas. If something feels wrong, it probably is. Trust yourself."

I was relieved to learn that being aware didn't have to mean that I was afraid. With that confidence, I could now follow my instincts.

Later, when I least expected it, instinct would serve me well again.

Eventually, Hugh and I enjoyed a family band with the girls. Shannon and Gina also formed a group with Frank's two little girls, called Peanut Butter and Jelly, with drums, guitar, and vocals. They performed all over Southern California.

I saved most of the money the kids made, for college or for whatever else they wanted to do as adults. Hugh and I had our worst disagreements over putting their money away, because he wanted to spend it to remodel the house. I guess he thought the work would last forever. But he was not a saver and didn't even believe in buying life insurance. Because there would be rough years ahead, it was a good thing I insisted on storing away their money. They would need it in the future.

CHAPTER 21

OPPORTUNITY KNOCKS

*Be anxious for nothing, but in everything by prayer
and supplication, with thanksgiving, let your requests
be made known to God. And the peace of God which
surpasses all understanding will guard your hearts and
minds through Christ Jesus.*
Philippians 4:6-7

WHEN I WAS SINGING WITH THE BAND and being their MC, occasionally people would come up
to me and say, "You have a very pleasant speak-
ing voice, have you ever thought about going into radio?" Even
though they meant it as a compliment, at first I found it an-
noying because I was so busy with the family that I thought a
radio career would never fit into my life. I also knew it was a
very competitive industry to break into and would require a lot
of training. Secondly, I still had a thick southern accent, which
would never be acceptable since most announcers come from
the Walter Cronkite era, with Midwestern dialects. But I was
flattered by their comments and filed the idea away for future
thought, possibly when the kids were older.

In those days, I was a crazy person, sometimes getting on the
210 Freeway and thinking, *Now wait a minute, where am I going?
Oh, yeah. Let's see. Pick Gina up, drop her off at gymnastics, go
back and get Shannon, drop her off at her piano lesson, and go back
and get Gina, then go back and get Shannon.*

On days when the girls had a recording session or an on-camera interview in Hollywood, I picked them up directly from school, prepared with a change of clothes and snacks ready for them in the car. I tried to make the trips fun by taking them out to dinner afterward to some special place. As long as the girls wanted to do these singing jobs and they kept their grades up, I thought it was a great experience for them. But I wondered later if we did too much.

Now I understood how Mrs. T must have felt when she happily hauled me around to so many activities, sometimes driving in the fog, or over the hills to Bradford to roller skate. The longer I was a mother, the more I revered her.

The difference was that before I came along, she had a quiet, serene life, riding her horse and enjoying friends. She did not have to do all that she did for me because I wasn't even her child. To take care of me with food, clothes, and a safe, loving home would have been generous enough by anyone's standards, but she went way beyond what I ever could have dreamed of.

When the girls were very young, I was eager to challenge their little minds. While they napped, I laid out Play-Doh, puzzles, and books, or cleaned house so that when they got up, they'd have constructive things to do and I could spend time with them.

Since I felt inadequate as a mother because of my background, I didn't want my girls to suffer from my faults. So, I haunted the educational stores for just the right toys and books. I understood now how Mrs. T was not only a mom to me but showed me some of what a dad might be because she was such a tomboy. Hugh would be a strong male influence in our children's lives and supportive to me. Other than that influence, I was just guessing as to how to be a good parent.

I realized, as I talked to other moms in the neighborhood, that I was more concerned about ordinary things that they didn't worry about, because they hadn't had my negative experiences. For example, even though we lived in a nice area, I rarely let my girls play out in front of the house unless I was right there with them. I feared someone would pick them up, so I was either out front with them or had the local kids over in our backyard. We bought the largest jungle gym, swing set, sandbox, and any other yard toys we could find, so our backyard was a playground. Gina could usually be found hanging upside down from the highest bar on the jungle gym.

When the girls started grade school, I often drove them to school so I'd know that they got there safely. After all, I couldn't see the building from our front sidewalk. When they did walk to school, I was uneasy. It's what I felt I had to do at the time, but perhaps I was overcompensating.

* * *

Do the right thing. It will gratify some people and
astonish the rest.
- Mark Twain

I still remembered the years in Memphis, with no breakfast and buying a stick of bubblegum to get me through the morning, so it was very important to me that the girls have a good breakfast. I actually enjoyed cooking bacon, eggs, and blueberry muffins or pancakes for them.

Hugh was a good dad in those early years, taking an interest in the girls' science projects, hiking with them in the local mountains behind our house, being proud of their music, and encouraging them in school.

When the children were eight and ten, the most fun we had was when we bought a used ski boat with another family. Even though our kids had had swimming lessons since they were toddlers, I wondered, *Shouldn't someone in the group know something about lifesaving?* I was a weak swimmer myself—I remembered how, in high school, I was embarrassed because I couldn't swim out to the raft at Cuba Lake when the other kids could—so I was concerned about safety.

Since no one else volunteered to do it, I went to our local YMCA and started taking beginner's swimming courses. I kept at it until I went through all their classes, learning the different strokes, and finally signing up for the Senior Lifesaving Class.

The joke was on me. I was in my thirties, 5'4" and 120 pounds, in a class of all teenage boys, 5'9" to 6'4", who wanted to pass the class and get a summer job as a lifeguard at the beach or a local pool. Athletically, they were tops. And I was, well, an out-of-shape housewife. But if I started something, whatever it took, I was determined to finish.

On the final test, we were each required to dive into the eight-foot-deep end of the Olympic size pool and bring up one of the other students from the bottom. We drew names and my guy was a big, strapping, 6'4" kid. It was Red Rover, Red Rover all over again for me; I flashed back to the streets of Memphis, determined that, no matter what, no one would break through my side of the line.

I dove in and down, down, down to bring him up. I didn't think I could hold my breath much longer as I grabbed this hulk under the arms from the back and pulled him to the top.

I passed. Whoo-hoo!

I never dreamed I'd be able to do something like that. I could mark that off my bucket list. I smiled to myself when I thought of how proud Mrs. T would have been.

This became a lifetime pattern for me: enthusiastically jumping into a new project, realizing it would be much harder than I thought, and persevering until I mastered it. Mrs. T used to say, "Make sure you're right, then go ahead." Eventually, I learned to examine new projects carefully before I dove in.

* * *

Therefore, we will not fear, though the earth be removed, and though the mountains be carried into the midst of the sea. Be still and know that I am God.
- Psalm 46:2,10

We woke up at 6:00 a.m. to the sound of screaming all over the neighborhood. A roaring sound, like a freight train, hit our ears. Hugh and I were jolted out of bed as our house shook violently. Had a bomb gone off? Was the house exploding? On February 9, 1971, Shannon and Gina had been asleep in their upstairs bedrooms across the hall from us.

Instinctively, Hugh and I ran to snatch up our daughters, who were ten and eight. We ran down the stairs and stood trembling by the open front door. Looking to the top of the mountain behind our house, we watched helplessly as dust and debris rose dozens of feet in the air.

Earthquake.

Would the mountain come down on us? The ground under us shook even more, over and over again, with aftershocks.

We held the girls close. Was this the end? We watched as cracks appeared in our living room wall. Our terrified dog whined and leaned against my legs. Later, we learned that the foundation of the house next door split in half.

Wanting to be strong for the girls, I said, "It's okay. It's okay," not, of course, believing my own words. *Was this all we get? Were our lives about to be over? Had I done enough to prepare our children for their possible entry into eternity today? Was this the day Christ returns? Would we be taken up into heaven with him any minute?*

After what seemed an eternity, the bad shaking stopped, and we walked through our house. Everything was on the floor— even the piano had moved halfway across the room. We had no electricity. It had been one of the most destructive earthquakes in Southern California's history. The news on the radio said the epicenter of the earthquake was in the San Gabriel Mountains, which included our hilltops. Sylmar had the most damaged homes, including a collapsed freeway. Eighty thousand people were evacuated below the Van Norman Dam in the San Fernando Valley.

The very next morning Hugh, with no warning or explanation of where he was going—and over my protests—packed up and left for a trip. *What?* More shocking than the aftershocks, I did not hear from him for weeks and was only told by his secretary not to worry, that she could not reveal where he was, nor could he call me, but he was safe.

What about us—his family? I felt abandoned both as a wife and mother at one of the most frightening times in our lives. Except for talking with friends and neighbors, the girls and I were left to deal with this upset alone.

I felt the urgency, as did my friends and neighbors, of living each day as if it were my last.

Weeks later, Hugh told me he had been on a top-secret mission for the government. The realization that he could leave us at any time with the ring of the telephone and with no consideration for our wellbeing undermined any security I felt for us as a family. Hugh never told me where he had been, except that it was to a foreign country. My trust in him as a partner in marriage took a dip. The knowledge that his work would always take priority over us, his family, undermined my belief in his loyalty to us. *Was I in this marriage all by myself? Was this how I wanted to live my life?*

* * *

Nothing in this world can take the place of persistence. Talent will not; Nothing is more common than unsuccessful people with talent. Genius will not; unrewarded genius is almost a proverb. Education will not; the world is full of educated derelicts. Persistence

and determination alone are omnipotent. The slogan,
"press on" has solved and always will solve the problems
of the human race.
- Calvin Coolidge, 30th President of the United States

This quote was on the refrigerator the entire time the girls were growing up. It embodied what Mrs. T and I believed. How she would have loved it. I passed Coolidge's profound words on to my daughters and any young people I worked with. I also believed that we needed God's help to be that persistent and to have determination in our lives.

Every year I thought about going back to public school teaching, but I knew it would be the end of my kids' afterschool activities. Several teachers in our neighborhood often had to stay after classes for faculty meetings and clubs. They called frequently, asking me to pick up their offspring and watch them until they got home. I could see that sometimes those children felt tossed around, and I wasn't willing to do that to mine.

As Hugh's demands at work became more intense because of his many promotions and added responsibilities, I was grateful that the girls and I had our music to keep us busy. He never minded my going out to a class or working with the band in the evening. Due to his severe insomnia, he was glad to be at home so he could read most of the night after the girls went to bed.

Before long, he also read in the daytime—every spare minute he was home. When Hugh and I were dating, his mother had tried to tell me that he read a lot. I thought that was a strange thing to say, since reading is a good thing. But now, I realized that it was his escape from the pull and tug of daily life. Ultimately, as he withdrew, he showed no desire to spend any time with me. Getting him to go out socially became almost impossible.

Due to the pressures he felt as he climbed the corporate ladder, Hugh became more solitary and distant. Often, I'd think his silence was caused by something I'd done to displease him. And since much of his work was classified as top secret, he couldn't talk to me about it. Except for the children, we no longer had much in common. His life was work and living by night, and mine was a life lived in the daytime with our daughters. Geniuses can often be loners and not necessarily happy people.

Was marriage supposed to be like this? Lonely? Or was something wrong with me? Could I live like this after the girls were grown?

Since I hadn't seen many happy marriages with companionship between husband and wife apart from the two years I lived with Daddy and Mama, I decided I should just be glad that Hugh was a good dad.

For many years, I had felt that I should start cultivating some marketable skills, since I was uncertain of what the future would bring. So, to develop my own talents, I took evening classes whenever I could.

* * *

Hope is the happy anticipation of something good.
- Joyce Meyers

Finally, in 1977, when the girls were fourteen and twelve, I got serious about planning for future employment. After all those years of training to be a teacher, teaching no longer appealed to me. Disappointed in what I saw in the local public high school, I watched as the principal did nothing to stop kids from openly smoking marijuana in front of the campus.

Why not try something new and exciting after so many years at home? Since I was at ease in front of a microphone, I investigated the possibilities of a career in radio. While the girls were at school during the day, I enrolled at KISS FM Broadcasting School on Sunset Boulevard. I took all the news and DJ (disc jockey) classes they offered, thinking that when the girls graduated, I could work in that field. Besides, I didn't want to be eighty years old someday and look back thinking, *Gee, I could have done that.*

I had already appeared in several little theater productions in recent years and had done some on-camera roles in several TV commercials and sitcoms after acquiring an agent. Finally, I was eligible to join SAG and AFTRA. But very soon, I realized I was competing for roles with women who had been in the industry for many years, and I knew the work would probably not be regular enough for me to make a solid living in the future.

In my radio classes, I realized that before I could make an audition tape, I had to get rid of the rest of my Southern accent. Even in the Deep South, the DJs and radio personalities didn't have southern accents, and there would be no jobs for me if I sounded like I was drinking from a Dixie cup.

So, I went to a diction specialist and spent two hours a day with a tape recorder, practicing how to speak correctly. I laughed because I could relate to *My Fair Lady* and Liza's struggle to learn how to talk properly.

Finding a job as a beginning news person or DJ in the major market Los Angeles area, which is loaded with talent from all over the country, is almost impossible. I learned you should start in smaller markets, perhaps somewhere in Nebraska or Iowa, build up a resume, and then hope to move on to a major market. But any job I got would have to be within driving distance to be compatible with my family life.

In the summer of 1977, I was thrilled to land a weekend gig as a DJ in the resort town of Palm Springs. Working Saturday and Sunday mornings allowed me to be home with the family during the school week.

With Hugh's encouragement, I made a special discounted arrangement with a small motel there. I drove down on Friday afternoons for my Saturday and Sunday morning shifts, which were from 6:00 a.m. to noon. The pay was minimum wage, but at least it was a start, and I'd have my foot in the door with something to put on a resume.

Hugh liked the idea. Since he wasn't with the girls as much as I was, he would have quality time with them while I was away. Having been a star gymnast in high school, he liked going to Gina's gymnastic events and having that in common with her. So, for a while, the weekends worked out well. In fact, sometimes he drove the girls down to Palm Springs for the weekend, and they'd enjoy the motel pool and the mountain gondola ride. They often rented horses and rode out into the desert to watch the sunrise.

My job was made easier because I had a knowledgeable background on most of the recording artists and could give interesting, succinct introductions to the songs.

Being the only one in the station on the weekends, I arrived at 4:30 a.m. All the downtown streets were dark at that time of morning, but even though I still had daunting memories of vagrants in Memphis, I walked up the shadowy staircase of the building to the station, determined not be frightened. When I unlocked the station door, I faced the most intimidating challenge of all: turning on the transmitter, which covered an entire wall. If I didn't pull the right switches, we wouldn't be on the air.

I had also gone to classes at Pasadena City College (PCC) and gotten what was then called a First-Class Engineering License for Radio, which qualified me to be the engineer on staff at any station. Having the license seemed ludicrous to me because I knew that if I ever had to fix a transmitter, I'd probably turn into a piece of bacon. To pass the test, I had memorized a bunch of formulas without really knowing what they meant. But every station always had to have such a person there to turn on and monitor the transmitter, so having the license helped me get the job. I found out later that I was the first female DJ in Palm Springs, and one of the only women in the state to have acquired that radio engineering license.

The trickiest part of my DJ shift—and it seems funny to me now—was figuring out how, in a six-hour shift, to find a four-minute break, long enough to run down the hall to the bathroom. I had to make sure I didn't lock myself out of the station. It involved putting on a record that would play for at least four minutes—of which there were few, because most records only run two-and-a-half to three-plus minutes. The unforgivable sin in radio is to let music or talk run out and have dead air. That meant instant firing, no questions asked. After I met some of the guys who worked a DJ shift there, they delighted in telling me they had every advantage over me. For their bathroom needs, they used the wastebasket in the studio.

Somehow, I couldn't bring myself to do that.

Over the weeks, as I got into my groove, I relaxed and loved not only airing the music, but reading dozens of live commercials. The large studio window looked out onto the desert, and as the sun came up over the mountains with blazing colors of orange and red, I always started the show with Cat Stevens's "Morning Has Broken." Awesome.

After nine months, being away weekends was finally becoming a strain on my family. Our marriage had not been going well for a long time, so I decided to stay home and see what I could do to salvage it.

CHAPTER 22

NEW BEGINNINGS

*Others can stop you temporarily. You are the only one
who can do it permanently.*
- Zig Ziegler

SHORTLY AFTER I LEFT THE WEEKEND JOB in Palm
Springs, in 1981, after twenty-one years of marriage,
Hugh surprised me by filing for a divorce. The girls were
eighteen and sixteen. Overcome with grief and disappointment,
I had promised myself that divorce would never happen to me,
as it had to Mother. Even though Hugh and I had not been close
for many years, the pain of realizing that our marriage had
failed was so overwhelming that I wanted to die. *What use was
there in going on?* I would never commit suicide, would never do
that to my kids—*but, God, couldn't you just let me not wake up in
the morning? Just let my heart stop?*

*What should I have done over the years to make us happier?
What had I done wrong?* Here we were, two intelligent, educated
human beings, and we couldn't make this work? *Why? Had we
lived like this for so long that neither of us cared anymore?* This was
not just our failure; somehow it must be my failure.

*If my life was a failure, what good was I on earth, especially for
my girls? What kind of a role model was I now? What kind of a human being was I now?*

It was too painful for me to attend our old church, where
we had been friends with other couples for over fifteen years.

Devastated and depressed, I started attending Church on the Way in the San Fernando Valley, a basic Bible teaching church.

As I walked into the service the very first time, they were singing "He Loves You with an Everlasting Love," based on Jeremiah 31:3. I sat in the back row and let those beautiful words wash over me. What great news to be reminded that He loves me. Unconditionally. Always had. *Had I forgotten that He forgives no matter what?* I asked forgiveness right then for all my failures, especially my failed marriage.

God, of course, knew what was coming with the divorce, long before I did. Once again, when I needed friendship at a crucial moment, He sent into my life an angel with a heart and wisdom, like Mrs. T, to help me. My girls' pediatrician, Hilda Berg, and I had become good friends. She attended our church in La Crescenta, was a born-again Christian, Jewish, and a Holocaust survivor.

She came to know Christ as her Messiah through extensive study of the Bible, especially Isaiah 53:5:

> *But He was wounded for our transgressions, He was bruised for our iniquities; the chastisement for our peace was upon Him, and by His stripes we are healed. All we like sheep have gone astray. We have turned, everyone, to his own way; and the Lord hath laid on Him the iniquity of us all. He was oppressed and He was afflicted, yet He opened not His mouth; He was led as a lamb to the slaughter.*

The words had been written by the prophet Isaiah over seven hundred years before Christ was born, and Hilda's rabbi could not explain it to her. A pastor and his wife, who were close friends of hers, showed her that this was a prophecy of the coming Messiah, Jesus. Hilda was a gentle soul, brilliant in her understanding of kids and one of the most popular pediatricians in the Glendale area.

She never married and had lost many friends and relatives in the camps from starvation and typhus, barely surviving herself as a child because of tuberculosis. Her miraculous story of coming to America and becoming a pediatrician, and yet being so humble and kind, was the stuff of inspiration to our community and even the nation, as she became a speaker and wrote a book.

Hilda was the one person in whom I felt safe to confide over the years as my marriage became more and more difficult. Her compassion for me and everyone was remarkable, considering what she had gone through. I had told her that I didn't think I had enough strength to face the coming years in this lonely marriage. I'll never forget her answer to me. "Of course, you don't have enough strength right now to face any of life's hardships that will come up. God just doesn't pour strength all over you when you don't need it. But when that moment comes, when you need it, He will provide it."

She directed me to the book of James in the Bible, chapter one, verse two: "My brethren, count it all joy when you fall into various trials, knowing that the testing of your faith produces patience." Also, Romans 5:3-5, one of my favorites: "Tribulations produce perseverance, and perseverance character, and character hope. Now hope does not disappoint, because the love of God has been poured out in our hearts by the Holy Spirit who was given to us."

Hadn't I had enough tribulation already? Couldn't I just live happily ever after from now on? Apparently not. I still had more growing to do—a lifetime project.

Hilda inspired me to trust God with whatever the future might bring. Still, I carried a black cloud of depression over my head. *How would we live now? Would I be alone the rest of my life? How would divorce affect my girls? They adored their dad. Could I get to work and find a decent place to live for the three of us?* I had no established credit to rent or even qualify for a mortgage loan to buy a small condo, and certainly no resume to apply for a decent job. I hadn't worked full-time in seventeen years. *What had I been thinking to stay home all that time?*

* * *

I've learned that people will forget what you said;
people will forget what you did, but people will never
forget how you made them feel.
- Maya Angelou

Hugh moved out of the house. I would have loved to get a good job right away and buy his half of the house so the girls and I could stay in the area, but that was impossible; lenders required that you not only be on a job two years to qualify for a loan, but also have a good down payment. I met neither qualification. Immediately, I returned to Pasadena City College in hopes of putting a news audition tape together because they had a good radio, DJ, and TV department.

One outstanding professor, Dr. Smith, had been an announcer on a major TV channel before retiring and becoming a newswriting instructor. On our first day of class, he announced, "After class, if you will, go into one of the recording booths and write and record a five minute newscast, which you can glean from the UPI wire," (United Press International), "and I'll personally review it with you."

A major professional would personally review my tape and coach me? I almost leaped out of my chair. What an opportunity! I was the first one out the door to grab a recording booth every day after class, where I taped a newscast and handed it in to him. In addition, on the campus radio station, I got to do a regular weekly DJ shift. (In fact, I was picking out my records for my shift the day John Lennon was shot. You know how that goes:

you remember the very spot where you were standing when you hear news like that.)

As much as I loved the DJ shifts and did well in them, I thought that at my age, my best chance in media was news. Even though I looked younger than I was, I'd be competing with kids in their early twenties.

At PCC, I had many opportunities to tape on-camera interviews on various subjects. Different professors and local officials sometimes requested me because they thought I was a natural on camera. But I quickly realized I couldn't cut it in TV news as a career because of my vision—I couldn't read the teleprompter quickly enough to keep up. So that left radio news. When the end of the semester came, Dr. Smith called me into his office. I was worried when I sat down with him to hear what he might say.

"You have a good news audition tape," he said. "And you're one of my most diligent students."

I smiled. *That's a good start.*

"So, I'm offering you first chance for an intern position with KBRT radio in LA. The internship is available right away, if the head newsman there likes your tape. There's another opening at a major station in LA but its union, and you'd never get on the air. You'd just answer phones and work around the office. Are you interested?"

"I'd like to know more about it."

"Well then, call Rich Buhler at KBRT and take him your tape. It's an unpaid job but would give you experience and could possibly lead to work later, if you do well."

I tried to remain calm and professional to hide my eagerness. I knew that with a huge, 50,000-watt signal all over Southern California, KBRT was one of the largest Christian stations in the country.

"Rich was a KFWB newsman for years," Dr. Smith said, "and is well known as a great guy. You might even get a chance to do the news on the air, after a while."

"I'd love to talk to Rich," I said.

With telephone number in hand, after a polite thank you, I flew up the stairs, two at a time, from his basement office, to get to a pay phone as fast as I could.

* * *

Why not go out on a limb? Isn't that where the fruit is?
- Vin Scully

Rich answered the phone himself in a warm, friendly voice, as if he was reaching through the phone and greeting me in person. I drove to Century City the next morning to interview with him.

To say we hit it off from the very first moment we met is an understatement. Of course, later I learned that everyone hits it off with Rich Buhler in the first five minutes they know him. I wondered how such a huge man, over six feet tall, who looked like a fullback from Notre Dame with hands as big as a football, could be so humble and kind, instead of intimidating. A blond, gentle giant, his nickname at Biola University had been Cotton.

After a brief introduction, he went into a recording booth and listened to my tape. When he came out, he said, "I like your resume and your news tape. The acting and singing experience you've had make you sound right at home when you read the news."

I smiled with relief.

"Can you start interning for me Monday? You'd need to be here by 5:00 a.m. to write the 6:00 a.m. newscast. I'd voice it on the air, of course, but you'd write the script, which I'd go over with you. That way, you can learn how to put together an even better newscast. You can also write for the seven, eight, nine, and ten o'clock broadcasts."

Was he kidding? Could I start Monday? Do birds fly? I'd like to do everything and anything that I possibly could. "Sure, Rich. I'd be grateful for the experience. I can be here at five." The station format was Christian music in the morning and taped programs throughout the day, so I could also do a DJ shift.

"Great. I'll see you Monday morning," he said. He gave me that compassionate smile with no pretense on his part, then a handshake, and I was engulfed in his big bear hug that became so famous. Once you've had a hug from Rich Buhler, you know you're accepted. It's safe to be you. I dared to think I'd found a place to start, maybe even a home. With that, he took me all over the station and introduced me to the entire staff.

Proud of me. Impressed with my work. Wow. How could this be? Is this answered prayer after all these months on my knees before the Lord asking for His help?

I floated from the fifth floor of the building to the parking structure. As I drove the hour and a half home to La Crescenta, it felt like my car levitated over the five freeways. I had a chance. He liked my tape. Maybe it would lead to a job someday in something I loved to do. And to work with people like that, who were so kind and helpful, would be more than I had dared to dream. All the way home, I thanked the Lord over and over. *I have a chance, Lord, thank you. I have a chance.*

Uh-oh. To get there before 5:00 a.m., to have a five-minute newscast ready by 6:00 a.m., meant leaving La Crescenta, in the foothills of the San Gabriel Mountains, by at least 4:00 a.m. Bedtime the night before needed to be 8:00 p.m. if I needed eight hours' sleep, and boy, did I.

I'd been warned in broadcast classes that if I ever got a news job, as a rookie I should expect the worst. Certainly, the news director would take one look at my script, and say, "This is a piece of junk." Then he would rip it up and tell me to start over. For good measure, and to put me in my place, he'd certainly curse a lot too.

Not so with Rich Buhler. Those early weeks when I was so raw and nervous, I'd write my five-minute newscast, and he'd kneel down by my desk, which put him at eye level with me.

"This isn't too bad, really," he'd say. "Now if you change this line that's down here, bring it up and make it the lead to your story, it would stand out more. Otherwise, it's okay. You're coming along fine." Then he'd make a few more suggestions.

He never knew that after he left the room, I'd choke up, so happy that my work was acceptable, that he was willing to train me, and he wasn't going to throw me out. He was one of the kindest men I ever met.

Just as Dr. Smith had hoped, in a few weeks, Rich had me voicing several newscasts a day on the air.

My strongest memory of those first few months, in addition to the challenge of the work, is of fatigue. Because I was excited and afraid that I'd oversleep in the morning, it was hard to get to sleep so early the night before. But I had my foot in the door and that was all that mattered. We were on the air on Saturdays, too. By Saturday night I was so tired that just getting to Church on the Way on Sunday, a half hour away, was about all I could handle, what with grocery shopping and other errands. But never mind. It was worth it, whether I was tired or lonely or not. I already knew what loneliness was, and I could deal with that for a career opportunity.

Rich also pastored a church in Long Beach and encouraged me to keep attending Church on the Way, where I later took classes whenever I could, beginning a lifetime of getting to know my Bible better, which helped me find peace of mind on a new level.

While I was still his intern, Rich asked me and several other close friends to pray for him because he hoped to convince the station owner to let him start a four-hour afternoon talk show as a host with guests and open calls—the first live Christian program of its kind in America. The owner flew out from the east coast for numerous meetings with Rich. It would take a big leap of faith on the part of Rich's boss to cancel four hours of paid programming and hire account executives to find advertisers to sponsor the show. Rich proposed calling the show *Talk from the Heart*.

According to Rich, his boss was one of the sharpest and most powerful businessmen in radio. With all that going for him, I was not only impressed, but also intimidated. At last, I got to meet him when he came for the final session with Rich. We exchanged the normal niceties and I scurried off to get my newscast ready. Rich had already told me what the meeting would be about. That day, the owner agreed to let Rich begin his own talk show.

* * *

Never let the fear of striking out keep you from playing the game.
- Babe Ruth

But who would they hire to produce the show? Who did they want to come in mornings, book the guests, plan the format under Rich's supervision, engineer the show, play the commercials, and screen the calls? In addition, the producer would do the news at the top of the hour, which they would prepare while Rich was on the air. In union stations, they hire a separate person for each of these jobs. Would they hire three different people? Then, would they no longer need me? *Did I have enough experience to be considered for the job?*

Rich told me later that he and the owner discussed hiring some well-known newsmen in the LA area, whose names I knew. While their discussion was going on in the conference room, I was searching the news wire for interesting stories for the day. In my tiny UPI room, I closed the door and got down on my knees to talk to the Lord.

216 • ANNIE FARRIS

"Lord, please. I need this job. I know I can do it. Please, I can't go on as an unpaid intern much longer. I'm running out of the little savings I have. Please, God, help me."

Almost immediately there was a knock on the door. Rich popped his smiling face in, full of concern.

"Ann, would you produce the talk show for us?"

Leaping up from my chair, I said, "Absolutely! When do we start?"

That was the quickest, most directly answered prayer I've ever had.

The owner and I shook hands, and so, our great adventure began. We had no way of knowing how life-transforming and successful the program would be for all of us.

The first day we went on the air was April 1, 1981. Dr. James Dobson was our guest. He was the well-known national broadcaster of "Focus on the Family" and author of many books. Since it was April First, we joked about it being April Fools' Day.

After interviewing Dr. Dobson, Rich said, "Okay, Producer Ann, let's open the phone lines and take some calls." *The courage this guy has. Would anyone call? What would we do if no one does? Is anyone really listening?*

I played a commercial break as I watched all the phone lines light up immediately.

Whoo-hoo! We had listeners. We had an audience.

In all our broadcasts, as I screened the calls while running the commercials, many callers did not want to use their real names. I told them the name wasn't important, but their question was. I said, "Why don't you call yourself George?" And so were born the hundreds of future Georges who could ask any question in the world and feel safe. One innocent caller asked Rich, "How come you have so many Georges calling you?"

The show was an immediate hit. As the weeks progressed, every morning the desk of "Producer Ann" would be inundated with piles of books from authors wanting to get on the program.

I'd put a yellow Post-it on the ones that looked good so that Rich could look them over when he came in. Of course, Rich already had various guests in mind, too. Then, I'd book the show per his instructions.

To discuss a wide variety of subjects, we booked many authors, counselors, musicians with new albums, and pastors, both in Southern California and nationwide.

I especially loved the interview that Rich had with a respected Catholic leader because the tone of it was, "Let's not talk so much about the differences between Catholics and Protestants, but our similarities, what we share in common, such as the sanctity of marriage, the basic beliefs of the Bible, and Jesus being the Son of God." The audience ate up every program like ice cream with chocolate topping.

I especially enjoyed the challenge on days when Rich would phone me a short time before the program was to start and say, "Producer Ann, find me such-and-such an official now, and let's get them on the air today." Even if they were in another country, I delighted in tracking them down like a detective and finding them through networking. The job was never boring, and I met tons of interesting people with knowledge on every subject.

One afternoon, Dr. Robert Schuller came to the studio to be Rich's guest. During a commercial break, while Dr. Schuller was waiting in the lobby to come on the air, Rich said to me though the intercom, "Ann, why don't you go out and tell Dr. Schuller about your experience when you were depressed and how his broadcast helped you?"

"Oh, no, I'm sure he's heard hundreds of stories like that."

"No, you go tell him. It will encourage him. I'll play the commercials for you while you go."

Feeling silly, I went out to the lobby and knelt by Dr. Schuller's chair. I briefly described how one Saturday night, right after my divorce, I was so depressed that I did not want to go on.

"Then someone on your program sang, 'Because He Lives, I Can Face Tomorrow,'" I said, "followed by a great sermon from you, Dr. Schuller. It changed everything for me, and I made the decision that very night that I would, and could, go on with God's help."

He gave me the magnetic, warm Schuller smile.

"Thanks for telling me, Ann. I need to hear that we are helping people. I know that wasn't easy to share.

Eventually Hugh bought me out of the house, and even though my paycheck at the station was minimum wage, I miraculously qualified for a loan to buy a small townhome for the girls and me. Across the approval letter from the lender, whom I didn't know personally, was handwritten, "Good luck and God bless you, Producer Ann."

As Daddy always said, "Well, what do you know about that?"

* * *

It's never too late to be what you might have been.
- George Elliot

Over the coming years, Rich and I discussed why the program was such an instant success. Even before shows like *Oprah* came along, Rich, with warmth and compassion, was covering, on air, many topics that were considered taboo at that time, not only in Christian circles but on secular radio as well. He conversed easily about alcoholism, drugs, child abuse, molestation, incest, rape, PMS, suicide, any form of victimization, homosexuality, divorce, dating, sex education in public schools, child rearing, why bad things happen to good people, dealing with loss, adoption, and many other issues. No subject was off-limits, as he handled it with kindness, wisdom, and tact. No wonder the listeners immediately loved and trusted him.

After several months on the air, while the station was still in Century City, he asked me if I'd like to have a talk show of my own on Saturday mornings. Since I had sat in for him occasionally when he was sick, he was confident I could carry my own program. He felt that I could be an encouragement to help other singles move on with their lives in the areas of dating, single parenting, surviving after divorce, forgiveness, keeping their values, where to go for fellowship, and other subjects. We called it *Saturday Singles*. My visibility on the air led to numerous speaking engagements for singles' groups in Southern California. It pleased me to think that some of the pain I'd been through could be used to comfort others and reassure them that they'd get through their issues, too. If I could build a new life for myself with God's help, so could they.

Just as Mrs. T had used the pain of her own divorce to steer me in the right direction and prepare me for the unexpected in life, I wanted to help do that for others, too.

Since I was producing Rich's show while also producing my own show, doing the news, and voicing some of the commercials, the six-day week became too much for me. After two years I finally had to end *Saturday Singles*.

I am still in awe that at such a crucial time, God sent Rich into my life. But why should I be surprised? He has sent someone to help me every time I've needed it. God was there for me as a small child when my blind grandfather taught me the 23rd Psalm. He was there when my sister Georgia and I were home alone and a burglar cut the screen. He sent Mrs. T to rescue me in the difficult years of my childhood. He had Hilda Berg, strong Christian and Holocaust survivor, come into my life in my darkest hour with biblical words of encouragement. And now He provided me with the exceptional opportunity to work with, be mentored by, and be close friends with the most humble, brilliant believer on the planet—the real deal, Rich Buhler. Rich was eight years younger than me, so, huge as he was, I called him my little brother. He joked that we would always have to be friends because we knew too much about each other.

CHAPTER 23

LIFE-DEFINING MOMENT

*So we may boldly say: "The Lord is my helper; I will not
fear. What can man do to me?"*
- Hebrews 13:6

WHEN WE WERE HELD HOSTAGE in May of 1981, in what we thought was a life-threatening event, our lives were tied together forever. Rich joked that because we thought we might be living our last hour that afternoon, from then on, we were permanently joined at the hip.

But for me, when I prayed and called the operator on that bright, sunny spring day, a feeling of calm had come over me. Though I hadn't planned on meeting my maker that day, if that was to be my destiny, so be it. I'd had a good life, and, in no small way, I had Mrs. T to thank for my many blessings, including this job I loved so much.

From that day forward, I became very much aware that we only have now to live for. *I only have now. Right now. This hour, this day. There are no guarantees of a tomorrow. Forget the past. It's now that counts and it's never too late for me to be the person I need to be. It's never too late to change course, never too late to find peace, never too late to learn to trust God more than ever.*

This was one of the most defining moments of my entire life and I longed to learn from it, to never forget that feeling of being trapped so suddenly, to remember that our lives could have ended in a moment, and to never forget that God hears even the shortest prayers. Just three words, "God, help me."

I am still aware of feeling God's presence that frightening day. I did not have to turn around in my chair and look. He was standing behind me. That's when the shaking stopped. Suddenly I knew exactly what to do. Seeing that I was the only one in the station with no terrorist hovering over me, I knew I must take action. I must try to get help for us. I felt almost detached, as if viewing the situation from outside my body; as if I was someone else.

I said out loud with certainty, "Okay, Lord, I may be with you in a few minutes. I know what to do now. It's okay. My kids are grown. I've had my turn. But Rich and Sam still have families to raise. So, Lord, help me, please."

Calmly, I put on my headphones and faced the console, hoping to look like I was getting ready to read the news. Out of the corner of my eye I quickly glanced left to Rich's booth, then right to Sam's. I waited until none of the men in black suits were looking my way. I quickly reached to my left and punched 0 for the operator.

"Operator, we're in trouble at KBRT Radio. We've been taken hostage. Please send the police right away. We're on the fifth floor, Century Boulevard in Los Angeles." I described the situation to her.

"How do you know you've been taken hostage?" She seemed cool and uninterested.

I saw one of the men glance at me and I immediately hung up. I didn't think the operator believed me.

What will they do with us when they're through? I wondered. *After all, we can identify them.*

A few minutes passed—minutes that felt like hours. There were muffled noises, quick movements in Rich's booth, and angry voices.

And then they were gone, out the door and down the stairway.

Would they be lurking in the hall or parking lot waiting for us when we got off the air?

Soon afterward, the police arrived. They rode up on the elevator as the terrorists escaped down the stairs.

Later, Sam told me that the operator did call back on the outside line, the one connected to his recording booth. He said that she had asked if we were in trouble.

He said, "I'm so sorry, ma'am, but we can't rent out any recording booths to you today. We're all filled."

She said, "I asked you if you are in trouble at the station.

"Well, you could call next week to book a recording booth."

Sam continued to give her nonsense answers to every question she asked. When she finally asked if the station had been taken hostage, Sam replied, "That's right, ma'am. That's perfect. If you call back tomorrow, we'll schedule you in for some recording time."

I asked how he managed to keep his composure. "The Lord was looking over me," he said.

I felt the same way. Surely the Lord was watching over me, just as Mrs. T had. Since we first met when I was six, Mrs. T was the one who always helped me feel less afraid. I was certain that's why she came into my thoughts at that moment, to help me once again overcome my fear.

Immediately after Rich and I went off the air at 6:00 p.m., reporters from the three main TV networks were waiting in the lobby to interview Rich. He asked why we were getting so much attention. The reporters explained that when terrorists want to take over a country, the first thing they do is try to take over the media. But this had occurred years before the word "terrorists" was known so well in America.

The next day, we had a lock put on the front door of the station. I wasn't sure how much that would help; people often stood in front of the glass window next to the door waving a tape they had come to deliver and, of course, the receptionist buzzed the door and waved them in.

For several days after the incident, Rich and I both went on the air taking calls from those who had heard the broadcast. We learned that listeners from all five counties—Los Angeles, Orange, San Diego, Ventura, and Riverside—had called the police to report that something was wrong at KBRT.

With them, Rich and I discussed the topic of forgiveness. Why forgive your enemy? Does it damage you if you don't? What does harboring hatred do to you? We explained that we forgave what the terrorists had done. After all, we reasoned, hatred would only harm us, not them. And if God forgives us on a regular basis, shouldn't we do likewise? Forgiving, we reasoned, does not mean we shouldn't have boundaries. Then, we discussed boundaries. It was one of the most intense broadcasts we'd ever had.

Several times over the next few months, Rich and I were called to the police station to see police lineups. Finally, the terrorists were identified and eventually convicted.

One year later, as I passed by the conference room at the station, I noticed Rich meeting with three men.

That's not unusual. He meets with clients that I don't know all the time.

But something seemed weird. I couldn't put my finger on it. *I guess I've just gotten paranoid. Overprotective of him.* So, I went on about my business.

Shortly after they left, Rich appeared at my desk.

"Producer Ann, did you recognize those men?"

"Uh, no. Why?"

"I'm glad you're sitting down. They were the men who took us hostage last May."

"Oh no! How did they get in with the door locked?

"We have a new receptionist so, of course, she didn't recognize them. They waved a tape outside the door window and she buzzed them in. Then, they asked to see me and I came right out."

"Do you want to call the police?"

"No. They've served their time. They got off easy after we identified them because we did not actually see a gun. They're out after only six months of jail time."

"What did they want? Did they threaten you?"

"No. Are you ready for this? They wanted to buy airtime and have a talk show of their own."

A long silence fell on both of us. Finally, we shook our heads incredulously. Then we howled with laughter.

"The nerve!"

"Yes. Fortunately, there will be no legal battle or accusations of discrimination on our part because I could honestly tell them that we are sold out and have no available time slots."

"Thank the Lord for that."

After all the excitement, I hoped and prayed my life would be calmer and free of drama, but that was not to be.

CHAPTER 24

A CHIP OFF THE OLD BLOCK

Being confident of this very thing, that He who has
begun a good work in you will complete it until the day
of Jesus Christ.
- Philippians 1:6

RICH WAS ADOPTED, so he loved to discuss the subject on air with experts in the field. His passion for the topic brought to our audience a new understanding and compassion for adoptees, and those who were missing closeness with a parent, and anyone who dealt with issues of abandonment. His affection for and support of adoption organizations led to many listeners adopting children.

I asked him how he kept such a busy schedule, since he and his wife had seven children. I knew the talk show lead to many speaking engagements for him, so he told me that in order to have individual time with each child he always took one of them with him on his trips, sometimes all over the country.

Even though he was adopted by a wonderful family, he longed to find his birth parents and siblings. One morning he came striding into the station all aglow, excited to tell me that he had found his birth sister, who lived in another state. Since her name was Martha, I started addressing all my memos to him as Richbom. He came to me, his eyes full of question marks.

"Why are you calling me Richbom?"

"BOM stands for Brother of Martha." He teared up with joy, so I called him that from then on. Eventually, he met some of his other birth relatives. They were like him in many ways, blond with similar senses of humor, and some were tall and left-handed like him. Finding his biological family was one of the high points of his life. When Martha visited Rich and his family several times here in California, I had the privilege of meeting her.

I encouraged him, as several others did, to write a book. I wondered how he found the time, but he told me that he'd get up at 4:00 or 5:00 a.m. to write for several hours before the household woke up. All his books were popular, as they hit a nerve in the Christian community.

Some of them included *Love, No Strings Attached* (1987), *Pain and Pretending* (1988), *New Choices, New Boundaries* (1999), *The First Book of Self Tests*, with Gaylen Larson (1993), and *Be Good To Yourself* (1994).

Meanwhile, Rich and I established a referral book off-air for our listeners who needed counseling, a church, or help of any sort. Eventually it grew so large that it served all five counties and became a lifesaver for thousands of people.

Amidst all our serious topics, we all needed some comic relief. Rich, ever the prankster, was notorious around the station for his jokes on all of us. Rich was well known as a popular guest speaker in many Southern California churches and organizations, and the pastors, well aware of Rich's humor, loved to call in on air, disguise their voices, and bait him with ridiculous and even embarrassing questions and pleas for advice. It usually took Rich a few minutes to realize that he was being fooled, but by then he had poured out his counseling heart in an effort to help the poor caller.

Meanwhile, those of us in the know giggled in the other rooms as he struggled to help the caller. Once the jig was up, he roared with laughter that he had been had.

So, naturally, the challenge was to see how far one of us could go in fooling him. Who better to do it than me, never suspecting that it could backfire?

That next April Fools' Day, we had our usual sales meeting with the account executives, our writer-partners, staff, and, of course Rich, who needed to know about the ad campaigns we were strategizing for his clients. The large conference table was full.

I entered the room with my most forlorn "actress" face. The rest of the staff had been clued into my prank ahead of time.

I sat down with my paperwork.

"What's wrong, Producer Ann? I've never seen you look so sad," Rich said, always the caring counselor.

"Oh, Rich, I have terrible news!" I said as my genuine tears began to flow.

"Well, what is it? Maybe we can help."

"Rich, I can barely bring myself to tell you! I just got off the phone with the FCC." (The Federal Communications Commission licensed the station.)

"Yes? Is there a problem?"

"Oh Rich," I cried, almost sobbing. "They are going to take your show off the air."

Flabbergasted, he said, "But why?"

I said, "They are doing away with any talk shows that have a religious element to them."

"What? What? What?" he shouted as he rose from his chair, red faced, almost knocking the table over.

"This ruins my life!" he shouted. He flew out of the room like a rocket, slamming the door behind him.

"Wait, Rich, please wait," I pleaded, as I chased after him down the hall. But because he was over six feet tall and I was only five-foot-four, I could not catch up with him. He barreled through the lobby, out the station door, and rushed down the five flights of stairs with me in hot pursuit.

"Please wait, Rich, I can explain!" But he was too far ahead of me to hear as he fled through the crowded main floor lobby, out to the huge parking structure.

Now, I really was crying real tears of horror.

What have I done.?

Suddenly, he turned, ran to me, with a big smile, laughing, arms outspread and swept me into a big bear hug.

"Gotcha, Producer Ann! I knew about your prank all along. Mark clued me in yesterday."

"Oh! Rich, I'm so sorry!"

"No apology needed. The joke was on you. But I must admit your acting was really good, I almost believed you."

Arm in arm, we returned to the station amidst the chuckles of the entire staff. Since then, I have never pulled an April Fools' joke on anyone. Not ever. And never will.

Lesson learned.

I produced Rich's talk show for two years. Since I was already in my mid-forties and didn't have much in savings and benefits, it became clear to me that I couldn't live on that minimum salary much longer, knowing that I needed to be socking away money for old age.

Rich was concerned about my future, too. Often, when we went to lunch to discuss plans for the show, he'd talk to me about going into sales at the station. That would mean going out and finding advertisers, developing an advertising strategy for them, and getting their commercials on the air. Depending on how well I did, the pay would be much better.

"Oh, yuck, Rich. I could never do that. My dad has been in commission sales forever and I vowed I'd never go into it because I've seen how hard he has had to work. Besides, I have no experience. Why would anyone hire me?"

"Ann, you'd do well; people like you. The listeners know your name and your voice. That would help you to approach potential clients." For months, he kept insisting that I should try it, try it, try it.

I assured him that I would never go into sales. Never. Never. Never.

* * *

But God has not given us a spirit of fear, but of power
and of love and a sound mind.
- 2 Timothy 1:7

Since Rich's audience was growing in listeners, the owner decided to hire a few more salespeople to find more advertisers. So far, all the account executives, as he called them, were men. The message went out over the air that applications were being accepted. Dozens of men responded. "Ann, you could at least apply for the job," Rich said.

I was finally starting to listen to him.

"Well, why not?" I said. "You're right. Even though I have no sales experience and I don't stand a chance, it won't hurt to try." I had to smile. Rich was Mrs. T all over again, confident that I could do almost anything. What a blessing to be believed in.

To get hired, applicants had to study a thick sales manual, and then take a long written test that covered the basic training and philosophy for selling created by the owner.

I had just finished the lead role in the play *Never Too Late* in a small dinner theater in La Crescenta. While most of the people who applied for the sales job assumed it would be a simple test, I decided I could not take that chance. I knew I'd have to do very well on the test in order to earn an interview with the owner and have a better chance to get the job. So, I memorized the entire thick study manual as if it were a script. What did I have to lose?

I studied the sales material like a marathon runner preparing for the most important race of her life. Consequently, I scored very high on the test. Some said it was one of the highest scores ever for the sales department, nationwide. *Aha. Now the owner would have to interview me, at the very least.*

Fear is a great motivator. The advantage of commission sales was that there was no ceiling to what I could make if I really applied myself. I had to admit I liked that idea. I knew the other applicants had an advantage because, in the years while I was home raising my kids, they had worked in some form of sales and had impressive resumes.

Clearly, I had to make a better living. I had to try. I must try. I would try. If God wanted me to have the job, it would happen. I'd do my part and trust Him with the result.

Several of my friends at the station and church were praying for me. The owner flew out from the east coast and interviewed those of us who passed the test. I spent the next week waiting to hear the final decision, half wanting the job and half wondering if I'd be able to fulfill the necessary requirements if I got it. The next week the call came.

I got the job. Whoopee! I could hardly believe it. I closed the door to the UPI room and danced around for sheer joy.

* * *

*Success is not final; failure is not fatal. It is the courage
to continue that counts.*
- Winston Churchill

Until then, I had thought my chances of getting the job were slim and hadn't imagined that I'd be hired even though I gave it my best shot. Now I had to get in my car, go out, and find advertisers anywhere in the five surrounding counties: Los Angeles, Santa Barbara, Orange, Riverside, and San Diego.

My first day on the road looking for potential clients was overwhelming. With a list of businesses on which to cold call, I parked down the street, away from a large retail store in Orange County, so they wouldn't see me. But I couldn't go in. As I sat paralyzed in my little Toyota, I said out loud, "I cannot do this, Lord." Then I remembered a speaker I had recently heard. He emphasized that we should visualize Jesus with us. So, I looked at the empty seat beside me and imagined Jesus in a long white robe, with a cord tied around his waist, sandals on his feet, long brown hair, and blue eyes, smiling at me. *I cannot do this, Lord. I cannot go into this store. What if they throw me out? What if they laugh at me? What if they ignore me?* Then, in my head I heard a voice clearly say, "You are not going in alone. It's okay. I'm going with you. If they throw you out, we'll go somewhere else."

An unexpected calm came over me.

Confidently, I walked into the store. The scripture that kept coming to mind was Philippians 4:13: "I can do all things through Christ who strengthens me."

The clerks were polite as I asked to speak with the manager. Immediately, he came out, interested in hearing what I had to say, and full of questions about advertising on the station.

From then on, cold calling became easier. I realized that most potential clients had great respect for the station, because we had something to offer them.

The station owner flew out every few months to go on the road with each new account executive to see how we were doing as we interviewed perspective clients, and how he could help us improve. Four meetings with each were required; we checked them out thoroughly before they signed a contract and their ads were written and put on the air.

He had trained hundreds of salesmen all over the country, so he knew what he was talking about. When it was my turn to go out with him, I was looking forward to learning a lot from him.

Even though I had been nervous just thinking about having him with me as we made our rounds, I had prayed ahead of time and that helped me to be calm. One of the meetings I had set up included a large counseling service of five PhDs in Pasadena who wanted to advertise. We drove there from Century City.

Completely at home with these sincere, experienced men, I thought the interviews went great. Our conversations were relaxed and informative as I answered all the questions they had about the station. We got back in the car and I drove us to several other appointments.

At the end of the day, driving back to Century City, the owner said, "Ann, I don't think you'll make it. You talk too much and you're too friendly with the clients. But we'll see how you do in the next ninety days."

* * *

You must do what you think you cannot do.
- Eleanor Roosevelt

I thanked him for his time and drove back to La Crescenta in tears. I thought that my friendly conversations with the potential clients had set them at ease—that not talking about sales every minute was a way to show interest in them. I let them talk and if they digressed a little, I followed their lead, gently bringing the conversation back to advertising.

Apparently, I was wrong. I had a lot to learn in a very short time or risk losing the job.

The goal at any of the stations was to get long term advertisers under contract for a whole year rather than, say, six weeks or a few months. Usually, it takes a new account executive twelve months or more to learn how to accomplish that.

In ninety days, the owner returned to go out with me again. When he got in my car, I quietly handed him a folder with five signed one-year contracts. Even though I knew I had done well, I was still intimidated because of what he had said before about my not making it. But he was surprised and impressed. So was

I. My work ethic had paid off: I would set up appointments with clients anywhere, anytime, in the five counties—even long after business hours, if that's when they could meet—because I just didn't know any better. Apparently other salesmen went home to their families at dinner time.

From the start, I did very well. I stayed in sales for ten years, living on the freeways, sometimes driving two thousand miles a month. But I was motivated by fear of failure. Rich was my greatest cheerleader and comforter. In this kind of high-stress commission job, where you're only as good as your last sale, his constant reassurance got me through. And here I was following the same career path as Daddy, which I had said I'd never, never do. *What do you know about that?*

I loved the adrenaline rush of radio, the immediacy and the deadlines. If we had to have a new commercial on the air by, say, tomorrow morning, my writer and I, regardless of how many hours we worked, would get it on the air, right on time—strategized, written, timed, and recorded. My very favorite writing partner and friend for the last five years of my job there was Allison. Talented, hardworking, and, incidentally, beautiful, she could have been a model. We were a great team. Sometimes, at 9:00 p.m. she'd call me to clear the ad she had written in the car while we had been on the road together that day. Allison made work fun. We often laughed at ourselves and I attribute many of our successful ad campaigns to her brilliant writing. We have been friends ever since.

In addition to having been Rich's producer for two years, I continued to work closely with him for ten more years, since most of the advertising I sold was primarily for his show.

But driving two thousand miles a month finally caught up with me. At one point my car was hit from behind on the 210 Freeway by a drunk driver who was going over ninety miles an hour. As my little Toyota spun out of control across four lanes of traffic, I was headed for a ten-foot cement wall just a few yards away.

I cried, "Jesus help me!" Immediately my car skidded around, and I hit the wall from behind. God provided that no one else hit me and I wasn't killed. A sweet Chinese lady pulled up behind me, crying, because she thought I must be dead. My car was bent in half from the back. Since there was no other way out, I crawled out the back window. The very next day, I rented a car and tried to keep my scheduled meeting with an attorney who advertised with us. As he was giving me a phone number, I struggled to write it down. He had to repeat each number numerous times. Finally, he said, "Do you realize that you're in shock? You need to go home and get to a doctor right away."

The doctor later told me that had I crashed head on, I would have been killed. Fortunately, all my injuries were soft tissue, but it took months of therapy to even be able to turn my head. I realized I couldn't live on the freeways forever, but for now, I didn't know what else to do.

Any client who wanted to advertise on Rich's show had to have his approval first. After I had checked them out, I'd arrange to take them and Rich to lunch, often at the Claim Jumper restaurant in Orange County, so they could get acquainted. If he was really enthusiastic about them, he could even endorse them and voice their commercials, so meeting them in person was important.

Most clients only had an hour for lunch to meet with us to discuss the advantages of being on his show. I had already informed them of many facts about the station, such as how large the audience was, but they wanted to ask Rich all kinds of questions about ad campaign strategies, how many ads per hour he'd recommend, and what kind of response they could expect from their investment. We would start lunch with a normal, friendly conversation, order our food and then—oh, and then—Rich would start talking about an entirely different subject: of all things, his fantastic annual fishing trips to the Alaskan Yukon. The clients couldn't wait to hear about these fishing adventures.

Over time, Rich invited some of the men to fly up with him on his next trip.

He'd tell his favorite story of how a fishhook got embedded in his cheek on the last trip and a well-known cosmetic surgeon who was with him, Dr. North, was able to take the hook out without having to use any painkillers. Then, Rich would wax eloquent about the size of the monster fish or tell some of his hilarious jokes as we all roared with laughter. *How could he remember such long stories?* I knew his secret. He had many of them in his pocket, on a little electronic gadget (this was long before iPhones).

But he would not leave the lunch until he knew the names of all the clients' wives and kids, as well as their ages and interests. Within ten minutes, they'd be pouring out the most intimate details of their personal lives to him with no regard at all to the time. Amazing. At exactly the right moment, he'd bring the subject back to advertising and answer the important questions.

Rich made the whole experience fun and pressure-free. We'd then go our separate ways without a word spoken to persuade the client to sign an advertising contract. Typically, I'd call the potential advertiser the next day to get their feedback. Most often, he'd say, "When can I sign up and how soon can I get ads on the air?"

I listened in wonder at Rich's natural, perfect sense of timing, observing his understanding of human nature and his enormous compassion. I learned from him never to pressure a client, or anyone for that matter. He demonstrated the importance of taking an interest in people as human beings, and not just objects for business. What I learned from him helped me the rest of my life, not only in a future career, but in my relationships with others. He genuinely loved every person he ever met. Everyone I ever knew who had known Rich for over ten minutes enthusiastically claimed that Rich was their best friend.

Lord, help me to be more like that.

* * *

It's easy to make a buck. It's a lot tougher to make a difference.
\- Tom Brokaw

All the dozens of seminars I've ever attended boiled down to a simple concept: just care about people. Even love them. That may seem naïve at first; in business, of course, your priority is to know your subject well and to know how to help the client, but that's a lot easier to do if you care about them as human beings. That's straight out of Scripture, and it just naturally oozed out of Rich's pores.

Not every client we worked with was an angel. Allison and I had one difficult client relationship that we watched Rich repair, as he taught us the art of forgiving and how to move on together. This client, Mr. Colton, was verbally abusive to Allison and me. Finally, when we couldn't take anymore, we confided in Rich.

He was angry that we were treated so badly. Actually, I'd never seen him so angry. The next day, he called the client into his office at the station. Allison and I stayed out of sight, a few rooms away. To my shock, we could hear Rich yelling from clear down the hall as he told Mr. Colton off. We'd never heard him raise his voice before.

"If you ever speak to Ann and Allison with such disrespect again, you will be off my show. Do you understand me?"

The client left Rich's office like a slick-eared puppy with his tail between his legs. *Had he thought we wanted his business and his bucks so badly that we'd put up with anything—even verbal abuse?*

The next day, Mr. Colton came back in and apologized profusely to Rich. They left for lunch, joking and laughing together, the best of friends, with Rich's arm around his shoulder.

From then on, the client sought Allison's and my opinion on every detail of the ad campaign we were doing for him, showing great respect. Our success was confirmed in that he stayed with us for years and we got along great. Rich knew how to draw the line and defend his staff, but he also knew how and when to forgive and move on together. No wonder he was able to write a book about boundaries and forgiveness.

With the help of the other account executives, we sold out Rich's show. Most advertisers stayed with us for many years, which was pretty much unheard of at the time. The majority of our clients were located in Orange County, so the station moved there in 1986 from crowded Century City. Since I had dreamed of living near the ocean all my life, I rented an apartment close to the station in Huntington Beach. Even so, I was still on the freeways a lot.

Finally, though, the stress and driving wore me down. I was doing well, but I needed a life. With my long hours there was little time left for friends and family. Shannon had graduated from college and was working in science and engineering, and Gina was pursuing her singing and acting career. What should I do now?

CHAPTER 25

A NEW ADVENTURE

Sooner or later the person who wins is the person who thinks he can.
- Napoleon Hill

IN 1991, RICH LEFT THE STATION. In 1992, the station and I parted ways. After all that driving, I longed to work locally. For several years, out of the corner of my eye, I had looked at real estate since I liked working one-on-one with people and had always been interested in every aspect of houses. My background in planning ad campaigns and marketing seemed like a good fit for selling people's property and helping buyers find a home.

As I studied for the real estate exam in order to get my license, I had to lie on the living room floor on my side because I had fractured my pelvis playing tennis. I enjoyed the game even though I didn't play very well. However, while running backward to hit a ball in a match, I caught my heel and with both arms in the air, tripped and landed right on my tailbone. *Ouch.*

Again, persistence would be my trump card. I didn't think that I had superior intelligence, but I did know how to hang in there. It reminded me of my old cheerleading days. But this time, as an adult, I had to cheer for myself.

During those painful months studying on my side, I again turned to my Bible for comfort, particularly Isaiah 40:31, one of my favorites: "Even youths grow tired and weary, and young men stumble and fall; but those who hope in the Lord will renew their strength. They will soar on wings like eagles; they will run and not be weary, they will walk and not be faint."

I wanted to pass this tricky exam on the first try. I had heard that many people had to take it several times, but I didn't want to waste time taking it again. The day I was notified that I got my real estate license was the day my grandson was born to my daughter Gina—two major blessings in one day.

In those first years of real estate, I often called Daddy in Memphis. From the start I'd tell him about each transaction. He'd say, "Hot dog. What do you know about that? I knew you could do it. I'm so proud of you." My path would mirror his, both as a choir director and in sales. In those adult years, I was pleased that we had reconnected, now having more in common. I knew in my heart that between Daddy's encouragement and the Scripture, "I can do all things through Christ who strengthens me" (Phil. 4:13), I could be successful in real estate. Even though changing careers was stressful, I felt I had all the tools needed to see me through.

* * *

Yea, though I walk through the valley of the shadow of
death I will fear no evil, for you are with me.
- Psalm 23:4

In 1993, while I was in my office, an unexpected call came. After a long bout with the flu, Mother had suddenly passed away. Mother and Tom had retired and moved to Ashland, Mississippi several years before, where living expenses were less than in Southern California. Georgia, her four grown kids, Shannon, and I all flew back for the funeral.

She had come back to La Crescenta a few months before her passing to visit Georgia for a few weeks. After having had a stroke when my girls were little, she was having heart problems.

I drove to Georgia's house to take Mother out to dinner. I prayed before I went up to meet with her, realizing it might be my last opportunity to see her. While I had usually found it easy to talk to a friend about God and eternity, I thought it might be daunting to try to talk to Mother, knowing that in the past she had not been interested. After dinner, when I took her back to Georgia's, I parked in front so we could visit privately.

"Mother, I don't know when I'll be able to get back to Memphis to see you again and you've been pretty sick."

"Yeah, I don't know how much longer I have. I'm tired out."

"How are you and the Lord getting along?"

"What do you mean?"

"Have you ever thought about where you will spend eternity when that day comes?"

"I don't know, but lately I think about it a lot," she said.

"Do you believe that Jesus is the Son of God?"

"Yeah, I do."

Annie and Real Estate Awards

"Have you ever invited Christ into your life and told Him you believe in Him?

"No. I don't know how."

"Do you want me to help you by leading you in a prayer to invite Him in?"

"Sure. Please." I took her hand and she repeated after me, "Lord Jesus, please come into my life. I believe you are the Son of God. I believe that you died for me and rose again and ascended into heaven. Please forgive me for anything I've done that is not pleasing to you and help me to know you better. Amen."

I hugged her. The years of resentment were gone. She was old, weak, and tired. We talked awhile and I assured her, with Scripture, of the decision she had made.

Even though it had been hard to bring up the subject with her, I felt the peace of God, and knew that He was there with us.

I never saw Mother alive again. I grieved over all that never was with us, but at least I could thank God that our relationship ended on a loving note, and I knew that God is more gracious than any of us can comprehend, so I had peace about leaving her in God's hands.

As for the long-suffering Tom, he told Shannon after the funeral, "Now I can go fishing. I even have $1,600."

* * *

For I am persuaded that neither death nor life nor
angels nor principalities nor powers nor things present
nor things to come nor height nor depth nor any other
created thing shall be able to separate us from the love
of God, which is in Christ Jesus our Lord.
(Romans 8:38)

Eleven months later, Daddy, who had been a champion athlete for years in Senior Olympics in swimming, golf, and tennis, went in for a stress test. The doctor found a blockage in his heart. I called the night before his open-heart surgery to encourage him but, as usual, instead, he encouraged me.

"Oh, honey, there's nothing to it. Sure, I know it's serious, but I'm just replacing parts like I did with my knee and the back surgery a few years ago." His positive attitude forever delighted me.

I couldn't be there because Gina, in a high-risk pregnancy, was ready to have their second child any moment. When Daddy came out of surgery, Mama, Liz, and Lynn waited for him to re-gain consciousness. We talked daily. Those hours were torture for me, wanting to be there, and needing to be here with Gina. We waited and waited for Daddy to wake up.

For nineteen days.

Gina delivered my granddaughter within the next two weeks. Because we had almost lost her in childbirth with the first baby, I stayed by her side. It was a rough delivery, but she and my grand-daughter were okay.

Daddy never regained consciousness. He died on March 3, 1994, when he was eighty-four years old. The doctor's opinion was that a piece of calcium had broken loose and gone to his brain. We all agreed after his death that God gave us the nineteen days to adjust to the idea of losing him. Charismatic and full of enthusiasm, he glittered when he walked into any room. Thank God, he had been happy for over forty years with Mama. In a heartbeat, he was gone, eleven months after Mother.

When I heard the news, I grieved about the decades I never had with him. *What would it have been like to have had a dad with me all my life, or, at least, in my childhood years? What would it have been like to have a dad to give me advice from a male perspective—especially when I started dating—to teach me about men, to have a dad to defend me and encourage me when I was small?*

We weren't close until after I was grown and married. *Where were the lost years that other women had?* Through my tears, I tried to thank God for the two years I did live with him and his family. Then I remembered Mrs. T and thanked God that she had been both mother and father to me.

I flew back to Memphis for his funeral. As I sat staring at his coffin after the other guests had walked away, I wanted to be grateful that, across the miles, he had at least been part of my life when I was an adult. How exceptional that we managed to stay in contact. Mrs. T had made every effort to keep that connection for me when I lived with her. And Daddy and I both made the effort to keep in contact in my adult years, so at least I always knew he loved me. In the end, that's all that mattered.

Many times, when Shannon and Gina were young, I had taken them to Memphis because I wanted them to know and love my family. I was also grateful that, because I knew he was getting older, I had flown to Memphis to be with the four of them for the last four Christmases. Those trips had also given me an opportunity to visit Mother, Tom, and Uncle Dan.

From left to right: Annie, sister Lynn, daughter Shannon and sister Liz.

One good thing came out of the nineteen days that Liz, Lynn, and Mama sat with Daddy. Lynn, who had been a professional musician for years, watched the ICU nurses and saw how rewarding their lives were. Even though she was in her forties, she decided to go to nursing school. Mama paid for it, and Lynn is now a successful nurse in Memphis. Daddy would be proud, just as he was proud of Liz, who is a schoolteacher and counselor in Jackson, Tennessee.

When Shannon and I returned from Daddy's funeral, I poured my life into real estate, just as I'd had to do as a new teacher, days after Mrs. T's funeral. With some hard work, I went on to become a successful realtor, and within the first two years of selling I bought a lovely three-bedroom townhome.

My job was rewarding because of the interesting clients I had the privilege of helping during one of the most important transitions in their lives. I loved the drama of real estate. Many buyers and sellers were fascinating, as they often shared the most intense details of their experiences with me. Each situation was different, and I enjoyed planning how I could help them by making this change in their lives as stress-free as possible. The radio years had prepared me for the negotiating and marketing I would do on their behalf, but I wondered if this was all there was. Was my career to be my whole life from now on?

I certainly wasn't going to count on a prince charming showing up with a glass slipper.

CHAPTER 26

WILL

Across a Crowded Room

IN THOSE BUSY YEARS, while working long hours, I did manage to visit singles' groups at St. Andrews Church in Newport Beach, and Mariners Church in Irvine.

Because I love to dance, whenever I could, I attended gatherings that singles organizations put on in elegant ballrooms around the county. One Saturday night, a big dance was held in Long Beach, but I was so tired from passing out real estate flyers all day I thought I'd rather have a root canal than scrape myself together and go out. But a close girlfriend called and said she would not go alone, so I went to keep her company. Once I got in her car, I thought, *This might be a mistake.* I didn't have my own transportation, so I couldn't leave when I wanted to. Worse yet, I thought I wouldn't know anybody there, and they would all be younger than me, anyway. With me in that negative frame of mind, off we went.

As we walked into the exquisite hotel lobby, we heard the band starting up. A crowd of over three hundred people were already circulating around. The dancing began immediately and, wonder of wonders, I recognized some of my buddies from Mariners and St. Andrews. Most were frogs whom I would never have an interest in kissing, but at least they'd be someone to dance with.

Then, across the crowded room, I saw *him.* Wouldn't you know it? Lots of well dressed, attractive women, obviously younger than me, were swarming around him like hormone-driven hummingbirds on the first day of spring.

Oh well, he's probably conceited. Why shouldn't he be? As I casually strolled by him, I caught flashes and bits of his humorous stories causing the ladies around him to chuckle. *No use getting excited about him, with all those women fluttering around.* I couldn't help but notice his broad shoulders, slim physique, blue eyes, and oh, that sweet beguiling smile.

Of course, he didn't have time to notice me. *I didn't care. Why should I? After all, I was having fun. Forget him. He's not the last boat out.*

Then, to my surprise, he cut through the crowd and asked me to dance. Even with the loud music, I caught that his name was Will. The first tune was a fast one, "In the Mood." We were so well matched it was as if we had been partners all our lives, but the melody ended much too soon. He thanked me and disappeared.

I thought I'd never see him again. We hadn't even had a chance to get acquainted.

After a while though, this Will person came back, and this time a slow song was playing, the romantic Nat King Cole favorite, "Unforgettable." He took me gently in his arms and drew me very close. *The nerve. I didn't usually like a stranger snuggling up to me so soon. But, oh, it felt so good to be next to him. Couldn't I stay here for just a few more minutes?* I couldn't bring myself to pull back into a proper dance position just yet. He was the perfect height for me so that, if I wanted to—in the future, say—I could easily nuzzle my nose into his warm neck. But, of course, I wouldn't do that this soon. Instead, we pressed our cheeks together.

Well, well, well. Yes, indeed. Might as well enjoy the moment. The tenderness of his embrace touched my heart. I've always thought that the way a man holds you when you dance tells you exactly what kind of a sweetheart he would be. If he jerks you around the dance floor and holds your hand hard, he is insensitive. I pulled back enough to observe his smiling blue eyes, his light brown hair—yes, he had all his hair. I smiled at him, hoping he'd get the message that I liked him.

A lot.

Now that the music was softer, we could hear each other talk.

"What kind of work do you do?" he asked, a typical ice-breaker question.

I wanted to put off his knowing that I was a realtor as long as possible, so we could get acquainted a little before he found out I worked weekends, which was a downer for a lot of guys.

"Oh, uh," I stumbled, "I'm in investments."

"Interesting. What kind of investments?"

"Uh, well, financial investments."

"Really. What kind of financial investments?"

"Well, real estate."

"How nice. Residential or commercial?"

"Residential. Well, okay I'm a realtor."

"Well, how about that? I'm a broker."

We had something in common. Maybe he would understand that my working hours were flexible. I relaxed a little, aware that, for the first time since we started talking, I could breathe.

He smiled. "I'm not a practicing broker now, but I was for many years."

We talked about the market. He wanted to know whether I preferred dealing with buyers or sellers and in what areas I worked.

"Unforgettable" was over, but I wouldn't forget him for a very long time, if ever. He thanked me and disappeared.

Oh, no. I couldn't go after him. My rule was, never, never go after a man. I needed him to chase me until I caught him, so I'd always feel wanted. Would he come back?

Annie, silly girl, get a hold of yourself.

Will did come back and asked me to dance again. I noticed how athletic and agile he was. And he smelled nice. With that light touch of men's cologne, he was almost irresistible.

I felt like laughing as I thought, *Should I get on with it and wrap my arms around his neck right here and now, or be more ladylike?* I controlled my feelings and acted casual and friendly instead.

"Say, Annie, could I have your number so I can call, and we can go for a walk on the Huntington Beach pier sometime?" he said. I gave him my business card. But how many times has a seemingly nice guy asked for my card and yet never called? We women never understood that. Did they go home and change their minds? Or did they just think that was the courteous thing to do, a way to say goodnight? It's hurtful when you never get the call.

With that the evening ended. Two weeks went by with no call from Will. *I knew it. He was just another smooth operator.* Finally, to my surprise, he called, explaining that he'd been out of town camping with his grown sons. *His grown sons? He likes his sons? He wants to be with them?* That's an admirable trait.

He lived more than an hour away, but his willingness to make the drive to see me pleased me. I'd thought he'd consider me "GU"—geographically undesirable. As we strolled on the pier, I hardly noticed how cold and windy it was. We walked and talked for hours and I loved hearing him tell how he enjoyed his family—his sons, his daughter-in-law, and tiny granddaughter Robin. He laughed as he told about the boys' surfing adventures and how they all loved camping. He explained that he'd become a widower over fifteen years ago and had been in several serious relationships since then. I felt drawn to his easygoing style, as if I'd known him for years.

Okay, Cool it. He can't be as nice as he seems. None of them ever are when the veneer wears off. Don't get too excited. Give it time and see where it goes. Get on with your life. The most important thing to focus on right now had to be my real estate career, which was doing well.

Within weeks, anytime we weren't working, Will and I were inseparable as we discovered many wonderful things to do together. We took picnics to the beach, hit golf balls badly at small courses, played ping-pong, enjoying that we were so well matched, and went dancing often. He was very in-tune with nature, having been raised on a farm in Canada where the winters were severe and the coming of spring a major event. Every bird, every tree, every sunset was a wonder to him. It became our little joke that he was so in awe of how the very tip-top leaf on a tree managed to get water through osmosis—a miracle against the pull of gravity.

He often came over early on Sundays, when I had open houses, to help me put up signs and take them down. Afterward, he'd take me out to dinner. We had so much to talk about; our points of view about life, love of nature, and even our love of God—all were in perfect agreement. He even made me laugh with his corny jokes. Will loved to cook and would sometimes come down early on a Saturday before we went out so we could prepare dinner together.

He called every evening for long conversations. After we had dated for four months, on several of those lengthy phone calls, he went on and on about how he and his family had camped in Sequoia every June for the last thirty years. Since he was quite the talker, I'd half-listen and work on the computer at the same time. *What was he getting at?*

Finally, he said, "You know, how 'bout you get away for a few days, and come up and join us? It's only a five-hour drive. Some of my kids will already be there and our campsite is right by the rangers' station. You'd have the big tent and I'd have a pup tent nearby. And if you'd come, I'd protect you from the bears."

It sounded tempting. *How well did I know this guy? Was it safe to be out in the wilderness with him? He could be an axe murderer for all I knew.*

Time to check him out.

The next day I called Marilyn, a well-known party organizer in Orange County. You couldn't get into her dances unless she approved of you. I asked her what she thought about this Will person. "I know him pretty well," she said. "He's been a widower for many years and is well-liked by the ladies. The gals who have dated him say he's a sweet guy, honest and trustworthy. You'd like him."

Still uncertain about going and armed with Marilyn's information, I called my daughter Gina and told her my story. Divorced with two children, she had dated a lot, and knew the scene much better than I did.

"What should I do?" I said

"Mom, go and have fun. You haven't been away for ages and you love to camp. He sounds like a nice guy. But, always, keep your pepper spray and your car keys in your pocket. One false move and you hop in your car immediately and head down the hill. Don't even go back to the tent to get your purse and stuff. Just leave."

That sounded reasonable and safe, so on the appointed date in June, I happily loaded up my little Toyota with lots of food, since I figured they'd be running low by now, and headed for the mountains. I also took some song sheets and my beautiful Ovation guitar. I hadn't played it in months and had missed it.

Most important of all, I took my pepper spray.

Will didn't know that I was a seasoned camper from way back, and I didn't know that that mattered to him. In addition to having been a camp counselor one summer in college, I had camped with my family for years as the kids were growing up.

I learned later from his sons that they had said, "Dad, if you want to find out what a woman is really like, take her camping. You'll see if she's fussy or picky and can't stand dirt or cold. Who is this woman anyway, that you're spending so much time with?"

When I arrived in the late afternoon, his kids were just leaving. Hmm. *What did that mean?*

A huge, old Taj Mahal of a tent was set up just for me. A separate room for sleeping was equipped with an air mattress and down blankets, and a curtained-off room with a small table, a mirror, and a large basin for washing up was ready for me. The tent even had a porta-potty, and all the creature comforts. I had never camped with such convenience. I named it the Will Hilton.

The campsite it-self was the most beautiful one I'd ever been in, with water-falls on two sides. The fresh smell of the stately Sequoia trees permeated the air beneath a sky of radiant blue. A fire pit, complete with

Sequoia, Close to Heaven

grill and frying pan, promised good cooking for dinner. When I arrived, the aroma of hot coffee brewing filled the cool mountain air. Impressed and grateful for the food I'd brought, Will was nevertheless surprised when he saw my guitar. I had stopped in Porterville, as he requested, and brought him a large container of live crickets to fish with. And, sure enough, a few campsites away, was the rangers' trailer.

And fish we did, pulling out trout almost as soon as we dropped in the line. He taught me where to find the fish and how to troll for them. I'd never learned before how to carefully take the hook out of the fish's mouth and gently lower it back into the stream if I wanted to set it free.

Each evening, when the sun went down, the cold closed in around us as a million stars, like 4th of July sparklers, invited us to reach out and touch them. The quiet of the woods and the sound of the rushing stream were a soothing contrast to the constant sound of traffic at home.

To keep warm after dark, on a chaise lounge by the fire, we cuddled up together under a blanket. We talked half the night about the wonder of God's beautiful handiwork that we saw all around us, as our ears bathed in the murmur of the stream and waterfall. We discussed our belief in Christ, how we wanted to live our lives, and our kids and our grandkids. In that tranquil atmosphere, it was almost as if we were in the very presence of God.

* * *

I don't know anything about music. In my line, you don't have to.
- Elvis Presley

Will was a practicing pharmacist, policing the drugs at a large hospital in LA. The real estate broker's license was something he had done years ago. To my surprise, he read some of his poetry to me. He amazed me that even with such a scientific background, he was also so creative, and I was pleased at how good his poems were. He asked me to set some of them to music and to sing them with my guitar. I used just simple chords but he, being unmusical, thought I was a genius. It tickled me to think he could be so easily impressed. *Me and Elvis.*

As the fire went out, we almost froze to death. We did not want to leave each other and go into our separate tents. The pleasure of meeting such a warm man, a romantic, who talked so easily and to whom I was so attracted, was an experience I hadn't had in years. But as the night got colder, even under a blanket, the air became so damp from the dew that we finally had to part. He shuffled off to his tiny, freezing, pup tent, while I snuggled under my warm down blankets and enjoyed my comfortable castle.

I woke in the mornings to the aroma of coffee brewing and bacon frying, the sound of the rushing stream, and the scent of the pine trees and Sequoias. As I came out of my tent, I found him cooking eggs, bacon, toast, and hash browns for us over the open fire.

When we sat fishing by the stream, I asked him to tell me his life story. "I was born and raised on a farm in Alberta, Canada. Eight of us kids plus our parents lived in a one-bedroom house with no telephone, no indoor plumbing, and in the winter, it was twenty to fifty degrees below zero."

"Wow." I shuddered. "I can't imagine living in such cold."

"I took my younger brothers and sisters to school in a sleigh. My parents were Ukrainian immigrants, along with all the other families in the small village of Myrnam. My Dad died a few weeks before I graduated from high school, so I headed out on my own to the big city, Vancouver, and worked my way through college by driving a taxi."

"Coming from such a small village," I said, "that must have been a stressful time for you."

"Yeah, it sure was. After college, I worked my way around the world on cargo ships. But my dream was to come to the United States. In graduate school, I managed to transfer to USC and finished there as a pharmacist. By that time, I was married, and we had the two boys. Their mom died of Lou Gehrig's disease when the kids were in their late teens. I've been single ever since."

"I'm so sorry for what you went through. It sounds like you've been a good dad."

He smiled that kind smile again.

"Annie, how did you end up being single?"

I briefly shared with him that I had been married to my college sweetheart for twenty-one years and had been divorced for the many years since.

Because I felt my life story was so different from his, I didn't want to go into why I had not been raised by my parents. His childhood seemed so wholesome and happy, and mine was so, well, different. If the relationship continued, I'd share more later.

The four days ended too quickly. No bears showed up for him to protect me from, but from that day forward I called Will my bear protector.

Back home, hopelessly smitten, I thought about him all the time.

We continued dating most weekends. I especially loved Saturday nights when we went ballroom dancing, because it gave me an excuse to be wrapped in his warm arms and nuzzle in his neck.

One Sunday after several months, he invited me to go to San Diego to visit his sons, Ryan and Darren, and Ryan's wife Marsha. Later, Darren married Corina and we attended their wedding together. All of them were friendly and gracious to me. I loved how well they got along, with lots of friendly kidding. Obviously, they loved one another and their dad.

At Christmas he came over to meet Gina and her two children, who were eight and six. He had already met Shannon, who lived with me part-time. It occurred to me how Mrs. T and Daddy would have loved him.

I'm not sure where this romance is going.
I only know I'm having the time of my life.

CHAPTER 27

A TIME FOR EVERY PURPOSE UNDER HEAVEN

...casting all your care upon Him, for He cares for you.
- 1 Peter 5:7

OUR CLOSE RELATIONSHIP THRIVED for three more years. My girlfriends thought I was lucky to have such a wonderful guy in my life, who seemed to love me, *at my age.* But I finally realized that I wanted more than just a charming companion to date. I wanted someone to spend the rest of my life with—in other words, marriage. I certainly wasn't going to propose to him, or any man for that matter, because I thought I would then forever wonder if he wanted us together as much as I did. *If what I want is a husband, am I wasting my time with him?*

One day, my sister Georgia, who still lived in La Crescenta, called. Except for a few holidays, we hadn't had much contact over the last few years due to my long hours and her being busy with four grown kids, two stepchildren, and seven grandchildren. She had joined a women's Bible study in Glendale and renewed her commitment to the Lord. She wanted us to get back together and be close again. After all, we had shared some difficult and important years of our childhood. I was delighted.

Being with her again was as if we had never been apart. Since she and Will were both outgoing and friendly, they hit it off immediately. We had some fun times with her and her husband.

She asked me on the phone, "Honey, Will's a keeper. What's going on with you two, anyway? What do you want from this relationship? Are you content to date him indefinitely?"

"Well, no. I'm interested in marriage, but I don't see us going in that direction."

A few weeks later, we met her and her husband Phillip at the Hollywood Bowl to hear Ray Charles perform. Georgia and I were moved as he sang his bluesy hit "Georgia on My Mind." It reminded us of our younger years in Memphis. We didn't know it then, but we wouldn't have many more times together.

On these visits, we always had to sit outside because they were chain smokers. Georgia still had the persistent cough that she had had for as long as I could remember.

One evening, in the fall of 2002, when Will and I went out to dinner, I thought it was time to have a serious talk. I asked him where he thought our relationship was going.

"I'm content with things as they are with us," he said.

"Okay. I understand," I said. "I'm really glad you told me, and I appreciate your honesty. That's fine, of course, if that's what you want. But it's not what I want for my life, so I think it's best if I pull back and not spend so much time exclusively with you anymore. Since there is no serious commitment between us, I'm sorry, but I need to get on with my life."

He looked surprised. An awkward silence followed.

"If you want to keep in touch," I said, "you can call me once a month."

It took all the strength I had to tell him this. He was everything I had ever wanted in a man, but I knew I could never chase after him. I needed to be pursued, not the other way around. After thinking it through for many months, I had decided I'd rather be alone than be with someone who did not want to spend the rest of his life with me. Even though the breakup was painful, I knew it was the right thing to do.

Meanwhile, Georgia and I burned up the phone lines catching up on our lost years. In every call we could go from deep, serious discussions, trying to make sense of our scrambled childhoods, to so much laughter that I was doubled up over the kitchen counter gasping for breath with "tears" running down my legs. It was as if we'd picked up right where we left off and God had restored all the years we had lost.

Georgia Makes Me Laugh

The first of the year, 2003, I was attending a Zig Ziegler real estate motivational conference when my cell phone rang.

"Hi, Aunt Anna. It's Nanci," (Georgia's second daughter). "Mom's in the hospital."

"What happened?"

"She's had bad headaches for weeks while she's tried to quit smoking, but the headaches got worse until she couldn't stand it anymore. They're running tests right now to see what's wrong."

"I'll be there as soon as I pick up Shannon," I said.

We raced to Verdugo Hills Hospital to sit with Georgia, Nanci, and Cindi, Georgia's oldest daughter, as the long hours passed waiting for MRI results. We made small talk to mask our dread that the news might not be good.

Finally, the doctor came in. "I'm sorry, but in addition to lung cancer, you have five large lesions in your brain. It's at stage four. You don't have long to live."

We were stunned. *Lesions? What were lesions? Surely there must be some mistake. If the lesions were cancer in her brain, why didn't the doctor use the word cancer? What did stage four mean?* We didn't understand. *Lung cancer? Can't that be treated?*

Georgia appeared to take the news calmly, while I felt as if a knife had been stabbed into my stomach. We tried to say everything we could think of to encourage her, explaining that they can do so much nowadays, and now that they've identified the problem, surely, they could help her. The bond of love we felt for each other that night, and the love of the Lord that penetrated the hospital room, would be remembered the rest of our lives.

We prayed together for her recovery.

We did understand that she was very ill, but still, I expected that if they gave her chemo, it would extend her life at least for a year or so.

* * *

When life is more than you can stand, kneel.
- Gordon B. Hinckley

When Will made his once-a-month call to me, I told him about Georgia's illness.

"May I come back into your life as your friend," he said, "and stand with you through this? I know what this is like and I want

to be there for you." He really loved Georgia, and the long, painful death of his wife from Lou Gehrig's disease fifteen years before gave him a special empathy for our situation.

I welcomed him. I could sure use a strong shoulder to lean on, and I had missed him terribly anyway. In the coming months, he drove Shannon and me to the hospital and Georgia's home several times. Chemotherapy only reduced her violent headaches

Georgia's Last Summer   for a few weeks. She didn't get better. Within two months, she was readmitted to the hospital and placed in hospice care.

Hospice care? How could this be? I could not believe it. Hospice usually means you have six months or less to live, and the goal is only to make the patient comfortable, not to cure them.

There must be something else they can do.

Finally, she became too weak to have any more chemo. At the hospital, the oncologist told her husband and me, "I'm sorry. We've done everything we can do for her."

Oh, no. Surely, she'd start to get better after all these treatments.

I stood outside her hospital room door, listening to make sure Phillip told her what the oncologist said. I knew she wanted to know the truth.

She took the news calmly and seemed to understand.

Denial is sometimes a protective shield from grief, but only works temporarily. Then, like ice water poured down your warm neck on a cold day, the awful shock of reality sets in. At least, that's what happened to me.

I stayed with her at the hospital every possible moment, as did her three daughters and Shannon. Here was my opportunity to be by her side at a crucial time, just as she had been there for me when we were little latchkey kids. One Friday afternoon when she and I were alone in her room, she was weak and exhausted, but coherent. I bragged to the nurse about what a great athlete Georgia was as a kid. "Why, the boys in the neighborhood would knock on our door begging her to come play baseball on their team because she could guarantee home runs for them. She was a slugger, a champ."

Georgia lifted one weak finger, wagged it at me and said, "You're a good sister." She had been such a good sister to me that, somehow, after being apart for so many years, her words were a great comfort.

Two days later, just as the hospice nurse had predicted, Georgia grew even weaker. Her three daughters, stepdaughter

Julie, Shannon, and I were gathered around her bed as her vital signs began to decrease. We prayed in the hall together.

"Lord, please send a miracle and let her live. She's only sixty-eight. Please give her a few more years. But if you don't choose to do that, and you're going to take her, do it soon so she won't suffer anymore. Don't let her linger in pain."

That was the hardest prayer I ever prayed.

That Sunday afternoon, as we all realized the end was near, Georgia's stepdaughter, Julie, and Shannon felt something urgent should be done. They both felt that we needed a chaplain or pastor to guide and pray with us. The nurses station said there was no one like that but there was a church next door.

They ran down the block to a small church that had lights on inside, dashed in, and returned to the hospital room with a wide-eyed, startled youth pastor in tow.

We all linked hands around the bed as he benevolently led us in prayer. That night, we held Georgia's hands as she slowly slipped away. When her spirit left her body, Shannon felt a jolt. Even though there was no breeze coming in from anywhere, the small flower vase across the room tipped over. Surely, she was with the Lord now, and even in the midst of our tears, that gave us some comfort. We stayed with her for hours after she died as other family members arrived. Then we all walked alongside the gurney as they took her to the hearse. We stood on the curb sobbing as they drove her away.

Shannon and I arrived at my house back in Orange County at 3:00 a.m., numb with grief. As I stood in the kitchen, I sensed the presence of my sister. In my head I heard her voice saying, "I'm okay. Don't worry. And Mother's here with me."

Startled and shocked, I didn't understand. *Was I hallucinating?* While I don't fully comprehend everything in the Bible and how it all works, I do believe that, to get us through, at special times when we need it most, God does extraordinary things. I only know what happened to me that night and how it gave me peace. Here we see through a glass darkly, and I accept that as part of the mystery until we get to the other side when we will understand everything.

I'm okay with that.

* * *

To be absent from the body is to be present with the Lord.
- 2 Corinthians 5:8

I relived Georgia's final moments over the coming days and months, but I had to go on, even though there were times when I could not hold up my head for crying. I grieved over our lost years together—my playmate and my protector as a child. I grieved that she had had such a hard life, with so little help, rarely seeing her own dad. I grieved that she did not have the opportunities that I had with Mrs. T. Worst of all, I grieved over the great times we would never have together again.

My best source of comfort was my Bible. "Let not your heart be troubled; you believe in God, believe also in Me. In My Father's house are many dwellings; if it were not so, I would have

Sequoia, Grandkids, Shannon

told you. I go to prepare a place for you. And if I go and prepare a place for you, I will come again and receive you to Myself; that where I am, there you may be also" (John 14:1-3). Even though, as a believer, I know Georgia is with the Lord, I have never stopped missing her. In the days before her funeral, Will called to comfort me. He attended her funeral. After that, I assumed he and I would return to our once-a-month phone call, if that. Too numb to care about anything, I didn't listen for his call.

In the coming weeks, his sons took him on their annual surfing and camping trip to San Onofre State Beach. He must have told them that our relationship had cooled because, unbeknownst to me, they said to him, "Dad, what do you intend to do about Annie? You can't let her get away. This isn't college dating. You need to marry her."

A few weeks after Georgia died, he called, saying he wanted to get together and talk. "Can I take you to lunch?"

"Will, thank you, but we've talked enough. There's nothing else to say. I need to get on with my life."

"No, I mean we need to talk seriously."

Long pause.

"Why? About what?"

"I realized when Georgia died that, well, we don't have forever. We're older now and life is short."

"Yeah, so?" *Didn't we already know that?*

"Well, uh, we need to uh, talk, uh, about mm...mm...mar—uh, well, marriage."

Interesting. I almost dropped the phone. I needed to let that one marinate for a long time—at least a half second.

"Well, I suppose I can at least have lunch with you."

On a sunny afternoon, in a quiet corner on the patio deck of a beautiful restaurant overlooking Newport Bay, we had a three-hour lunch.

I will not let him mess with my head. If he is going to talk marriage, there will have to be a ring and a date or I'm not having any of it. No more wasting time with this guy.

He explained how much we had in common, how we loved each other's kids and how his kids loved me. "And, well, I realize that I love you," he said. "And I want to spend the rest of my life with you."

Sweet. But what does it mean? I knew that it didn't necessarily mean marriage. "Thank you. But unless there is a ring and a date, I have to move on."

"I understand that now. I don't want to lose you. Okay? Will you marry me? We can go to LA next week and pick out a ring. Let's set a date for the wedding."

I smiled and wrapped my arms around his inviting neck. I didn't need a glass slipper on my foot to know that he was my prince. We kissed right there in the restaurant.

"I love you, too, Will." I suspect that I had loved him from the first moment, but not knowing if it would work out, I had held myself back.

CHAPTER 28

LOVE BEARS ALL THINGS, HOPES ALL THINGS

Though I speak with the tongues of men and of angels, but have not love, I have become as sounding brass or a clanging symbol...Love suffers long and is kind; love does not envy; love does not parade itself, is not puffed up; does not behave rudely, does not seek its own, is not jealous or boastful; it is not arrogant or rude. Love does not insist on its own way; it is not provoked, thinks no evil. Love bears all things, believes all things, hopes all things, endures all things. Love never fails.
- 1 Corinthians 13:4-7

ON A BEAUTIFUL SATURDAY MORNING, May 8, 2004, on a bluff overlooking Laguna Beach and the peaceful Pacific, we were married. Forty family members and friends grouped around us as we stood in the center of an outdoor gazebo. My twelve-year-old grandson, David, walked me down the aisle, and my granddaughter, ten-year-old Dina, carried the ring cushion. Will's three tiny grandkids were flower girls. Will's sons stood beside him and my two daughters and my half-sisters, Liz and Lynn from Memphis, read selected Scriptures. Will's sister, brother-in-law, and niece were there from Canada.

Georgia's daughters Cindi and Nanci stood right behind Will's shoulder in tears—a bittersweet moment for all of us. I knew they were thinking that Georgia should have been there as my maid of honor. It had been more than a year since she died.

Our Families Together

As I turned to hold Will's hand to take our vows, I could not believe how incredibly handsome he was. This funny, humble guy who never thought of himself as good looking was slim, tan, fit, smiling, and finally all mine. My husband. Surely, God had blessed us beyond what we ever could have hoped.

The celebration with our guests continued for three days. Since between us we already had everything we needed for the house, we didn't want any presents—we just wanted to have a good time with our friends and family. So, instead, as a gift to all of them, Will and I rented fifteen ocean-view rooms, right on the water, for two nights at Laguna Riviera Resort.

Everyone checked in on Friday afternoon. I had had a disc jockey put together a CD of our favorite tunes to dance to on the large deck as we served food both Friday and Saturday nights.

We wanted each side of the family to get to know each other and this might be the only chance they had.

As we began our great adventure, I vowed privately to the Lord that I would do my best to keep Will happy and take good care of this gift from God. I wanted to make up for the difficult years he'd had, nursing his first wife until she died. He had been a good dad all that time, encouraging his sons through college and staying close to them. Someday I hoped to see their mom in heaven, and I want her and the Lord to say that I did a good job filling in for her, being Grandma Annie to the little grandkids.

After the wedding in the gazebo, we adjourned for lunch right next door, in the gorgeous sunroom of the Las Brisas Restaurant overlooking Laguna Beach. Then we all went back to the Laguna Riviera, put on our bathing suits, and frolicked in the surf. As the sun set over the Pacific, we put on dry clothes, went back out on the big deck with our CDs, and danced some more.

What a perfect day.

Sunday morning was Mother's Day, so all of us went back to Las Brisas for a buffet. Liz and Lynn had to leave to get to LAX and fly back to Memphis for work Monday morning. Their coming made a clear statement to me that they would always be there for me. What a privilege to have them as sisters. We hoped it had been a three-day vacation for everyone.

The next day Will and I flew to Maui, Hawaii for our two-week honeymoon in paradise.

* * *

Don't wake me up, I'm dreaming.

My sweet husband. Gee, I liked that word. Husband. *My* husband.

Even though Will hadn't had any experience in the ocean where he couldn't touch the bottom, he was eager to learn to snorkel. When he was a child, his mom had cautioned the eight kids to stay away from ponds and rivers when they wandered over open fields near the icy lakes in Canada. No wonder he was afraid of deep water. So, I thought he was brave to want to snorkel, especially at his age. Fortunately, the cove right outside our hotel in Kaanapali Bay was a perfect place to start, because we could stand waist deep, lean over with our masks on, and see all kinds of beautiful fish. I have humorous videos of Will placing only his face in the water and quickly pulling back. Each time he'd stay facedown a little longer. Pretty soon he was lying flat, floating and following the fish. Finally, we went out on several snorkeling boat trips to Lanai.

Did God want to give me a special welcome to Hawaii? That's the only way I can explain what happened to me one beautiful, blue, sunny morning as we were snorkeling right off the beach by our hotel. Swimming close to the rocky shore, gazing at the dozens of schools of fish— yellow, black and yellow, black, and gray and white, marveling at what God had created, a different kind of fish approached me. My family and friends know that turquoise and blue are my favorite colors. In fact, I have joked that the whole world should be blue or turquoise since it practically already is, what with the sky and water taking up two-thirds of the planet.

Coming right at me was a very large fish, over a foot long, staring at me as if to say hello. He actually paused, eyeball to eyeball, with his magnificent, radiant turquoise face almost touching my mask. Then, with a flip of his majestic turquoise and purple tail, he turned and sped away. I had never seen such a fish before—or since—that day. For a while I thought it must have been a dream. I finally concluded it was just another little personal note from God saying, *I know you're there. Aloha.*

In our two weeks in Maui, we were ecstatic that we could do so much, including sunset dinner cruises, visiting Lanai, hula lessons, a class in making leis, lots of dancing, and a luau. Maybe that is one of the benefits of being older: deciding to *do it now*.

I loved that Will was a doer. "Come on, honey," he'd say. "Let's drive up the coast to a new beach." Before I even got out of bed in the morning, he was on the phone making dinner or evening cruise arrangements.

I expected that the euphoria of the honeymoon would wear off over time. But, the longer I knew and loved him, the more I respected and delighted in him.

One sunset evening while we were enjoying dinner along the beach I said, "I've always regretted that I never learned to surf."

"Why don't you take a lesson here?"

Honeymoon in Maui

The next morning, he was on the phone arranging a lesson with a robust surfing teacher who would meet us at a local beach. When we arrived at the appointed time, the instructor showed me, on shore, how to stand and balance. Then we paddled out, waiting for just the right surge. On the first good wave, he gave me a shove. I felt like I was flying at least a hundred miles an hour and fell off almost immediately. But with the second breaker, before I crashed, I had one of the biggest thrills of my life and actually stood for a short time. I got up several more times until I was too exhausted, just from paddling back out with my board, to continue. I wish I had started to surf earlier in life. It's pretty close to heaven to be out there, in a whole different world—to feel that power under your feet, hear the roar of the ocean, and be surrounded by the beautiful turquoise and blue water.

After we arrived home, my grandson's birthday was coming up and he wanted a boogie board. Will said, "We might as well get one for each of us, too. The boys can teach us how."

"Really?" We were both in our sixties. *Was it too late to be so frisky?*

I had avoided going into the Pacific most of my life because, in my opinion, the water in California is too cold. But when we bought wet suits, that changed everything. Off to San Diego we went, where Darren and Ryan cheerfully waded out with us and taught us how to catch a wave.

Frequently, we saw teenagers sitting on the beach watching us waddle out, looking like two awkward ducks, in our black wetsuits and flippers. Inevitably, some of them would politely come up to us and ask, "Uh, excuse me, ma'am, but, uh, we were wondering, just how old *are* you?" For years, we laughed over that.

* * *

Growing old is mandatory. Growing up is optional.
- Chili Davis

Even though I thought I knew him well, I had no idea what fun being married to Will would be. We both had birthdays in October, so we celebrated all month. In fact, since we knew we probably wouldn't live long enough to be married forty or fifty years like some couples, we decided to celebrate an anniversary every month as if it marked a whole year.

Mischievous, like Daddy, Will was full of pranks. He knew that since I liked lemon juice on everything, I had always wanted a lemon tree. But my townhome only has a small patio. So, for my birthday, he bought me a miniature lemon tree covered with tiny buds in a lovely redwood pot. We expected that it would be many months, maybe even a year, before it bore any fruit. I came home from an appointment a few days later and stepped out onto the patio to relax. My tree was covered with large, fully grown lemons. Immediately suspicious, I looked closer and saw that he had carefully wired fully grown lemons onto the little tree. I laughed and thought, *I'll fix him.*

He couldn't resist calling me from work. I didn't say a word about my discovery. Finally, he couldn't stand it. "Annie, did you go out to water the patio today?"

"Yes, Honey. And it's amazing. My tree is covered with large fully-grown lemons—at least a dozen of them. In fact, I just called the Orange County Register," (our large county newspaper), "and a reporter is on his way over right now with a photographer. I told them that it's some kind of strange miracle because we could document that you only bought the tree a few days ago."

I had him.

"Oh, no, no, sweetheart," he said. "You don't need to do that. Call them right away and cancel the appointment." Then he confessed to his little hoax.

* * *

A happy marriage is the union of two good forgivers.
                              - Ruth Graham

In the evening, rather than watch television, we sometimes liked to read to each other. One chapter at a time, we read Rick Warren's bestseller, *The Purpose-Driven Life*. Over and over in the book, the point is made that our lives are not all about us, not all about me, but about loving and serving others.

Okay. We got that.

When we went to bed one night after reading a chapter, I was half asleep when Will cuddled up to me and whispered, "You know, Annie, it's not all about you."

"Umm-hmm."

"You're sure you understand that? It's not all about you."

"Umm-hmm."

Why is he waking me up to tell me now?

"That's because it's all about me." Half asleep, I almost fell out of bed laughing.

Ever the romantic, he continued to write poetry and give me roses on many occasions. In addition to lovely mushy cards, he'd slip in a fun one occasionally, such as, "Roses are red. Violets are blue. Some poems rhyme, this one doesn't."

More than any man I'd ever known, Will noticed and complimented me on every outfit I put on, no matter how old it was. "Look at her. She's the prettiest woman in town. You look great."

"You're not exactly chopped liver and onions yourself," I'd say.

Marriage spoiled me, or rather, Will did. In addition to all his charms, he was our master chef. He had cooked some when we were dating, but now he turned into my fearless maniac, making up his own recipes. The ten pounds I gained the first year of our marriage were a testament to his culinary talents.

By marrying late in life, we quickly became young at heart, as the song goes, appreciating each other more and more. Blessed more than I could have imagined, I knew Will was not perfect, of course, but he was just perfect for me.

We traveled a lot in those early years, and figured you have to have four components to make it happen: the time, the desire, the health, and the money. With careful planning, we went to the Grand Canyon, looking down over the edge as the birds flew below us, and drove through the Canadian Rockies, on our way to the farm where Will grew up in Myrnam, Alberta, Canada.

We flew to Nashville and drove through to Jackson, Tennessee, to see Liz, then on to Memphis so Will could meet Mama—who adored him immediately—and see Lynn and her husband. After visiting Graceland, we drove to Elvis's original home in Tupelo, Mississippi, where the concierge and I exchanged stories about his early years. Then we made a sobering visit to the Civil War battlefield in Shiloh, where over 100,000 men were injured including 23,746 who died. Finally, we drove across the state to Augusta, Georgia, where we used Mama and Daddy's lifetime tickets and enjoyed the Masters Golf Tournament. Closer to home, we visited the Reagan Ranch in the mountains above Santa Barbara, saw Elton John in Las Vegas, sunned in Palm Springs, and boogie boarded in San Diego with the kids.

But most precious of all for me was an unexpected return to Olean.

CHAPTER 29

FULL CIRCLE

Home is the place where, when you have to go there,
they have to take you in.
(Robert Frost)

I RECEIVED A CALL FROM BETH, my old friend from first grade and my roommate at Geneseo with whom I had come to California. She now lived in Woodland Hills, in the San Fernando Valley. After being widowed for several years, she had married the guy with whom she had gone to our high school junior prom in Olean.

I had not been back to Olean in forty-five years, since I attended Mrs. T's funeral in 1960. Now it was time for our fiftieth high school reunion.

"You should go, Annie," Beth said. "You've never been to any of them."

I told Will about it and, for some unknown reason, choked up.

"We're going," he said.

I had mixed feelings, because for all those years the thought of Olean without Mrs. T had been too painful. The town reminded me of all the happiness I'd had with her, and the sadness of losing her. Besides, I didn't think anyone would remember me after so many years anyway. But Will felt it was important for us to go.

It didn't take long, with the help of Classmates.com, to contact some of my cheerleading buddies. Seven of the eight came for the three-day reunion. Driving into Olean from the Buffalo airport with Will was a thrill. He enjoyed seeing what I had described to him for years, the gentle green mountains, so different from the west, the main street, which was almost the same, the four-story high school building, the Allegheny River, and finally, *my* old neighborhood.

Mrs. T's youngest son, Paul, and I had reconnected by email after many years. He urged me to go knock on the door on York Street and ask to see the house, which a contractor had bought and remodeled.

Finally living his dream, Paul owned a stunt flying school in Florida and had flown with the United States Aerobatic Team in world competition twice, where he won two silver medals. The two books he had written on the subject had become the standard for teaching aerobatics.

John Thompson and his wife had lived in Arizona for many years after the family business was sold. I was sad to learn that he had passed away in his fifties, twenty-five years before the reunion. I regretted that I had lost contact with him.

On that cold, drizzly June morning, Will and I drove up the hill into the neighborhood that I loved, which still looked like a Currier and Ives painting. We pulled up in front of the house.

My home, with *my* mountain in the backyard. Surprised that my hands were trembling, I knocked on the front door.

"Hi. My name is Annie, and I grew up in this house when I lived with the Thompson family and..." Then the tears I tried so hard to hold back began to flow.

I was home. I never thought I'd be here again.

"Please come in and look around," the owner said. It was almost as if he and his wife had expected us. Even though I had been in the house when I returned for Mrs. T's funeral when I was twenty-three, the house seemed smaller than I remembered. The corner in the living room where the baby grand used to sit stirred wonderful memories for me.

I stood in the very spot where Mrs. T had said to me, "Annie, do you realize you can be anything in this world you want to be, if you're willing to work hard enough?"

How right she was.

We walked through the large country kitchen, all remodeled now, where the old refrigerator with coils used to stand. As the mist fell around us, we strolled around in the backyard. We lingered next to the tall pine trees that climbed their way up the hill. I felt like I was living in a dream.

After thanking the friendly owners, we left.

We picked up some flowers at a florist shop and drove to the cemetery in the rain. After searching around the hillside, I found the familiar spot—her grave, where she was buried beside her infant son who had died before John and Paul were born.

To give me some time alone, Will waited for me at the curb by the car.

My tears of gratitude mingled with the cold rain as I knelt and tenderly hugged her tombstone. *How could it be such a joy to hug a cold, wet gravestone?* But it was.

I whispered, *Dear God, please tell her how much she meant to me, how much I loved her and still do. Tell her that she has never been forgotten. Tell her that she planted the roots that made my life blossom with success and happiness.*

Please, Lord, tell her everything that I was not able to put into words when I was a child, and that every year, as I've grown older, I have appreciated her more.

And God, please grant that someday I will see her when I arrive in heaven and I can thank her myself.

Now sobbing, I turned my back so Will couldn't see my face. Then, overcome with gratitude and peace, I dried my tears and walked back to the car where Will was waiting for me with a big hug.

At the reunion I was overjoyed to see so many old friends— and pleased that they remembered me. They came from all over the country, but most lived in the state or nearby states. Reuniting with my cheerleading buddies was a blast, with lots of laughter and fun memories in addition to catching up on where they were in their lives now. I had an opportunity to thank Mary Jane for showing me around that very first day of school in the eleventh grade, and for inviting me to work out with her to try out for cheerleading. She hadn't realized what a difference that gesture had made for me.

That evening a dance was held at a beautiful local hotel outside of town. I was approached by a handsome guy whom I recognized as someone I'd had a big crush on in high school. He was popular—a basketball player then, and a star in my young eyes. I had admired him from afar but thought I wasn't in his league and not qualified for his attention.

"Hi Annie. Wow. You haven't changed much."

"Oh, aren't you kind," I purred.

"You know, I had a crush on you in high school and wanted to ask you out."

"Why didn't you? I had a crush on you, too," I said, laughing.

"I didn't because I thought you were that rich girl that lived on the hill and I wasn't in your league."

"That's too funny," I said as I explained my family situation and being raised by Mrs. T.

"Yeah, well, anyway, by the time I got up the nerve to approach you, you were Jamie's girl."

Oh, the twisted ironies of life. "Oh, what a tangled web we weave..."

To make matters worse, he was as handsome now as he had been in high school. Well, I missed out on that one—because at the time, I was eating my heart out over Jamie.

The next morning, Will and I drove out of town to see if I could remember how to get to Sunny Acres, where Mrs. T rode her horse Minky and I had ridden the Tennessee Walker, Flaxon. The daughter now lived there but wasn't home, so I left her a note. But the farm and surrounding area was just as beautiful as ever. The last afternoon, after having lunch with friends, we drove away from Olean in our rented car. I realized I'd probably never be back.

With so much to live for, our happy lives must continue somewhere else.

From Olean, we drove to Niagara Falls and had a romantic two-day visit, almost a honeymoon all over again. The thundering beauty of the falls as the ground shook under our feet was another reminder of the power and presence of God on this beautiful planet. Come to think of it, it's that same awareness of the power of nature as when you ride a boogie board, sometimes rapidly, sometimes gently, into shore, with the surge of the waves carrying you along.

We drove to Geneseo, where we met for coffee with my old friend Evelyn. The campus had grown so large that we had to have a student guide help us find the original quad. There we found Bailey Hall where Beth and I were roommates that first year. I even found the old mop closet I had climbed in to hear the news from Mother that Georgia had had her first baby, Cindi.

On the flight home, Will said, "You know, Annie, I always felt there was something missing in your life, an important part that you needed to connect to. And that was it. You needed to go home to Olean."

I loved him all the more for seeing what I could not see for myself. I felt somehow complete as I laid my head on his shoulder and dozed off to sleep.

* * *

Music is a precious, worthy, costly treasure given to mankind by God.
- Dr. Martin Luther King

Shortly after we arrived back in Southern California, I listed a beautiful home in South Huntington Beach for sale. I loved the tract because of the unusual architecture, with two-story, floor-to-ceiling glass windows. For over a year, I had coached the owner, Marla, an older woman, on how to stage the house in preparation to sell. We had become friends.

In the living room sat a gorgeous, white baby grand piano, which she didn't play anymore. She and I often joked about our dads, who were musicians, rushing into the room when we were kids practicing the piano, shouting, "No, no. It's B flat, not B natural." She told me that due to its size, she would not be shipping the piano back to Alabama when she moved, and she wanted to get rid of it. I offered to put a sign on the piano during open houses saying, *Piano Negotiable*. Because it looked so eloquent there by the window looking out on her beautiful garden, I was sure a future buyer would want it. No one did. So, I offered to call various non-profit organizations to see if they might want it.

"No. I'm giving it to you," she said.

Speechless for a moment, I spoke carefully, hating what I knew I must say.

"Thank you, Marla. That's very kind of you, but I don't think it would be appropriate for me to accept such a big gift from a client."

"Fine," she said. "If you don't want it, I'll put it out on the curb for the trash."

She continued to insist that I take it.

"I don't think it will fit in our townhome living room, anyway," I finally said.

"You can at least go home," she said, "and measure to find out if it will fit."

At my town house, I told Will the story, and he immediately went into the garage and returned with a measuring tape. The space needed was five feet by five feet, a perfect fit by the big bay window in the living room.

Yippee! Finally, without hesitation, I accepted the generous gift.

God amazes me. He sprinkles special blessings down on us sometimes, even when we have not asked for them. He remembers the desires of our hearts. It had never occurred to me to ask Him to let me have a baby grand piano. After all, it was not an essential, like, say, a refrigerator. It was almost as if He was giving me the piano from Mrs. T's, when I didn't feel right about accepting hers. What a wonderful reminder of those precious years with her. He remembered because He was there all along. I smiled to myself as I realized He would always be there listening.

CHAPTER 30

JOY AND SORROW

Delight yourself also in the Lord and He shall give you
the desires of your heart.
(Psalm 37:4)

SOON AFTER WE WERE MARRIED, Will and I visited several local churches, since we believed fellowship was important and we wanted to grow in our beliefs. We settled on attending a vibrant church—the First Christian Church of Huntington Beach—as often as possible, because the sermons were balanced and based on scripture, plus the pastor was not only gifted, but hilarious. Getting there was not easy, especially if I had an open house that day. That meant going out very early, before church, putting up fifteen to twenty open house signs, and rushing out afterward to grab lunch so I could start the open house by twelve or one o'clock.

From our first visit, the more we studied the Bible, the more we talked about going to Israel someday to see where all this history happened. I had been lucky enough to have seen some of the United States in my life, and Will had worked his way around the world as a young man, but when we discovered that we both wanted to go to Israel, we investigated cruises and found some to be affordable. We planned to see as much as possible in the area while we were there. So, in August of 2009, we fulfilled the dream of a lifetime: a Mediterranean cruise—which would include Israel.

Rich Buhler and I had talked about that trip many times because he had been there often. Will and I were invited to go with him and a small group, but we weren't able to because we couldn't work out our schedules.

We mentioned to our family that we wanted to see the Holy Land.

One of my daughters said, "No, no, Mom. Don't go. You could be killed. There are terrorists there who hate Americans. A tourist bus was blown up there last year."

"Good," I said. "What better place to die than Israel?"

Will, among his many skills, was a licensed travel agent. We went online, planning which cruise to take and deciding ahead of time which excursions to choose.

"We really are in God's hands, aren't we?" Will said as he looked out the airplane window when we flew over the vast Atlantic. We landed in Rome. We were astounded at the amazing art throughout the city. Because I had taught *Julius Caesar* in a high school English class, standing in the Roman Forum, in the very spot where he was assassinated, was especially meaningful. When we toured the Vatican, the Sistine Chapel, and St. Peter's Basilica, I had to admire the Catholics for their dedication to telling Bible stories through art. I asked our tour guide, "What are all those dozens of statues that stand on top of the wall outside of the Vatican courtyard?"

Her answer blew me away. "Those are the martyrs who died for their faith."

From the cruise ship, we toured Naples, Capri, Sorrento, Athens, Rhodes, Ephesus in Turkey, Bethlehem, and then Israel itself, including Jerusalem. With police escorts often in front of our tour bus, we felt secure during the entire trip.

One of the highlights for me, personally, was our tour of Ephesus. John, one of Christ's apostles, is buried there. As I have studied scripture, I have come to believe that Christians should be known not only for their love of everyone, but, because we are family, especially by our love for each other. But I'd realized that not only did I not love everyone, I did not love all Christians. In fact, there were some Christians I didn't even *like*. Love them? I'm not so sure. And the command to love my neighbors as myself? Well, I liked the ones I knew, but *love*? Maybe not. Sure, if their house was on fire, I'd do everything I could to save them as a human being, but was that love?

But then, walking among the ruins of the church built to honor John, the apostle whom Jesus loved, I actually tripped over his tombstone. As I looked down at it, God spoke clearly to my heart. "*This* is your family."

In awe, I got it. Finally. When we returned home, I never felt the same way again about other believers, the neighbors, and humanity in general. Since that moment, I've had a new love for people.

I have hungered most of my life for family, since mine was so broken, and here they were, all around me. I just hadn't seen it clearly.

Until that day.

In Ephesus, we were inspired and humbled by the sight of the ruins of the huge amphitheater where the apostle Paul had courageously stood and told thousands about Christ being the Son of God and about his relationship with Him. Surrounded by huge temples to the different gods, as he spoke, he knew his life was in danger. Eventually, he died as a martyr for his faith.

In Jerusalem, our tour bus took us to one of the most revered sites, the Garden of Gethsemane. Many of the tourists on our bus were men. I figured they must be pastors or church leaders on the trip of a lifetime.

Before the thirty of us were guided through the garden, our guide said, "Would anyone like to read the account of this from the Bible out loud for us?" No one volunteered. My head was bursting inside. *I want to read it.* But I made myself remain quiet, thinking I did not want to rob anyone else of the opportunity.

After our guide led us around for an hour, he paused at the entry point and said once again, "Doesn't anyone want to read this account to us out loud from John 18:1? I have it right here from the Bible."

Silence. I waited. Finally, I couldn't stand it anymore and said, "I'll read it."

He handed me a Bible with very tiny print. Not a problem. I whipped out a magnifying glass I kept in my fanny pack for maps and in a loud, clear voice I read the account. What a thrill that God allowed me to stand near where Jesus might have stood and give testimony to that evening in Gethsemane when Christ prayed before being crucified the next day. Another God thing to me—as if the Lord was letting me know that He knew I was there and knew how much I loved Him.

One day, we stood knee deep in the Jordan River, possibly near where Jesus was baptized by John the Baptist, which looked just like the paintings we've seen in the backs of our Bibles since our childhood. I'd love to go to Israel ten more times, but I am forever blessed to have seen it even once, so we will see what the future brings.

Finally, our cruise took us to Egypt, where we rode camels and went inside the pyramids. Then we had one complete day and night at sea as we circled back to Rome.

In the middle of the night, with no land in sight, we stood out on the balcony of our cabin. All we could see was a black sky sprinkled with millions of winking stars, as if inviting us to reach out and touch them. The only sound was the water sliding by the ship. With no horizon in view, and no apparent separation between earth and sky, we felt as if we could walk right on up to heaven. That experience alone was one of the most memorable and astonishing adventures of our lives.

We spent two more days touring Rome and recuperating in the hotel and spa, and then took the long flight home. We had seen where it all happened over two thousand years ago, and yet it had come alive to us as if it all occurred yesterday.

* * *

I have been driven many times upon my knees by the overwhelming conviction that I had nowhere else to go.
- Abraham Lincoln

I couldn't wait to call Rich when we got home to tell him about our trip. I still thought of him as my little brother and we had stayed in touch, remaining good friends even though our lives had gone in different directions. His career had continued to grow. Ten years after he had chosen to be off the air from KBRT, he had opened a recording studio—Branches Communications. Meanwhile, he had suffered through a painful divorce. That first summer, I gave a surprise birthday party for him at my home so the old KBRT gang and the family could get together. He wondered what God had next for him, but the difficulties he had been through only made him an even more compassionate and understanding counselor. So, for a while, he hosted a program on KKLA called *Table Talk*.

Eventually, he reconnected with an old friend from his Biola University days. They fell in love and married in 2005. Will and I were married the year before, so we were happy for each other and shared our joy at how the Lord had so unexpectedly restored our lives.

Rich returned to KBRT and resumed his talk show, *Talk from the Heart*. In July of 2010, several months into the program, his wife called and said that Rich was seriously ill in the hospital and wanted to see me. The prognosis wasn't good. I rushed to see him the very next day.

After a hug and some small talk, he said, "I went into the hospital with a side ache and found out I'm a cancer patient. Its inoperable pancreatic cancer and the doctor said I have only three months to live." His calm demeanor comforted me.

"Only God can decide that," I said.

He smiled but looked tired and worn out. We were both aware this might be the last time I'd see him alive. I needed to tell him how much he meant to me before it was too late.

"Rich, I want you to know that just by watching how you've lived your life day to day over the last thirty years, you've been the greatest influence on me as a believer. Even at times at the station when we were under a lot of pressure, you showed me how to trust the Lord.

Rich Buhler and Annie

Remember the time when we were on the air, that you insisted that I go out in the lobby and tell Dr. Schuller how watching his program *Hour of Power*, had encouraged me? I had wanted to die after my husband divorced me, but someone sang *Because He Lives* I can Face Tomorrow and it turned my heart around and gave me courage to live? You knew that Dr. Schuller would love to hear my story, so out I went, knelt down by him, embarrassed, and spoke with him. He was delighted knowing how he had helped me.

All along, you gave me so much courage. When I was a beginning news intern, you helped me at a crucial time in my life and you convinced me that I could do well in sales, even when I didn't think so. You've stood by me as a brother and friend through all these years and believed in me at times when I didn't believe in myself."

His eyes welled up as he smiled.

"I thank God for placing you in my life at exactly the right time," I said, "when I felt I was down for the count. In those crucial years, I don't know what I would have done without you. I know hundreds of people have said this kind of thing to you before, but I want you to know that here is yet another life that you have changed for the good."

"You've been like a sister to me, Ann. We had some good years, didn't we? Don't worry. Cancer is the enemy and I intend to fight it as long as I can."

We parted with a warm hug. When I got to my car, I could at last release the sobs I had held back all day.

Within a month of his diagnosis, while Rich was still living, a large celebration of life was given in his honor, with hundreds attending, offering many pastors, radio listeners, clients, and friends of every denomination an opportunity to thank him publicly for his impact on their lives. He was lauded by many Christian leaders as the father of Christian talk radio.

A celebration like that while the person is still alive is one of the best ideas I've ever seen because people don't get to hear all the good things that are said about them at their funeral. I wish we could have done this for Mrs. T.

With the help of chemotherapy, and thousands praying for him—including nine rabbis at the Jerusalem Wall whom he had befriended—his tumor shrunk, and he actually lived for another year and a half, which was a miracle in itself. He returned to the airwaves during most of that time, often joking that if he was at all forgetful, he was suffering from chemo brain. Ironically, while he was fighting for his life, his wife was battling breast cancer, which she survived. Both of them had such an honest, upbeat attitude that, even in this, they were an inspiration to everyone.

He went home to be with the Lord in April 2012, at sixty-five years of age.

CHAPTER 31

RHUBARB PIE

*God can use anything to reach people. But who knew
that God can even use rhubarb pie?*

IN ISRAEL, WHEN WE WALKED where Jesus walked, and
at home, when we watched Georgia and Rich's valiant and
courageous fights to live, Will and I came to have a different and sobering perspective on our own lives. We were never
the same. Our faith and our love of the Bible had deepened.

For many reasons, we desired more than ever to get involved
in a small Christian group. First, we wanted to get to know other
couples in the area who were our age. Secondly, we wanted to
study the Bible more and have fellowship with other believers so
that we would grow in our faith. Our church had dozens of small
Life Groups that gathered in individual homes one night a week
to not only study the Bible, but to cultivate close friendships. By
keeping the size of the group at ten to twelve people, it was easier
to get to know each other. At these gatherings, there were also
prayer requests, which were confidential, followed by conversation and snacks.

Even though Will and I had good times with our kids, none of
them lived close by, so we didn't get to see them very often. Will
and I were social people, but since most couples our age had been
married for many years and had enough close friends already,
some, it seemed, didn't need any new friends. Like interlocking
Legos, their lives were already full.

So, we prayed that God would put us in a Life Group that would bring us the fellowship we desired and new friends who would become like extended family.

* * *

Don't rob me of the blessing of helping you.
- Don Brown

One Sunday morning we sat in the downstairs video café at church, where people could have coffee and donuts while they watched the service on a big screen. Sitting at our table was a cheerful guy with black eyes that radiated with friendliness. We introduced ourselves and he struck up a conversation with Will before the service began.

"Say, Will," he said, "do you like those donuts?"

"Oh, sure," Will said, ever the extrovert. "But we love rhubarb pie even more."

"Rhubarb pie? Why, I've got a backyard full of organic rhubarb. When can you come over and pick some? Today after church?"

Uh, who was this guy? We'd never been invited to someone's home the very first minute we met them. We made some lame excuse and said we'd come over some other time. But Don was not the kind of man to take no for an answer. This conversation continued for weeks until we couldn't say no anymore without hurting his feelings. So, a month later, after church, we arrived at his house.

Oh, wow. He and his wife Diana did have a huge organic garden, including avocado trees, cucumbers, tomatoes, every kind of vegetable, all kinds of fruit trees and flowers, and, of course rhubarb. They both made us feel right at home, and Don sparkled with his enthusiasm for his Garden of Eden.

Before we knew it, we were attending Don and Diana's Life Group on Tuesday nights, which had grown to eighteen people. *Why would they invite us when the group was already so large?* We figured it must be a God thing.

After Don introduced us around, he said to us, "Now, this is not my house. This is God's house. If there's anything here you need, my car or truck or anything at all, just come on over and get it."

We'd never heard such talk.

From then on, we loved to kid him, saying, "Good. We'll back up a truck tomorrow and pick out the furniture we want." Most of the group had been together for many years as close friends and yet, right away, they made room in their lives for us. We had found our hearts' desire, a Christian group like a family that really seemed to love us. And we loved them.

It didn't take long to learn that Don had been a computer expert for Walt Disney in the 1960s. Because he offered to assist me by phone whenever I got stuck on my computer, I called him numerous times for help. But, finally, one day when I was stuck once more, I called to ask for his expertise and apologized, afraid that I might be imposing.

"What?" he said. "Don't you dare rob me of the blessing of helping you." I had never thought of help that way. I have used that wonderful phrase ever since when I want to help someone.

Friends Who Became Family

Now, there were over twenty in the group. Most homes were not large enough to host that many people, so Don and Diana ended up having us there every week instead of rotating host houses. That didn't seem fair to them, even though they never complained. We almost wore out their wood floors with our many Bible studies, socials, and potlucks. In addition, both of them were gourmet cooks, so we joked that, "We eat, and in between, we study the Bible." *But shouldn't someone start a new group to give them some relief?*

It didn't seem right to ask any of them to break off and form a new, smaller fellowship because they'd been together for so long. So, after much prayer, Will and I started a separate group with our new friends. Soon there were twelve of us.

It must have been a God thing because we hit it off instantly. We all wanted the same thing—to be family to each other. And oh, the fun we've had. Will and I invited some of them over to our community pool on Tuesdays under the pretense of exercising, but in reality floating around on Styrofoam "noodles," visiting and joking. We named ourselves The Noodle Group, often having lunch on our patio after the pool.

Most of all, we've been there for each other, not just for the happy times, but through the most painful, difficult moments that happen when you least expect them—the slings and arrows of outrageous fortune, as Shakespeare said.

We kept a prayer journal so we could remember the blessings and answered prayers that God has brought into our lives

In fact, sadly, when one of the husbands in our group passed away at 2:00 a.m., within half an hour most of the group arrived at the house to give support and spend the night. That's *family*. They stayed all night with the new widow.

That's how we are. That's what we do.

* * *

Life is like a coin. You can spend it any way you wish, but you can only spend it once.
- Lillian Dickson

In our Life Group, I met Delores. From the first moment, the joke between us was how very much we have had in common our whole lives. Who knew? We quickly became as close as sisters and, meeting every week, have been prayer partners for over five years. For two summers, Delores and her husband Jake joined our family, along with Shannon and her dog, on our annual, week-long family trip to Sequoia. Now they are part of our ex tended family.

We never would have met any of these won- derful people had we not been proactive, prayed, and sought out fellowship time and time again until we found it. The good- ness of God never ceases to amaze me as He never forgets the desires of our hearts.

Best Friend, Part Sister, Delores

An unexpected blessing came my way in 2013. After reaching the point in life where, even with my astigmatism and congenital birth defect, I was grateful for the vision I had, my Kaiser oph- thalmologist told me about a new eye surgery. When I had the procedure done, my astigmatism was decreased by at least 80 percent. I'm seeing better now than ever before in my life, at an age when vision normally decreases. How fortunate that I have lived during a time in medical history when that's possible.

Despite my difficult beginning but because others have prayed for me, God has had His hand on me. I believe that my grandpa's prayers brought John Thompson and Mrs. T into my life. A total stranger, why should she take me in when I had been told there wasn't much promise for me, that I'd never make it past third grade? What was in it for her?

Even after I went to Geneseo and California, she stood by me. Why? I was not her daughter. Or maybe I was, after all—because your real mother is the one who believes in you, is devoted to you, and loves you.

Mrs. T—That One Person who changed the course of my life—set my values, my drive, and, by her example, encouraged my love of God. She affected my attitude about every decision I'd ever make. No one had ever talked to me the way she did. And I was never the same again.

It wasn't that Daddy and even Mother didn't love me in their own ways, but they were caught up in their hectic lives. They did not have the ability, somehow, or the time, to spend with me. Perhaps I came along too soon for them.

But God took care of that by blessing me with Mrs. T.

Over my lifetime, no matter where I was, God has sent other people to be that one person—some for only a short time—when I needed them. While it started with John and Mrs. Thompson, the blessings continued through Hilda Berg, Rich Buhler, and now my Life Group.

If she could see me now, Mrs. T would smile at the successful careers I've had, all because she told me, "You can be anything in this world you want to be if you're willing to work hard enough."

Sequoia, Shannon, Fiona and Annie

She would be proud of my happy life, since she knew what I wanted most was a family to love and be loved by. God has given me not only my own family, including my two daughters, two grandkids, and two great-grandkids, but also Will's two sons, daughters-in-law, and four granddaughters.

Most of all, Mrs. T would be pleased at how my faith has grown from the time she took me to church as a small child, and how I have learned to trust Him through the ups and downs of life.

Having been told when I was a little girl that I had no future, I am amazed and grateful to God for bringing Mrs. T into my life—  that one person who believed in me and made all the difference. Because of her, I live a happy and fulfilling life. Any of us can choose to be that one person for someone—sometimes in big ways, as it was with her, or in small, day-to-day ways, by helping others. All we need to do is be on the lookout, willing to take the challenge when we see it and, in some cases, allowing our lives to be interrupted or even turned upside down.

Mrs. T was right when she said, "If you have just one person in this world who loves you and believes in you, you are very, very rich."

Having received so much, it's my life's challenge, with God's wisdom and His direction, to be that one person to others and to make them just as rich as I am, in any way I can. I challenge you to do the same. Keep paddlin'.

THE END

ACKNOWLEDGEMENTS

I would like to thank all those who heard my story from the time I was a child until now and encouraged me to write. Special thanks to the Southern California Writers Conference, my first contact in this writing journey. Editors who coached me along the way are Marla Miller, Maralys Wills and her writing class, Jean Jenkins, Stacey O'Brien, Mark Malatesta, my Life Group from First Christian Church, Huntington Beach, my prayer partner for many years, Dee Ransom, Laurey Venn, and sisters Janis and Linda.

My special thanks to Pat Boone who was so supportive in his endorsement, to Bill Nelson, Founder of Fresh Beginnings Ministry, to Ph.D., LMFT, ordained pastor and counselor Scott Grooms

Thanks to Rich Buhler, my mentor, role model, and pretend little brother who encouraged me during those wonderful years working so closely together as I learned more about what God's grace and compassion are all about.

Thanks to my dedicated publisher, CrossLink, and Rick Bates who worked tirelessly on this project.

Most of all, I am particularly grateful for Mrs. T and her son Jim who are the reason for my story. I owe them my life, because they believed in me long before I believed in myself. They were that one person from whom I learned the basics of life ...how to overcome the difficult times with perseverance, faith, hope and love, and trust in God. They equipped me to live a happy life and even how to be that one person for others.

Printed in the United States
By Bookmasters